MASTERING CSS
with Dreamweaver CS3

Stephanie Sullivan
and Greg Rewis

New
Riders

VOICES THAT MATTER™

Mastering CSS with Dreamweaver CS3

Stephanie Sullivan and Greg Rewis

NEW RIDERS

1249 Eighth Street
Berkeley, CA 94710
(510) 524-2178
Fax: (510) 524-2221

Find us on the Web at www.newriders.com
To report errors, please send a note to errata@peachpit.com
New Riders is an imprint of Peachpit, a division of Pearson Education
Copyright © 2008 by Stephanie Sullivan and Greg Rewis

Editor: Wendy Sharp
Production Editor: Kate Reber
Technical Editor: Dori Smith
Cover design: Aren Howell
Cover photograph: Brownie Harris
Interior design: Mimi Heft
Compositor: WolfsonDesign
Indexer: FireCrystal Communications

ISBN 13: 978-0-321-50897-3
ISBN 10: 0-321-50897-1

9 8 7 6 5 4 3 2 1

Printed and bound in the United States of America

This book is dedicated to our four boys—Cameron,
Hunter, Devin, and Noah—we love and adore you.
Anything's possible in this life. Follow your dreams.

Table of Contents

Acknowledgments   vi

Introduction > > > > > > > > > > > > > > > > > >   **viii**

Who Should Read this Book?   x

How is the Book Structured?   x

Files and Reference Material   xi

About the Authors   xi

Chapter 1: Laying the CSS Groundwork > > > > > > > > > > >   **2**

The (X)HTML Document   5

The CSS Document   10

Manipulating the Natural Flow   27

Chapter 2: Using the Fixed, Centered Starter Pages > > > > > >   **46**

Beginning to Build   48

Using Shorthand Properties in CSS   55

Using Background Images   59

Creating the Header   64

Rounding the Side Column   70

Adding the Bottom of the Page   74

A Bit About Floating and Clearing   81

The Issue of Source Order   85

Fonts and Final Styling   88

Drop Caps—Simple Page Interest   94

Completing the Footer   96

Bust the Bugs   96

Declaring Media Types   100

Wrapping It Up   103

Chapter 3: Migrating a Table-based Layout to CSS > > > > > >   **104**

The CSS Issues   107

Cleaning Up the <table> Mess   119

Rebuilding the Page Header   138

Continuing the Cleanup Process   144

Removing the Final Table Markup   149

A Final Review   153

Chapter 4: Using the Liquid CSS Layouts > > > > > > > > >   **154**

Simplifying the CSS Selectors   156

Creating the Header   159

Creating the Horizontal Navigation Bar   163

Laying Out the Main Content Area   175

Getting to the Bottom of it—Styling the Footer   191

**Chapter 5: Creating a More Complex Design
with Elastic Layouts** > > > > > > > > > > > > > > > >   **198**

The New Document   201

The Significance of the Em Unit   207

The Visual Transformation   214

The Main Content   224

The Main Site Navigation   228

Creating and Styling an Em-Based Form   240

Creating and Styling Accessible Data Tables   252

Chapter 6: Building a Gallery Site with CSS and Spry > > > > > >   **262**

Selecting the Proper Starter Layout   264

Building the Initial Framework   266

Lights, Camera, Content...   269

Directions, Please...   277

Combining Two CSS Layouts for Use in a Single Site   290

Building the Gallery—Part One   296

Progressive Enhancement—Making the Gallery "Cool"   304

Getting the Validation Gold Star   323

Index >   **336**

Acknowledgments

I was just inspired by this year's Oscars—"I'd like to thank the academy." Well, maybe not the academy, but a variety of wonderful people that have offered help, input, and support toward the completion of this book. Most important are my boys, Cameron and Hunter, who have endured almost a year of "mom gone missing" while cooking easy, and probably boring, stuff. Thanks so much, guys. I adore you both. You're amazing men and my life wouldn't be the same without you. I wish you the best as you embark on your own life journeys. To Timothy, thanks for picking up the slack with the boys during this year of travel and writing.

There were many direct contributors as well. Thanks go to Dori Smith for jumping in and tech editing for us. You relieved my mind. Great job, Dori! To Joann Lavrich—much love and gratitude for all your support this year, in so many different ways. I've sincerely appreciated your tireless beta testing of every chapter, at every step. You've been an angel. Hopefully, the errata will be minimal! To Sheri German and Vicki Stanton—kudos for helping us pull a couple of the chapters together. As we traveled and taught all over the world this year, your assistance was truly a lifesaver.

Linda Rathgeber, Scott LaPlant and Robert Chafino all contributed to the designs we were graciously allowed to mutilate and simplify for our purposes here. You're all extremely talented and I'm sorry we couldn't allow your full creativity to shine. Thanks for pitching in and being such great sports! Much love also to Brownie Harris—world-class photographer and good friend. Your willingness to shoot this cover was definitely above and beyond. We're not in your usual John F. Kennedy Jr. or John Edwards league, but hey, you've now got another book cover credit anyway. Thanks go to Dionne Stokely for the photo retouching. None of us are perfect, are we? Darn.

To Wendy Sharp, our editor at New Riders—thanks for your eagle eye editing. You've made this a much more succinct book. Thanks also to Kate Reber, our production editor, for her patience and persistence and fine eye for detail; to Mimi Heft, for the lovely interior design; to Owen Wolfson for his hard work on making the pages perfect; and to Emily Glossbrenner, for an excellent index. To David Fugate, our literary agent—you're a great negotiator and the most amazing, positive person. Thanks for all you continue to do.

Thanks also to the many people in the biz that led the way, mentored, advised, and steered me—too many to list here—you know who you are. To my friends Molly Holzschlag and Eric Meyer—you continue to inspire me. To Ray West, who gave me both my first full-time writing opportunity at Community MX (www.

communitymx.com) and my first speaking opportunity at TODCon (www.todcon. org), you are most awesome, sir! Thanks for your vision in our industry and your belief in my abilities to contribute to it. I'm forever in your debt. And going back to the very beginning—kudos to Stuart Nealy for convincing me not to learn C++ as planned. You knew the score, dude! Thanks for believing in me, getting me started in HTML and supporting me through some tough times.

Finally, to my co-author Greg Rewis—I have immense admiration and respect. You rock. Thanks for taking this journey with me. May it last a very long time and expand to many more horizons. You are, indeed, the kettle. And to you patient readers, thanks for waiting for, and buying our book. I hope it helps you learn, focus and hone your skills in our ever-morphing industry. Remember, life is about learning. Always improve—always force yourself to stretch—always grow. Ciao.

This has truly been an incredible journey—one that started too many years ago and has seen a several costume changes along the way. And yet, it seems like just yesterday that I began hacking my first web page together and viewing it in Mosaic (the idea of a site at that time was non-existent). Little did I know that I would owe so much to that fledgling technology. Since that time I have had the good fortune to make a career of working with cool software and traveling around the world to show it off. And of course, the side benefit is that I have gotten to know so many great people along the way. I obviously can't thank each of you by name—after all there is a page limit to this book—but a few of you absolutely deserve special notice.

In addition to all of the folks Stephanie has already mentioned, I want to thank my guys, Devin and Noah. The two of you are the brightest spot in my life and the reason that I keep doing what I do. Thanks for "missing Dad" and being there with a hug after yet another long trip. Thanks as well to Gabriele. You are an amazing mother to our boys, as well as a talented painter. Thank you for letting us use your pictures in the book. And Frederic, I hope you like the new site—thanks for letting us build it.

On the professional side, I'd be remiss if I didn't thank Andreas, whose amazing entrepreneurship got this whole thing started. And to Beth, who "had to have that guy at Macromedia"—and no, I still don't wear an XXL. Thanks also to all of my colleagues at GoLive, then Macromedia, and now Adobe—but most importantly to the Dreamweaver team. To say you all are amazing is an understatement. Thanks for such a great product.

Finally, to Stephanie, what more can I say? Your passion and pursuit of excellence are truly inspirational. Thank you for finally letting me wear you down. aota.

Introduction

DEAR READER,

Welcome to *Mastering CSS with Dreamweaver CS3!*

Adobe Dreamweaver (DW) is the leading web authoring tool on the market; Cascading Style Sheets (CSS) is the recommended method of separating presentation from content to make site upkeep simpler and faster, as well as friendlier to search engines. Yet it's a common misconception that it's tough to use Dreamweaver to build accessible, standards-compliant page layouts using CSS.

We're here to show you how easy it really is. Who are we? Greg is the Group Manager, Creative Solutions Evangelism at Adobe and has been involved with Dreamweaver since version two. He demos and teaches it weekly, including its CSS capabilities. Stephanie codes CSS for a living as a consultant and trains corporate web departments in CSS techniques, best practices and web standards. She's the co-lead of the Adobe Task Force for WaSP (formerly the Dreamweaver Task Force) and wrote the CSS layouts in Dreamweaver CS3 under contract from Adobe.

We wrote this book because we felt our combined knowledge about Dreamweaver and CSS could help you, our reader, grasp these tools in combination—the way we use them every day. And we wanted the opportunity to really discuss the CSS layouts contained in Dreamweaver CS3, showing you how to use, extend and really put them to work.

Who Should Read this Book?

We wrote the book with a fairly specific reader in mind. We explain each concept on first encounter, so you don't need to have extensive knowledge of either Dreamweaver or CSS, but we do expect that you have at least a little familiarity with both. We're also assuming you have some rudimentary working knowledge of (X)HTML.

On the other hand, if you're a power user of either Dreamweaver or CSS, this book will hopefully expose you to that "other" side and open your mind to some new workflow possibilities. Stephanie even learned some new tips as she edited Greg's writing, and if pressed, Greg will admit he learned some new tricks with CSS. In the pages of this book, you'll hopefully have several "gee, I wish I'd known that on my last project" moments.

How is the Book Structured?

Each chapter of the book is a stand-alone project. You don't have to do them in order, but they do build on each other, so starting at the beginning is probably best. Throughout the book, we'll try to show you different options of ways to use Dreamweaver and CSS, so you can figure out the best way for *you* to work.

We begin with a review chapter: Chapter One covers the basic principles of CSS, as well as giving an overview of Dreamweaver's CSS tools. Chapters Two, Four, Five, and Six each begin with a different type of CSS layout and walk you through building the initial page structure for a web site with it—just as we ourselves do during a typical work day—all while teaching Dreamweaver and CSS concepts. Chapter Three covers transforming an existing table-based layout to a CSS-based layout using Dreamweaver. The beginning of each chapter gives a bit more explicit instructions, but as you progress, we assume you remember what was done earlier and we don't waste space with minutiae.

We hope, when you finish each chapter, you feel like you've had a personal coach by your side pulling you through it. And this book costs a lot less than your local fitness trainer charges you for a personal trainer!

Files and Reference Material

The files for this book are housed on Stephanie's website— w3conversions.com. They're contained in, you guessed it, the "book" directory (http://www.w3conversions.com/book/). The web site includes the reference links found in the book as well, so you can simply click instead of typing while reading the book (some of the link names are really long). Also, if any links change (if you encounter a 404, let us know), we'll be able to keep the site updated.

We suggest you start by going to the site and downloading all the necessary files. From this page on, we're going to assume that you have the files you need, rather than directing you to download files in each chapter. So let's get started!

About the Authors

Together Stephanie and Greg have over 20 years of experience in the web industry and are both recognized experts within the web community and their respective areas of expertise.

About Stephanie Sullivan

Founder and principal of web standards redesign company W3Conversions, Stephanie Sullivan is a CSS, accessibility and XHTML expert, whose services are in demand by top firms across the United States. She regularly works with clients, large and small, to troubleshoot problems, train their web team, or to work behind-the-scenes transforming their in-house graphic designs into functioning standard-based web sites. Stephanie serves as co-lead of the influential Web Standards Project (WaSP) Adobe Task Force and is a partner at Community MX, a site currently offering over 2,500 tutorials to web developers seeking to increase their skills. She's an Adobe Community Expert, beta tester and Dreamweaver advisor.

A tireless advocate of web community education, she is "List Mom" for the long-running WebWeavers discussion list for professional web designers, and a moderator of the search engine marketing discussion group SEM 2.0 run by Andrew Goodman. She answers questions almost daily in the forums at Community MX, where she also writes a widely-read blog. She's a sought after speaker and lends her voice to a variety of events each year, including Adobe MAX, An Event Apart, South by Southwest, HOW Design Conference, Voices That Matter, Web Design World, and many more.

Stephanie headquarters her business by the beach in Wilmington, North Carolina, where she lives with her two teenaged sons. Though an admitted workaholic, she escapes as often as possible from the little people inside her computer to get sandy playing beach volleyball. Her hobby, if only she had time? Studying brain function. Her guilty pleasure? 80's music. Nina Hagen anyone?!

About Greg Rewis

Greg is a true "old-timer" in not only the web industry, but the computer industry in general. Having completed his studies at Louisiana State University in 1983, Greg sought out new adventures in Europe and ended up working for the US Army, attached to the National Security Agency. Little did he know that one of the systems he would be working on would later come to be known as the internet.

Fate led him to an industry tradeshow in 1990 where he met "a couple of German dudes" demonstrating their new desktop publishing system, P.INK Press. A few conversations later and Greg was the Product Manager for P.INK, which eventually spun off into a new start-up, GoLive Systems. When Adobe acquired GoLive, Greg left for the "greener pastures" of chief rival Macromedia. Greg wore a variety of hats at Macromedia—from sales engineer to Technical Product Manager for Dreamweaver to Evangelist.

With the acquisition of Macromedia by Adobe, Greg took on the role of Worldwide Web Evangelist. Through his role at Adobe, Greg has had the good fortune to travel around the world (more times than he cares to count) and talk with users of Adobe's products at seminars, conferences and trade shows. Greg is now the Group Manager for Creative Solutions Evangelism at Adobe, leading a team of worldwide evangelists as they spread the word about Adobe's creative products and technologies.

You can follow Greg's adventures at http://blog.assortedgarbage.com.

CHAPTER 1

Laying the CSS Groundwork

N   *If you already have a strong understanding of basic CSS concepts, you may choose to move on to Chapter Two. Or simply use this chapter as a review to find any cracks in the foundation of your CSS knowledge. On the other hand, if you're new to CSS and find the chapter overwhelming, relax— by the end of the book, you'll be able to return to this chapter and feel comfortable with all the concepts discussed.*

OUR GOAL IN THIS BOOK is to give you lots of handy techniques that'll help you quickly create beautiful sites that conform to Web standards and are accessible to everyone, using the CSS layouts and tools of Dreamweaver CS3. But before we can really jump into projects, we want to be sure we're all on the same page (metaphorically) as far as understanding the terminology of CSS and the interface of Dreamweaver. This chapter, then, is a quick-and-dirty CSS primer, with some hands-on Dreamweaver exercises that'll get you up and running and familiar with Dreamweaver's CSS tools and the CSS layouts.

We'll start by introducing the basic concepts of CSS. We'll then create an equal height, two-column layout with header and footer that is similar to one of the CSS layouts in Dreamweaver—basically going through the very process that Stephanie used as she wrote the CSS layouts. By the end of this chapter, you should be able to look at the code of any of the CSS layouts included with Dreamweaver and understand most of what you see.

Before we begin, let's save a new page based on the two column fixed, left sidebar, header and footer layout in the CSS layout list in the New Document dialog box. We'll use this document as an example as we examine the concepts of web standards.

1. Launch Dreamweaver and select File > New. Select the Blank Page category. Select HTML under the Page Type category. Select 2 column fixed, left sidebar, header and footer from the layout category.

   In the far right column we can see a graphical representation of the layout and a description of its specifications.

2. Leave DocType set to the XHTML 1.0 Transitional default. Leave Layout CSS on the Add to Head default. Click the Create button.

3. Save the document as concepts.html in the root folder of your site.

FIGURE 1.1 Choosing the 2 column fixed CSS layout

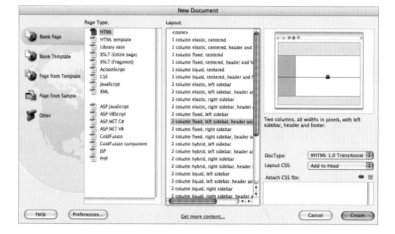

The Content/Design Equation

In order to understand solid standards-based design, you need to understand the two halves of the content/presentation equation: (X)HTML (for content) and CSS (for presentation).

In the early, early days of the web—yes, that means before YouTube and Facebook—HTML pages were simple. The few tags available were used to semantically define what the content was. For example, the h1 tag indicated that the enclosed text was a heading, and thus important. But during the wild days of the web in the late 90's, many designers applied values, such as weight, size, and color, directly to the text. They obviously wanted the text to take on a certain look, or presentation. But the fact that our *eyes* could see that the text was larger, bolder or a different color was useless to search engines and assistive technologies!

Today, our (X)HTML documents should include the page content, marked up in **semantic elements**— tags that actually describe the type of content contained within them. When our content has semantic meaning, the user agent (the browser in most cases) doesn't matter.

What are Web Standards?

In a nutshell, what we're calling web standards in this book are really just best practices for building web sites. Building sites in this manner means following three principles:

Separate content and its presentation. If you create the essential structure of the document in the (X)HTML page, you can code the information once, and output to many different devices.

Use Cascading Style Sheets for the design. If you've been around the web long enough, you'll remember the wretched days of using browser-sniffing JavaScript to determine how to display content based on which browser and platform someone was using. Or the endless search for a printer-friendly version of a page (which we unfortunately run into even today). Or creating text-only versions to minimally satisfy accessibility requirements. When you use Cascading Style Sheets to design your pages, these resource-consuming, economy-draining activities are a thing of the past. The simple text document known as a CSS file gives the (X)HTML document its look with a few well-crafted rules.

Design for universal accessibility. Not everyone on the web can access, or see, our pages in exactly the same way. The goal is to give everyone the same content, in a reasonably acceptable presentational style, without crashing the system. Standards-compliant browsers will render the pages one way. Buggy browsers, such as Internet Explorer 6 and earlier, will need adjustments to render correctly. Assistive technologies (AT) will have access to all our content without the presentational markup getting in the way. And older browsers will still present the essential content, although with fewer presentational enhancements.

The (X)HTML Document

Several concepts are essential to understanding proper, well formed (X)HTML documents: the doctype, character encoding, document flow, and inline versus block elements.

The Doctype

At the beginning of each web standards compliant document, the **Document Type Definition** (also called DTD or doctype), declares the document standard to which the file conforms. The nice thing about document standards is that there are so many of them—especially on the web! To this end, there are a number of different doctypes, each with its own set of rules for the standards with which it aspires to comply.

Take a moment to look at the various doctypes listed in the drop-down list of the New Document dialog box.

Dreamweaver uses the XHTML 1.0 Transitional doctype as its default. Unless the site has more specific requirements, this is a good doctype to use because of its backward compatibility with older web pages and its forward compatibility with the future of the web (we hope). XHTML 1.0 Transitional allows **deprecated elements**, which are mostly presentational elements and attributes such as font, `align`, and `bgcolor`. The XHTML 1.0 Strict or HTML 4.01 Strict doctypes do not allow those elements to be used.

Let's take a look at the page we just created. Open concepts.html and look for the following code at the top of the page. (Switch into Code view if necessary.)

```
<!DOCTYPE html PUBLIC "-//W3C//DTD XHTML 1.0 Transitional//EN"
"http://www.w3.org/TR/xhtml1/DTD/xhtml1-transitional.dtd">
<html xmlns="http://www.w3.org/1999/xhtml">
```

What this code is telling us is that the page uses XHTML 1.0 Transitional and will be compared against its rules as provided in the URL that follows. If you **validate** the page—check that it's free of errors—at the World Wide Web (W3C) consortium validator, the W3C would use that particular doctype as the basis of its tests.

Unfortunately, many web designers have neglected to include the doctype in their pages—and, in fact, even our beloved Dreamweaver included an incomplete doctype for several earlier versions. When this happens, pages will render in **quirks mode** instead of **standards mode**. In other words, they will render according to the methods of older, more forgiving browsers. This means our carefully constructed CSS might not display as we expect.

Character Encoding

Go back to the two-column CSS layout and look at the code beneath the doctype. The code should look like the following:

```
<meta http-equiv="Content-Type" content="text/html;
charset=UTF-8" />
```

This is the **character encoding** for the page, which is the system whereby each character we type is turned into computer bits. Until fairly recently, developers used character sets that expressed a limited number of languages, such as charset=ISO-8859-1 for Western

T   *To learn more about doc-types and the various rendering modes, read the article, Rendering Mode and Doctype Switching http://www.communitymx.com/ content/article.cfm?cid=85fee by Holly Bergevin of Community MX. The article includes a list of doc-types, as well as a list of resource links for learning everything you ever wanted—or didn't want—to know about doctypes.*

European languages. When the developer wanted to add a special character, such as a copyright symbol or an accent mark, they used a **character entity**. An example of this would be the character entity á that we use to represent the French accent acute.

More and more developers are using a universal character encoding called Unicode. In essence, Unicode allows us to use characters from almost any writing system in the world. The Dreamweaver CS3 default for both CSS and XHTML documents is a flavor of Unicode called UTF-8, which has backwards compatibility with ASCII. Because of the increasing internationalization of the web, as well as the ability of browsers to support Unicode, UTF-8 is a solid choice for character encoding.

The Natural Flow of the Document

Another important concept to understand is the natural **document flow**. The flow of the document is what you see if you remove all CSS control from a page. We'll view this in real time, using the concepts.html page.

1. Right-click on the top of the document to verify that the Style Rendering toolbar is displayed.

2. Click the Toggle Displaying of CSS Styles (the world icon) to turn CSS styles completely off.

3. View your page in Design view.

In the absence of any positioning techniques, page elements will flow one after the other in the order that they appear in the source code of the document. Be sure to toggle your styles back on for the rest of the chapter.

Inline Versus Block Elements

When you place text, images and other content in an (X)HTML page, each element flows one after the other in the natural order in which you insert it in the source code of the document. But another variable within the flow affects how elements behave: their status as a block or inline element.

Block elements are 100% as wide as their parent container and stack vertically on top of each other. It's as if there is an inherent line break between each element. Look, for example, at the **h1** text labeled Main Content at the top of the concepts.html document. It occupies its own block of space. The next element, the dummy text that sits in a paragraph, flows underneath it. Block elements do not, by default, sit next to each other.

Inline elements, on the other hand, flow horizontally and only require the amount of space they use (instead of the set width of block elements). Starting at the left, text characters, links, and images (all examples of inline elements) flow one after the other until all available horizontal space runs out. The next inline element then moves down to start a new line, just like the wrapping effect in your word processor. The browser calculates how many elements are going to fit on a line and then makes an invisible box that is tall enough for the highest elements in the line.

FIGURE 1.2 Inline and block elements within the natural flow of the document

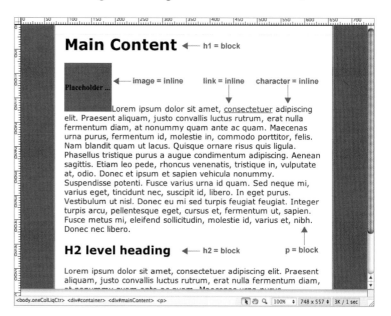

Building with Divs

The **div** is a generic empty box that lets you divide a page into discrete areas. For example, a developer might divide a page into header, sidebar, content, and footer sections, using divs with descriptive names such as header or footer. Look at any of the CSS layouts and see if you can locate this code:

`<div id="mainContent">` or `<div id="header">`

The div gives us yet another element that we can use to divide and style unique areas of the page. It has an intrinsic behavior however, that confuses new CSS coders: although the div is a block element, it ends when the content within it stops flowing vertically. If you look at the light gray background color on the `sidebar1` div in the concepts.html document, you can see how its outlines end when the content within ends. Dreamweaver's default method of outlining page elements makes the end of the div very clear.

FIGURE 1.3 A div ends when the content within it ends

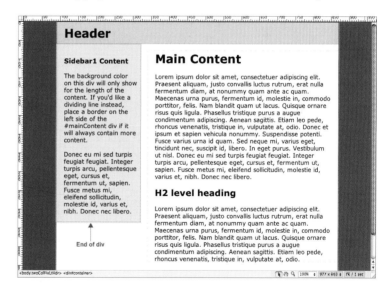

This behavior presents challenges when we try to extend background color on a column so that it goes to the bottom of the layout. We will explore the **faux column** technique, a common method to give the illusion of two equal height columns, in later chapters of this book.

The CSS Document

The (X)HTML page is not just pure content but has semantic markup (such as the **h1** of our earlier example) that describes the content's meaning. This markup provides the "hooks" to use CSS (Cascading Style Sheets) to style, and sometimes shift, the content.

CSS Syntax

Style sheets are made up of CSS rules that contribute to the design and placement of elements. Each CSS rule is made up of a selector and a declaration block. The declaration block, in turn, is made up of one or more declarations, each of which is a property with a value. Let's break this down by referring to Figure 1.4:

FIGURE 1.4 The anatomy of CSS syntax

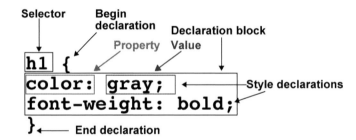

The **h1** element is the **selector** (a tag in this case) that we want to style. Next comes the **declaration block**, which is the series of property and value pairs such as `color:gray;` and `font-weight: bold;`. As you can see in the example above, the declaration block begins and ends with a curly bracket. Each individual property and value pair within is a **declaration**. For the first declaration, the **property** is color and the **value** is gray. Each declaration ends with a semi-colon.

Many people, as well as Dreamweaver, use the terms tag and element interchangeably. However, the text inside the h1 *is actually the element. The* <h1> *and* </h1> *surrounding it are the tags. Thus, tag selectors and element selectors are referring to the same thing. Since they're more commonly known as element selectors, we'll be using that terminology more often in the book.*

CSS Selector Types

When working with CSS in Dreamweaver, the New CSS Rule dialog box gives you three CSS selector options—Tag, Class and Advanced.

TAG SELECTORS (ALSO CALLED TYPE OR ELEMENT SELECTORS)

The most basic option is a selector that redefines the look of every instance of a specific tag or element. Returning to the **h1** example, if you want the color of your **h1** text to be gray instead of black, you could write a rule for the **h1** element. Redefining an element is a global operation that affects every element of the same type on the page.

As you can see in the image below, once you select the radio button for Tag, a Tag drop-down list appears that lists all HTML tags in alphabetical order.

FIGURE 1.5 The tag selector and its drop-down list

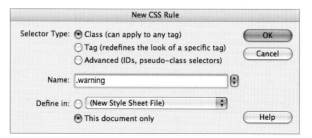

CLASS SELECTORS

The class selector applies to anything on the page that includes its attribute in the (X)HTML code. Classes are used on an as-needed basis, and should be applied sparingly. If you've ever worked with styles in a word processor or page layout application, classes work in the same way. For example, you might add a class to a paragraph element:

```
<p class="warning">
```

In the style sheet, the class might include these properties and values:

```
.warning {
  font-weight: bold;
  color: #FF0000;
}
```

FIGURE 1.6 The Class Selector

Selectors for class names begin with a period and then use a descriptive name, referring to the purpose of the class, not its appearance (although many a new CSS designer has been guilty of creating a `.boldRed` class!) We can use a class as many times as we like within a page to give elements consistent styling. For instance, we might want all of the important text within a paragraph to have the same visual properties and thus define a class called `warning` to set the appearance of the crucial text within the paragraph.

ADVANCED SELECTORS

The Advanced selector type, as it is known in Dreamweaver, is used most often for **IDs**, **pseudo selectors** and **descendant selectors** (though Dreamweaver allows you to type anything into this box, including child and sibling selectors). Let's look at what each term means.

Identifiers IDs are often used to identify a specific area of the page, such as the `mainContent` div in our example:

```
<div id="mainContent">.
```

In the CSS, you might create a rule that moves the `mainContent` div 225 pixels from the left side of the page.

```
#mainContent {
  margin-left: 225px;
}
```

Note that in the style sheet, selectors for IDs begin with a hash mark or octothorpe (#). Each ID name must be unique, and unlike classes can only be used one time on each page.

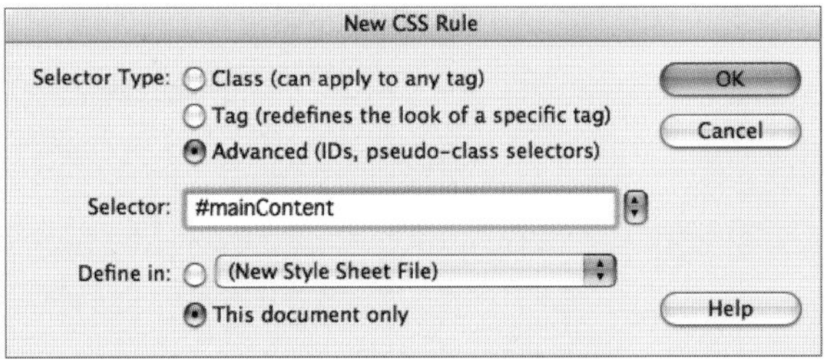

FIGURE 1.7 The Advanced ID

T *When you want to apply the same properties and values to a number of selectors, you can group them, by writing them together and separating them with a comma and a space. This is called a compound selector. Don't place a comma after the last selector in the list. Because Internet Explorer does not use the a:focus rule for keyboard navigators, but instead uses the a:active rule, we always group :hover, :active, and :focus together so that all types of users will see the same hover-type state when activating a link. We place :focus last to be sure IE keyboard navigators see the :hover style we intend.*

Pseudo Selectors The most common examples are the `a:link`, `a:visited`, `a:hover` and `a:active` anchor/link styles that we see listed in the drop-down list next to the Advanced selector option. These represent various link states: `a:link` is the initial state of the link; `a:visited` is the state of the link after the user has already visited it; `a:hover` is the interactive state of the link when the visitor passes the mouse over it; and `a:active` is the state of the link when the user clicks the link but has not released the mouse button. There is also the `a:focus` state which behaves much like the `a:hover` state and is activated by those who are using a keyboard rather than a mouse to navigate through links (and indicates that a link can accept keyboard events). While this pseudo class does not appear within Dreamweaver's drop-down list, it can simply be typed into the field as `a:focus`.

We can use CSS to style these link states to display their differences visually. The one thing that must be remembered with these specific pseudo selectors is that they must follow a specific order in the style sheet:

- `a:link`

- `a:visited`

- `a:hover`

- `a:active`

- `a:focus` (when included)

FIGURE 1.8 The Pseudo selector drop-down list

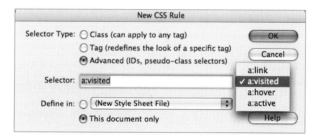

Descendant Selectors Understanding the document tree—the structure of the (X)HTML document and the relationships between the elements—is the first step in writing highly efficient and compact CSS. The document tree is similar to a family tree with ancestors, siblings and children. Learning to target an element using its descendants is a powerful tool.

Let's use the example of a document containing the body element with a container that holds `mainContent` and `sidebar1` divs. In `sidebar1`, we have some nested unordered lists creating the navigation. In `mainContent`, we have `h1`, `h2`, and paragraph elements. Visually, as a family tree is rendered, it might look like this:

FIGURE 1.9 All elements are descendants of the body.

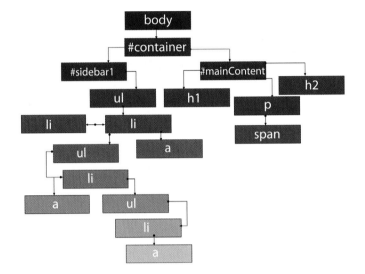

Earlier we mentioned that redefining the look of a specific element or tag is a global operation. If **h1** is defined as gray, every **h1** on the page will be gray. But what if we need to create different looks for the same element in different areas of the page? For example, we may want **h1** to be red in the sidebar, but green in the main content. If we set the ID of the main content div to `mainContent` and the ID of the left column to `sidebar1`, we can set individual looks for the **h1** tag by writing the style in context. A rule addressing `#mainContent  h1` will target the **h1** tag only when it is in the content area of the page. And a rule for `#sidebar1  h1` will target the **h1** tag only when it is in the sidebar area of the page. (Note the use of a space between the ID and the element name.)

FIGURE 1.10 The descendant selector targets elements within a specific context.

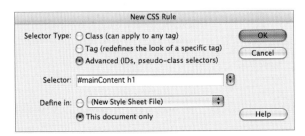

T   *To read a complex descendant selector, always start at the end of the selector and work backwards. For instance, `.twoColFixLtHdr #sidebar1 li a` selects any anchor (link) element contained in a list item that is contained within an element with the ID of sidebar1 that is contained within an element with the class `twoColFixLtHdr`. If you need help figuring it out, the selectoracle at http://gallery.theopalgroup.com/selectoracle/ can help.*

N   *The CSS layouts in Dreamweaver CS3 only use descendant selectors; however, the CSS specifications allow for other advanced selectors. These selectors, such as the adjacent sibling and the child selector, aren't consistently supported yet, but are available in IE7 (among other browsers). You can familiarize yourself with more selector types at the W3C: http://www.w3.org/TR/REC-CSS2/selector.html*

There are many varieties of CSS layouts available to us in Dreamweaver, and we may want to use more than one within a site. For example, we might want to use both a two column and three column layout within the same site. In order to give different values to the `mainContent` div in the two column page versus the `mainContent` div in the three column page, each CSS layout has a class assigned to the body element.

In the code below, you can see the class attribute that the CSS layouts add to the body of the two-column fixed-width page and the three-column fixed-width page:

```
<body class="twoColFixLtHdr">
<body class="thrColFixHdr">
```

The code below shows how we add a class prefix to the `mainContent` for each layout creating a descendant selector.

```
.twoColFixLtHdr #mainContent
.thrColFixLtHdr #mainContent
```

Now each rule that has a class prefix will maintain unique styles for different page types within one style sheet. We'll take a closer look at combining the style sheets for several CSS layouts later in this book.

Now that you understand basic CSS syntax and selector types, let's look at the kinds of style sheets in which we might use them.

The Cascade

There are many ways in which rules can be applied to our document. Though it may seem a bit mundane, it's important to understand the C in CSS, which is, of course, the cascade—the order in which rules are applied—and how it affects the page.

N   *Doesn't this seem rather counterintuitive? We give the user the ability to create their own styles, but as authors, we can override their preferences. Sad, but them's the rules, pardner!*

Style sheets operate in a hierarchy in which certain sheets take precedence over others. In the absence of any other style sheet, the browser style sheet determines how the page looks. But users can create user style sheets and set them as the defaults in their browser preferences, and those styles will take precedence over equivalent browser styles. Finally, author style sheets that we designers and developers create for our pages have the final authority over the look of the page.

THE BROWSER STYLE SHEET

T *There are a variety of ways to zero many defaults at once. We won't try to set any universal rules, but will simply zero values out as needed in the exercises, in order to keep the steps clear.*

Browsers apply default style sheets that set the presentation of all HTML elements. Formats such as the large size on level one headings, the gaps between paragraphs, the indents on lists, and other basic style information give the page a minimal design.

Though the different browsers use similar values in their default style sheets, they are, unfortunately, not exactly the same. As we start to create our own custom rules, we don't have a level playing field—the changes we make can affect users differently depending on which browser they're using. In order to create a style sheet that looks the same to every user, we should start by "zeroing out" margins, padding, and borders on many (X)HTML elements in order to override the default browser values. With everything set to "0", we can then go on to set our own values expecting that the effect will now be the same in each browser.

THE USER STYLE SHEET

N *Though the W3C recommends using the* `!important` *operator to force a value in the user style sheet to take precedence, not all browser manufacturers have implemented the operator at this time. In the browsers where it works, however, the* `!important` *operator tells the browser that this declaration, no matter where it comes in the cascade, should be honored. It is written as:* `font-size: 45px !important;`

The next style sheet in the hierarchy comes from a user who adds a style sheet that overrides some browser styles. This style sheet may designate a larger font size, for example, to make it easier for a person to read the text. Most browsers allow users to set a custom user style sheet in the browser preferences. These preferences override the browser style sheet, but not the author style sheet.

THE AUTHOR STYLE SHEET

The top dog in the hierarchy is the style sheet created by us, the web page authors. But there are three different ways in which our rules can be organized and applied: as external, embedded and inline styles. The closer to the element we get, the more precedence a style takes. Inline styles take precedence over embedded style sheets, and embedded style sheets take precedence over external style sheets.

External style sheets are exactly what their name implies: they are separate, or external, documents that include all, or a portion of, our CSS rules. The file name ends with the .css extension, and a link to this external CSS document goes in the head of the (X)HTML document.

If we were to create a new document based on a CSS layout in Dreamweaver CS3 and select the Create New File option in the drop-down list next to Layout CSS, you would see code like this in the head of the (X)HTML page:

```
<link href="twoColFixLtHdr.css" rel="stylesheet" type="text/css" />
```

There are several different ways to create a link to a file in Dreamweaver. If you're selecting a CSS layout, you can choose Create New File or Link to Existing File. You can also link to a CSS file from within an existing (X)HTML document by clicking the Attach Style Sheet icon at the bottom of the CSS Styles panel (it looks like a link in a chain). Or you can link the style sheet from Text > CSS Styles > Attach Style Sheet. And of course lastly, you can do it the most boring way—you can manually type it in the source code!

Embedded styles are placed within the head of the document. If we view concepts.html in Code view, we can see the opening and closing style tags, some HTML comments to hide the CSS rules from older browsers that don't understand them, and nested with that, the actual CSS rules.

> **T** *Some designers use the @ import notation rather than linking style sheets. This is another way to reference the style sheet in the head. One of the advantages of importing is that older browsers do not understand it and will ignore the style sheets. This is often preferable to the wacky way they might otherwise render (or attempt to render) the styles. This way an older browser will get a plain, but readable page, simply showing the normal flow of the document.*

Single rule shown for simplicity

```
<style type="text/css">
<!--
.fltlft {
    float: left;
    margin-right: 8px;
}
-->
</style>
```

Embedded styles only apply to the single page in which they reside. Many developers embed styles while experimenting with the layout, and after they are satisfied with the result, they export the styles to an external style sheet. (Dreamweaver CS3 provides an easy way to export styles to an external style sheet that we'll use later.) When creating a new document using a CSS layout, it's easy to embed the rules in the head of the document. Simply set the Layout CSS drop-down list to Add to Head (which is the default). When creating a new rule, choose "This document only" in the New CSS Rule dialog to embed the rule in the head.

When using Dreamweaver's CSS Styles panel, you can view the source of a rule in the All view. If the CSS is embedded in the head, it will be shown indented under `<style>` and if it's in a CSS document, it will be shown indented below YourPageName.css. Inline styles are not shown in the All view, but are shown in the Rules pane as `<inline style>`, which you can see if you hover over the selector while in the Current view.

Inline is a style that we apply directly to an individual element within the markup of the page. To style an h1 element, for example, we could add the style attribute along with the appropriate values:

```
<h1 style="font-size: 160%; color: red;">Inline Style</h1>
```

While arguments can surely be made for the use of inline styles, we rarely use them, as there's no easy way to update them.

CONFLICT RESOLUTION

When there is only one rule for a given element, we know which properties the browser will apply. But what if there are conflicting rules for the same element? What if we have two **h1** rules, for example, in one style sheet? In situations where rules have the same degree of importance, the rule that comes last has the final say: whichever **h1** style comes last in the style sheet wins.

But what if those two **h1** rules exist in different style sheets? In that case the browser follows the hierarchy of the kinds of style sheets. If you were napping, author style sheets take precedence over user style sheets, and user style sheets take precedence over the default browser style sheet. Now try to stay awake!

Again, the order of precedence is as follows:

- Browser
- User
- Author
- External
- Embedded
- Inline

In other words, unlike the real world, it's good to come in last!

If the two **h1** rules are in different author style sheets, the browser loads the author style sheets in the order in which they appear in the source code. So, whichever **h1** rule is loaded last (according to which sheet it is in) will win.

If one of the **h1** rules is in an external sheet while the other is in the head, the embedded style takes precedence over the external style, and any inline styles take precedence over the embedded style. The style closest to the element wins.

And Now for Something Really Confusing…Specificity!

Even though we just said that the last rule wins, sometimes rules have greater **weight**, regardless of where they appear. This means that even though they may not be last, they still win!

Let's consider two rules that define the color of text in a paragraph:

```
#mainContent p { color: blue; }
p.warning { color: red; }
```

The `#mainContent p` rule states that the text is blue, and the `p.warning` rule states that the text is red. Which one wins? How is their weight, or importance, calculated? The W3C considered this scenario too, and came up with a conflict resolution technique called specificity.

We calculate specificity by counting the number of ids (=a), classes (=b), and element names (=c) in each selector. The digital scheme displays as three hyphenated numbers (a-b-c), although it can also be written in comma-delimited style (a, b, c). You can basically read the value as a number: rules with higher numbers win. Let's look at an example.

`#container #mainContent ul` has two IDs and one element name. Using the above formula, a=2, b=0, c=1 so we get the specificity of 2-0-1.

In our paragraph color example, the specificity of `#mainContent p` is 1-0-1, while `p.warning` is 0-1-1. As a result, the text would stay blue, even if we applied the class of `warning` to a paragraph within it. In order to "beat" the specificity of `#mainContent p` and make the text in a paragraph red, we would have to make a more specific rule such as: `#mainContent p.warning.` This would give us a specificity of 1-1-1. And you thought high school algebra was complicated!

In our example, p.warning is not the same as the descendant selector p .warning. The space matters! The p .warning rule selects any element with the class of warning that is within, or a descendant of, a p element. The p.warning rule would select any p element with a class of warning placed on it.

Zoe Gillenwater of Community MX wrote an article that goes into detail on the subjects of inheritance, cascade, and specificity. You can find it at http://www.communitymx.com/abstract.cfm?cid=2795D. The article includes a complete listing of the properties that elements inherit, and those they do not.

Inheritance

Inheritance is the process by which the value of a CSS property on one element passes down to a child element.

A general rule of thumb is that child elements inherit text-related properties but not box-related properties. But before that makes sense, we should probably discuss the box model.

Understanding the Box Model

The box model is an essential CSS concept—with some associated problems. Remember when we discussed inline and block elements? Each block element generates a box—invisible by default—that can be given padding within to push the content away from the edges of the box, borders on its edges, and margins to hold it away from other elements. The values for these properties can be applied as global values for the box or as individual values for each side.

Inside the padding is the actual content area where we place our page elements.

By default, the width of the box will be 100% of the width of its parent container. (The parent container could be a div or even the body element.) The box will expand enough vertically to enclose the content within it, but no further. Of course, we can also assign a width and even a height to the element. Seems straightforward, right?

Unfortunately, Internet Explorer 5 and 5.5 render the page using a broken box model and many of us initially learned to code our pages using this incorrect math. Internet Explorer 6 (and even 7) will emulate the broken box model rendering when there is no doctype or an incorrect doctype. This is known as **quirks mode**.

The W3C specs state that to determine the overall width of a box, we should add the padding and border values to the width we specified for the content within our box. But in quirks mode, that crazy Internet Explorer squeezes the padding and border into the width given to the content, arriving at a much different overall size. Margins do not have an effect on the calculations—they are always an additional value and simply hold the box away from other elements.

Other browsers, including Firefox, Netscape, Opera, Safari and IE7 (with a correct doctype) are standards-compliant, and follow the guidelines of the W3C. However, documents with no doctype also trigger quirks mode, which varies from browser to browser.

Let's look at an example: If we set the width of a box to 200 pixels and then add 20 pixels of padding and 2 pixel borders to each side, a standards-compliant browser will read the total space that the element occupies as 244 pixels. Internet Explorer, in quirks mode, will stuff the padding and borders into the box content width—so the element would only take up 200 pixels of space on the page! Let's give the Internet Explorer team some credit—the broken box model makes logical sense, but it's not what the spec says, and it's not what we work with in standards mode.

T   *The box model problem also applies to heights. But since the box by default expands vertically as long as there is additional content, this does not usually create problems like those that occur with explicit widths. Heights should rarely be used since in most cases it's better to allow the page to flow.*

FIGURE 1.12

Standards compliant browsers:
200 + 20 + 20 + 2 + 2 = 244px

Quirks Mode:
200 (20 + 20 + 2 + 2) = 200px

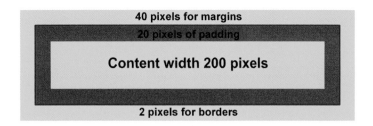

40 pixels for margins
20 pixels of padding
Content width 200 pixels
2 pixels for borders

John Gallant and Holly Bergevin of Community MX wrote an in depth article about the box model and its problems and solutions. You can read the article at http://www. communitymx.com/abstract. cfm?cid=E0989953B6F20B41.

With layouts that need to be pixel-precise, especially when using fixed widths, we may run into undesired results in browsers rendering in quirks mode. We need to have a way to render the box in both older and standards compliant browsers to the same width. This brings us to the unsavory topic of methods to deal with the challenges of the browser minefield.

Browser Anomalies

As you know, older versions of Internet Explorer pose more CSS challenges than standards-compliant browsers such as Safari, Firefox, Netscape, and Opera. Let's take a look at how the box model problem is corrected for IE in the two-column CSS layout.

INTERNET EXPLORER CONDITIONAL COMMENTS

Because Internet Explorer has so many *unique* ways of rendering CSS properties, we're fortunate that the Microsoft engineers had pity on us. As a workaround for all its quirks and headaches, they created something called the **Conditional Comment**. It allows us to set up conditions under which we can feed unique rules to targeted Internet Explorer versions. You can target all versions of IE, or just specific versions such as 5, 5.5, 6 or 7. You can even target less than a version or greater than or equal to a certain version using a specific syntax.

What follows is the basic syntax for Internet Explorer Conditional Comments (IECC) that are added to the head of the document. First, we set up the conditional statement that sniffs out a targeted version of Internet Explorer (highlighted below). Then we code a certain set of styles or a link to a style sheet containing those styles.

N *In the example we have one style block within an IECC and one linked CSS file within an IECC. Either can be used. The CSS layouts use a style block due to certain development limitations, but we like to move those styles into a separate style sheet that can be applied to every page for ease of updating. Who wants to update each page later if something changes? Not us! Dreamweaver does not yet have the capability of automating this process so you'll need to move these styles by hand.*

The following IECC selects all versions of Internet Explorer:

```
<!--[if IE]>
<style type="text/css">
Rules for all versions of Internet Explorer go here.
</style>
<![endif]-->
```

The following Conditional Comment targets Internet Explorer 6 and below:

```
<!--[if lte IE6]>
<link rel="stylesheet" type="text/css"
href="ie6andLessDocHere.css" />
<![endif]-->
```

When targeting anything other than a single, specific version of IE, the basic targeting syntax opportunities are as follows:

- `gt`: greater than the version number specified

- `gte`: greater than or equal to the version number specified

- `lt`: less than the version number specified

- `lte`: less than or equal to the version number specified

T *You can go to Microsoft's site to view the proper syntax for IECCs. Or you can download Paul Davis' IECC extension for $10 from Community MX. It will add the proper syntax to the head of the page for you using Dreamweaver. http://www.communitymx.com/abstract.cfm?cid=C433F*

Let's open the concepts.html document in Code view. We are going to look at the IECC containing the box model fix for the `sidebar1` div. In the style sheet, the `sidebar1` rule's content has a width value of 200 pixels. The left padding is 20 pixels, and the right padding is 10 pixels. In standards compliant browsers, the total will be 230 pixels. Browsers rendering in quirks mode will include the padding in the total, and compute the final overall width as 200 pixels. We need an IECC that targets Internet Explorer 5 and gives it a value of 230px so that when it includes the 30 pixels of padding, the overall box will be 230 pixels like the standard box model.

Locate the following code in the head of the document:

Place css box model fixes for IE 5* in this conditional comment

```
<!--[if IE 5]>
<style type="text/css">
.twoColFixLtHdr #sidebar1 { width: 230px; }
</style>
<![endif]-->
```

The CSS Styles Panel

The CSS Styles panel has two modes: you switch between them by selecting either the All or Current buttons at the top of the panel.

In All mode, the panel has two panes. The All Rules pane shows all the rules that affect the document, no matter how they are applied. Whether the rules are embedded, linked or imported, they appear in this pane. When you select a rule in the All Rules pane, its properties and values appear in the Properties pane.

In Current mode, the top pane shows a summary of all the properties and values that are affecting the element that's currently selected. This allows us to see the effect of the cascade on our element. When an element isn't doing exactly what we think it should and we need to troubleshoot, this comes in handy! Perhaps the text is red when we think it should be black: we can look in the Summary for Selection, find the color property, hover over it, and see what rule is overriding the red color.

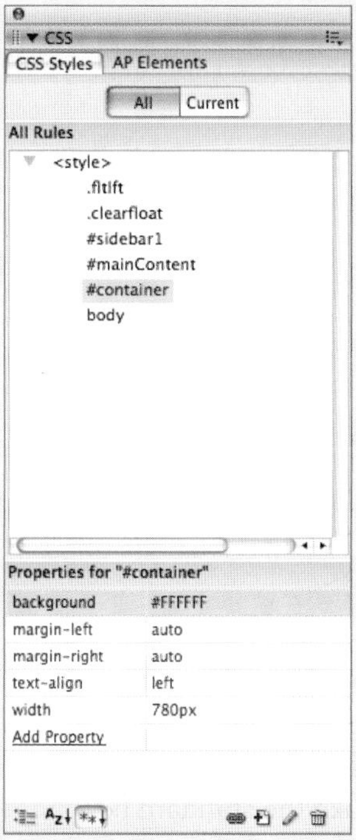

The middle pane of the Current mode has two sections—About and Rules. These are followed, just as in All mode, by a Properties pane showing all property/value pairs set on the currently selected element. If you select a property/value pair (declaration) in the Summary for Selection area, the About pane shows what rule contains the declaration as well as the CSS document in which it resides, and the Properties pane changes to show the specific rule.

Switching the middle pane to Rules view shows the cascade, from the body to our currently selected element. This is a handy way to move up and down the cascade viewing the various declarations in the property pane. Hovering over a rule shows us where the rule is contained as well as its specificity. This is another great troubleshooting tool since we can see when one rule is overriding another and if the latter needs to be made more specific to affect our element.

In the Properties pane, we can select an element and then use the Rules pane to move up the cascade to see what is affecting the element—or not affecting it. If the rule isn't inherited, Dreamweaver draws a line through it. When we hover over the rule, Dreamweaver creates a pop-up that explains why its property is not being applied.

With so many ways to utilize the CSS Styles panel, we find ourselves practically living there sometimes, usually in Current mode with the Rules pane selected.

FIGURE 1.11 Below the All Rules pane, the Properties pane shows the properties and values from the rule currently selected.

The hasLayout Property

In addition to its funny math in calculating the box model, Internet Explorer has a mysterious property called **hasLayout**. No such property exists as part of the CSS specifications, and no other browser uses it. It's the cause of many, many bugs.

So what is it? In general, think of **hasLayout** as a way in which Internet Explorer creates boundaries between, and relationships among, all page box areas. It's not a tangible property so much as an effect on surrounding objects and a way of calculating dimensions that economizes browser resources.

Some elements, such as the body, have **hasLayout** set to 'true' by default. Some properties trigger **hasLayout** when we use them in style sheets. Height, width and float directions all add **hasLayout**. Sometimes **hasLayout** needs to be triggered deliberately to fix an Internet Explorer bug.

Look again at concepts.html and locate the following code:

Place css fixes for all versions of IE in this conditional comment

This proprietary zoom property gives IE the hasLayout it needs to avoid several bugs

```
<!--[if IE]>
<style type="text/css">
   .twoColFixLtHdr #sidebar1 { padding-top: 30px; }
   .twoColFixLtHdr #mainContent { zoom: 1; }
</style>
<![endif]-->
```

N   *If you want to read a comprehensive reference on hasLayout, you can find the definitive guide at http://www.satzansatz.de/cssd/onhavinglayout.html—we'll warn you though, you'll need a lot of coffee—it's heavy reading!*

The #mainContent rule is adding a declaration to trigger **hasLayout** in Internet Explorer so that it draws the relationships among the divs more accurately. We are using the proprietary IE zoom property, a common way to fix bugs relating to a lack of **hasLayout** in the document. Don't ask us why (it's beyond the scope of this book)—it just works—and by using an IECC it validates and affects no other browser.

Positioning Techniques

CSS positioning properties allow us to manipulate the natural flow of the document and arrange boxes on the page into a pleasing and user-friendly design. This is the final concept you need to understand before we can dig in to actually creating a CSS layout.

The different positioning types (static, absolute, relative and fixed), as well as the use of floats for positioning, cover most layout situations. After we explore how each positioning type works, we will do some exercises to put some of them into action.

STATIC POSITIONING

Static positioning is the page default; the elements flow one after the other, filling the browser window with block and inline elements in their source order. Static positioning basically means that the element has no position—just the regular page flow.

Though it is the default, it's sometimes useful to explicitly set a layout to static positioning when we need to reset elements that have another kind of positioning applied to them. For example, printers can have trouble with pages with any kind of positioning; only one page may emerge from the printer or elements may be cut off. We can create a print style sheet that resets positioned elements to static so that they print properly.

RELATIVE POSITIONING

Relative positioning lets you give an element position in relationship to its static place in the flow of the document. If you set an element to relative positioning, but don't set values for the top, right, bottom or left property, the element remains in exactly the same place in the flow of the document as if it were using static positioning. But once you set these properties, the element will shift away from its natural spot in the page by the defined amount. The space it filled in the flow however, remains. Thus, if you give the element a 50px top and 50px left declaration, it will shift 50px in each direction, but there will be 50px of white space above and to the left of it. Nothing will fill that area.

N *You can also use negative values for these properties.*

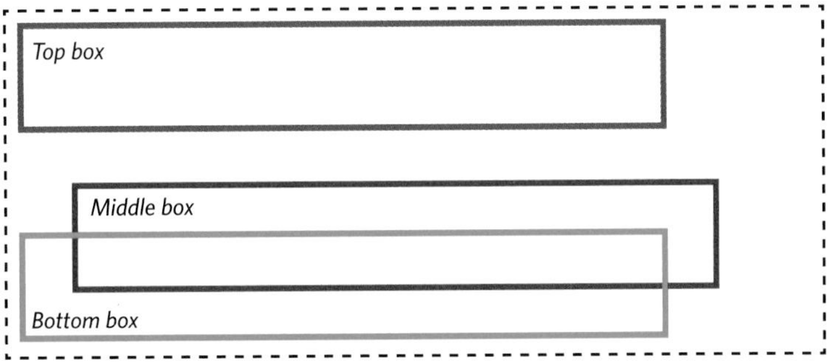

FIGURE 1.13 A relatively positioned middle box with the white space shown

Top box

Middle box

Bottom box

ABSOLUTE POSITIONING

Absolute positioning (AP) can be used to place objects on the page at precise X (horizontal) and Y (vertical) coordinates. The values of the AP elements derive their starting point from the last positioned parent element. This may not be the immediate parent: If the AP element's parent uses static positioning, it's not considered positioned, so the AP element looks farther up the document tree for a positioned ancestor. It may work its way all the way up the document tree to the body element (which is considered positioned) and set the X and Y coordinates from that point.

If you want your absolutely positioned element contained within a specific parent element, be sure to set the value of the parent element's position to relative. As stated above, relative positioning with no assigned values doesn't affect the element except to give the element a position that its children can use to figure their own position values.

Once the parent element has positioning, we can set values for top or bottom, and right or left for our absolutely positioned element. (We don't use both right and left, or both top and bottom, because these coordinates would fight each other, and that's such an ugly sight!)

Remember that (X)HTML provides a natural flow for the elements that begins at the top left of the browser window. Although we shift the elements around with CSS, the flow defines the ways in which they relate to one another. That is, except for AP elements. AP elements aren't very friendly. They're loners. Although they derive their position from a parent, they're outside the natural flow on the page; other elements can't relate to them and don't know where the AP elements begin or end. This can result in content overlapping and other unsightly messes unless the use of AP elements is carefully planned. You will see this in action in the exercises that follow.

FIXED POSITIONING

Like absolute positioning, elements with fixed positioning are set at a specific X and Y coordinate on the page. However, the position is always set in relation to the visible area of the browser window, known as the **viewport** (not the parent element like AP elements). When the visitor scrolls the page, the fixed content remains in an exact location on their screen.

Fixed positioning can be creatively used for background images, or navigation areas. Even when you scroll to read more content, the navigation area remains in the same place. Unfortunately, the only version of Internet Explorer that supports fixed positioning is the latest, Internet Explorer 7 (and the sooner that's adopted, the sooner we're all in better shape). Advanced CSS designers use scripts to force earlier versions of Internet Explorer to simulate the effect of fixed positioning, however in our experience this can often result in a stuttering scroll or flashing page refresh. If you're targeting early versions of IE, a lot of thought (and testing) should be used before deciding upon a fixed positioning solution.

Manipulating the Natural Flow

In this exercise, we are going to change the natural behavior of an image so that text wraps around it.

Floating Images

1. Open starter.html from the sample files for this chapter. This page has text very much like that used in the CSS layouts.

2. In Design view, place the cursor in front of the first paragraph of dummy text in the `mainContent` div, which begins with Lorem Ipsum.

   We are going to add a dummy, or placeholder, image to the page.

3. From the Insert menu, select Image Objects > Image Placeholder. Use the following values in the dialog:

   - Name: `Placeholder`
   - Width and Height: `200`
   - Color: `#CCCCCC`
   - Alt text: `Placeholder`

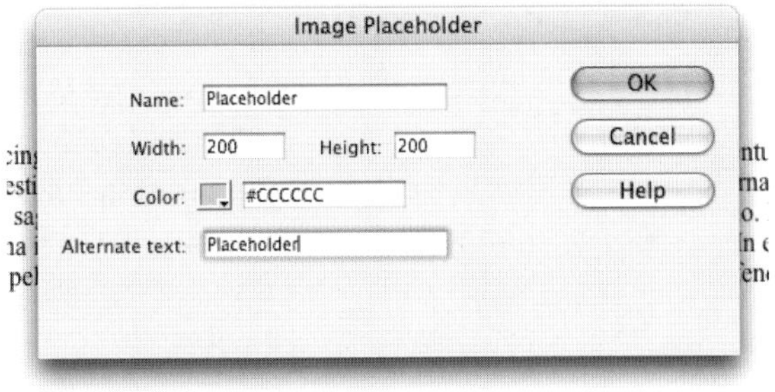

FIGURE 1.14 The Image Placeholder Image dialog box

N *Remember that class identifiers begin with a period. If you select the Class radio button in the New CSS Rule dialog however, Dreamweaver will automatically add the period for you.*

By default, images are inline elements. Thus, the placeholder image will appear at the baseline of the first line of text.

4. Click the plus button at the bottom of the CSS Styles panel to bring up the New CSS Rule dialog box. Select the Class radio button next to the Selector Type. In the Name field, type `.fltlft`. For Define in, select the radio button for "This document only".

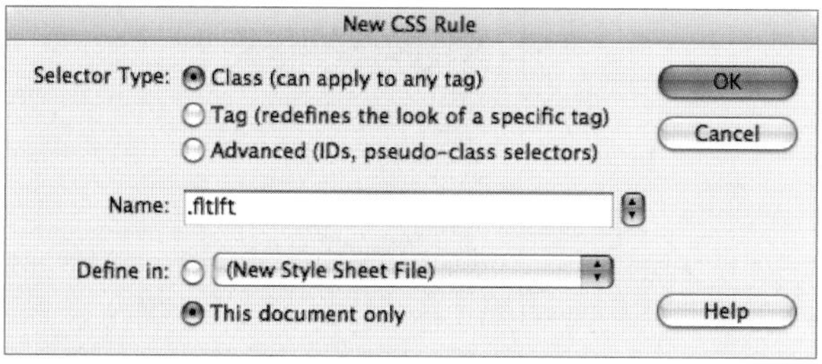

FIGURE 1.15 Rule definition for the left floating image class

New CSS Rule	
Selector Type: ● Class (can apply to any tag)	OK
○ Tag (redefines the look of a specific tag)	
○ Advanced (IDs, pseudo–class selectors)	Cancel
Name: .fltlft	
Define in: ○ (New Style Sheet File)	
● This document only	Help

As we mentioned earlier, many designers develop their pages by first embedding the styles in the head of the document, and then later, after the layout is complete, they export the styles to an external style sheet. Add to Head is the default method in the Layout CSS drop-down list for the CSS layouts.

5. When the CSS Rule definition for the `.fltlft` dialog box appears, select the Box category. Select left from the Float drop-down list. Deselect the "Same for all" checkbox under Margin. In the Right field, type 8. Leave the unit of measurement at pixels.

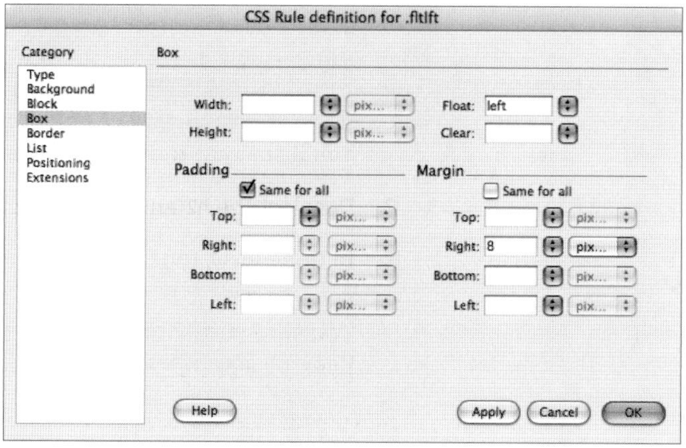

FIGURE 1.16 Float properties

CSS Rule definition for .fltlft		
Category	Box	
Type		
Background		
Block	Width: [ ] pix...	Float: left
Box		
Border	Height: [ ] pix...	Clear: [ ]
List		
Positioning	Padding	Margin
Extensions	☑ Same for all	☐ Same for all
	Top: [ ] pix...	Top: [ ] pix...
	Right: [ ] pix...	Right: 8 pix...
	Bottom: [ ] pix...	Bottom: [ ] pix...
	Left: [ ] pix...	Left: [ ] pix...
	Help	Apply Cancel OK

6. Click OK.

7. Click the image on the page to select it. Select the `.fltlft` class from the Class drop-down list in the Property inspector.

FIGURE 1.17 After applying the `fltlft` class to the image, the text wraps around it.

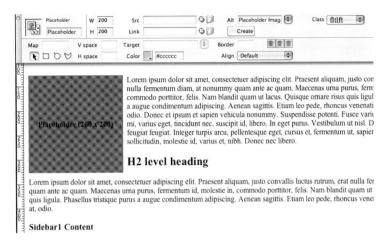

The text now wraps around the image. However, the next heading and its paragraphs wrap around the image as well. Sometimes this effect is what we're after, but other times we want to make the next heading and its text appear below the image. This is a job for the CSS `clear` property.

Applying a Clearing Element

1. Select the **h2** text "H2 level heading." Click the Split button in the document toolbar to enter into a split screen with code and design views.

You'll see that the **h2** text is also selected in code view.

2. Deselect the **h2** and place the cursor right above it.

3. In Code view, type a **br** element to create a line break and give it a class of `clearfloat`. Since we are using the XHTML Transitional 1.0 Doctype, add the space and forward slash before closing the element.

```
<br class="clearfloat" />
```

FIGURE 1.18 Adding a class to the br element

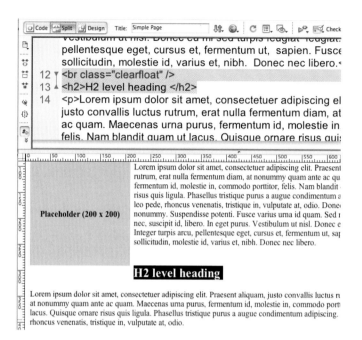

The break will provide a "hook" to add some properties via CSS that will clear the float while making sure it doesn't add any dimension to the page. Remember that browsers add their own default styles to elements, and thus add space that we may not want. In this case, the break is only there for the purpose of stopping the float effect so that the text that starts with the h2 doesn't wrap around it. There are various elements (such as a div) and other methods we could have used to clear the image, but this way is stable with older browsers and gives us a reusable element (with a class) that we can later apply to clear a floated column. (This method does add non-structural markup to the page to clear the float, and as such, some disagree with the method, but we do not yet live in a perfect web standards world!)

4. Click the plus button in the CSS panel to create a new rule called clearfloat.

5. When the New CSS Rule dialog box appears, select the Class radio button next to the Selector Type. In the Name field, type clearfloat. For the Define in option, make sure that the radio button for "This document only" is selected.

6. When the CSS Rule definition for .clearfloat dialog box appears, select the Type category.

7. For Size type 1 and leave pixels as the default. Give the Line height a value of 0. Select the Box category. Assign a value of 0 to Height. In the Clear drop-down list, select both. For the Margin, type 0.

FIGURE 1.19 Removing sources of dimension that the browser style sheet might add

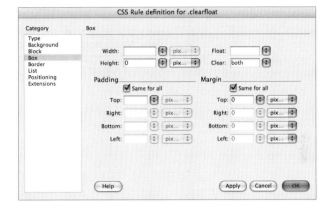

By making sure that the browser doesn't add any height, margin space, or line-height, and by setting the size of fonts to only 1 pixel—giving it that tiny size to prevent the break element from collapsing all together—we ensure that the break does the job of clearing the float without distorting the design with any unexpected dimension. By using `clear:both` instead of `clear:left`, the same class can be used for right or left floated images or columns.

8. Click OK.

The **h2** text and its paragraphs should now appear beneath the image.

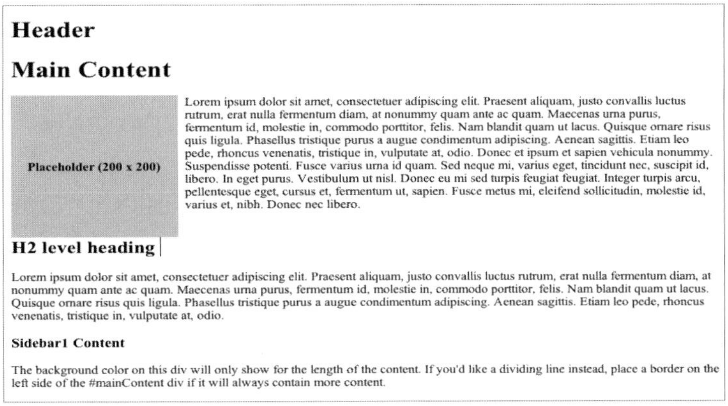

FIGURE 1.20 The result of applying the clearing element

Header

Main Content

Placeholder (200 x 200)

Lorem ipsum dolor sit amet, consectetuer adipiscing elit. Praesent aliquam, justo convallis luctus rutrum, erat nulla fermentum diam, at nonummy quam ante ac quam. Maecenas urna purus, fermentum id, molestie in, commodo porttitor, felis. Nam blandit quam ut lacus. Quisque ornare risus quis ligula. Phasellus tristique purus a augue condimentum adipiscing. Aenean sagittis. Etiam leo pede, rhoncus venenatis, tristique in, vulputate at, odio. Donec et ipsum et sapien vehicula nonummy. Suspendisse potenti. Fusce varius urna id quam. Sed neque mi, varius eget, tincidunt nec, suscipit id, libero. In eget purus. Vestibulum ut nisl. Donec eu mi sed turpis feugiat feugiat. Integer turpis arcu, pellentesque eget, cursus et, fermentum ut, sapien. Fusce metus mi, eleifend sollicitudin, molestie id, varius et, nibh. Donec nec libero.

H2 level heading

Lorem ipsum dolor sit amet, consectetuer adipiscing elit. Praesent aliquam, justo convallis luctus rutrum, erat nulla fermentum diam, at nonummy quam ante ac quam. Maecenas urna purus, fermentum id, molestie in, commodo porttitor, felis. Nam blandit quam ut lacus. Quisque ornare risus quis ligula. Phasellus tristique purus a augue condimentum adipiscing. Aenean sagittis. Etiam leo pede, rhoncus venenatis, tristique in, vulputate at, odio.

Sidebar1 Content

The background color on this div will only show for the length of the content. If you'd like a dividing line instead, place a border on the left side of the #mainContent div if it will always contain more content.

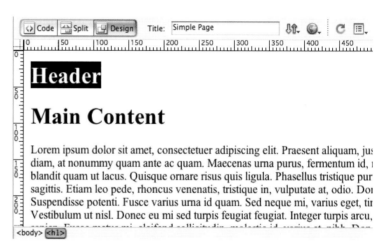

The tag selector is the bottom area of your document window. It contains the hierarchy of our page all the way to the element we've selected. For example: `<body><div#mainContent><h1>` When we say to click an element in the tag selector, be sure not to confuse that with the selector type that Dreamweaver identifies as a Tag selector (the one we prefer to call an element selector). When the tag selector is referenced, click the tag specified on the bottom of your document. Yes, it's quite confusing!

FIGURE 1.21 Using the tag selector to select the complete h1 element

Inserting a Div Tag

Continue using the page from the previous exercise (and delete the image holder and break element from the HTML, leaving the clearing class we created in the head), or use **create_div.html** from the Chapter 1 files. In this exercise, we will divide the page into different sections such as header, footer, and sidebar. The `div` element will be the building block to which we will give descriptive names that have semantic meaning.

1. Select the **h1** text Header. Click the <h1> in the tag selector at the bottom of the Document window to make sure that Dreamweaver includes both the opening and closing tags for the text.

FIGURE 1.22 Clicking the Insert Div Tag icon

The Insert Div Tag dialog box appears.

2. From the Insert toolbar, with the Common category selected, click the Insert Div Tag button.

3. For Insert, leave the menu at Wrap around selection.

    You want the opening Div tag to go before your selection, and the closing Div tag to go at the end of your selection so that it encloses all the text within.

4. Leave the Class field empty, and in the ID field, type header. Click OK.

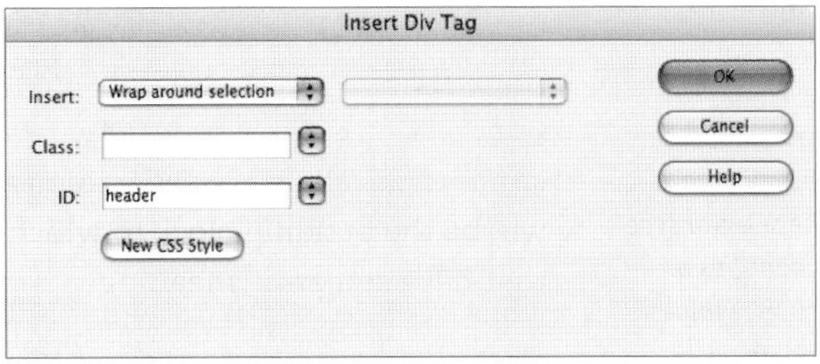

N *If you do not see the dashed line, you may have turned off the CSS Layout Outlines under Visual Aids (the Eye icon) in the Document toolbar.*

N *Dreamweaver has a tendency to exclude the opening and/ or closing tags of your selection, so it is a good idea to click the Split or Code view button and make sure the opening h1 and closing p are also selected.*

FIGURE 1.24 Ensuring that Dreamweaver includes opening and closing tags

Dreamweaver adds a dashed line around the area around the div or division of the page. The line is just a visual effect to help you see where each div on the page lies. You will not see this line in a browser.

5. Select all the text from the Main Content h1 title to the closing p tag of the paragraph after the h2 level heading.

```
27 ▼ <h1>Main Content </h1>
28   <p>Lorem ipsum dolor sit amet, consectetuer adipiscing elit. Praesent
     aliquam,  justo convallis luctus rutrum, erat nulla fermentum diam,
     at nonummy quam  ante ac quam. Maecenas urna purus, fermentum id,
     molestie in, commodo  porttitor, felis. Nam blandit quam ut lacus.
     Quisque ornare risus quis  ligula. Phasellus tristique purus a augue
     condimentum adipiscing. Aenean  sagittis. Etiam leo pede, rhoncus
     venenatis, tristique in, vulputate at,  odio. Donec et ipsum et
     sapien vehicula nonummy. Suspendisse potenti. Fusce  varius urna id
     quam. Sed neque mi, varius eget, tincidunt nec, suscipit id,  libero.
      In eget purus. Vestibulum ut nisl. Donec eu mi sed turpis feugiat
     feugiat. Integer turpis arcu, pellentesque eget, cursus et, fermentum
     ut,  sapien. Fusce metus mi, eleifend sollicitudin, molestie id,
     varius et, nibh.  Donec nec libero.</p>
29   <h2>H2 level heading </h2>
30   <p>Lorem ipsum dolor sit amet, consectetuer adipiscing elit. Praesent
     aliquam,  justo convallis luctus rutrum, erat nulla fermentum diam,
     at nonummy quam  ante ac quam. Maecenas urna purus, fermentum id,
     molestie in, commodo  porttitor, felis. Nam blandit quam ut lacus.
     Quisque ornare risus quis  ligula. Phasellus tristique purus a augue
     condimentum adipiscing. Aenean  sagittis. Etiam leo pede, rhoncus
   ▲ venenatis, tristique in, vulputate at, odio.</p>
31   <h3>Sidebar1 Content</h3>
```

6. From the Insert toolbar, again click the Insert Div Tag button. Leave the menu set to "Wrap around selection" as before. In the ID field, type mainContent. Click OK.

7. Select the Sidebar1 Content heading and the two paragraphs that follow it.

Again, use code view to make sure that everything from the opening of the first h1 to the closing tag of the second paragraph is included in the selection.

8. Click the Insert Div Tag button on the Insert toolbar and keep the same settings. In the ID field, type `sidebar1` and click OK.

9. Put your cursor within the text that reads Footer and select the `<p>` tag that appears in the tag selector at the bottom of the document window.

10. Insert a Div Tag from the Insert toolbar as before. This time, name the ID `footer` and click OK.

Your finished page will have four sections, each with dashed lines around them to provide a visual representation of where each div begins and ends.

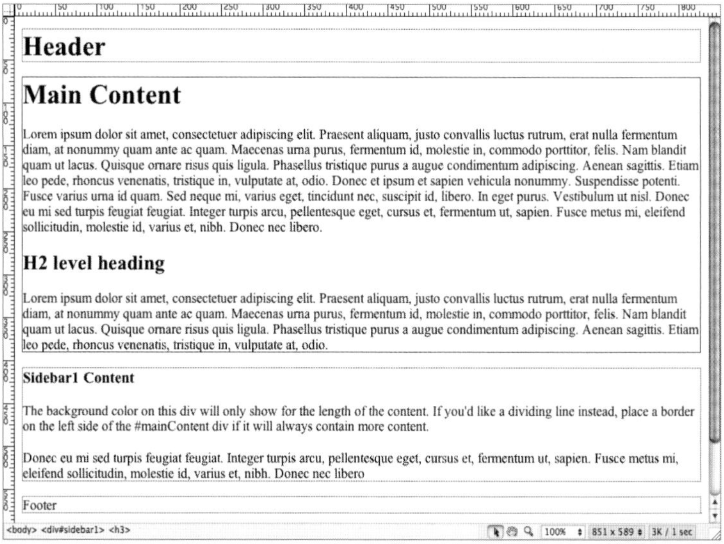

FIGURE 1.25 The page divided into divs

Columns with Absolute Positioning

Now that you have the page divided into sections, you can manipulate these by using different kinds of positioning techniques. Make sure your CSS Styles panel is open. If you do not see it on screen, go to Window > CSS Styles.

1. Continuing with the same file, click the new rule icon at the bottom of the panel.

The New CSS Rule dialog box will appear.

2. Select the radio button for Advanced (IDs, pseudo-class selectors). You will be making an ID style based on the name you gave the `sidebar1` div of the page.

3. In the field next to Selector, type `#sidebar1`. ID names always begin with the number sign (also known as a hash mark), and must be unique on the page.

4. For Define in, select the radio button for "This document only." Click OK and the CSS Rule definition for `#sidebar1` dialog box will open.

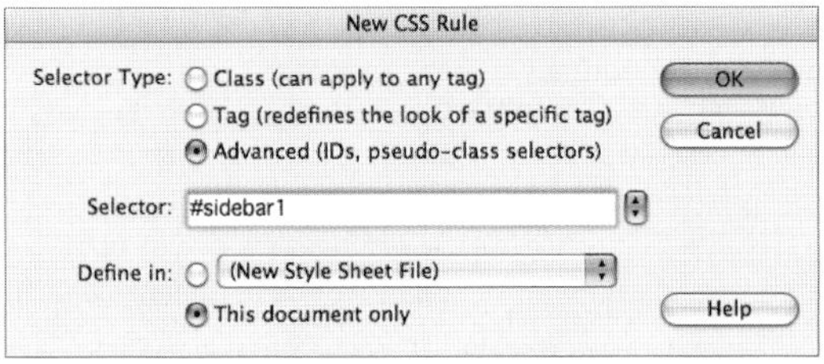

FIGURE 1.26 The `#sidebar1` rule

5. Select the Background category. In the Background color field, type #ebebeb. Select the Positioning category. For Type, choose absolute; for Width, type 200 and choose pixels (the default) as the unit of measurement. In the Placement section, for Top, type 80 and for Left, type 10. Choose pixels for the unit of measurement for both fields.

   The values for top and left are in relationship to the body, since that is the last positioned parent container of the `#sidebar1` div.

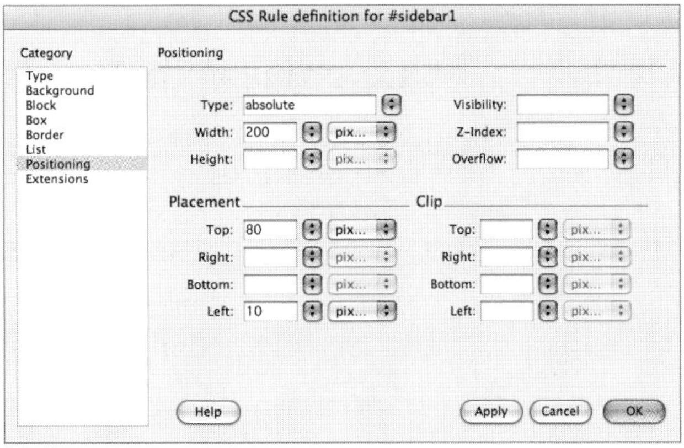

FIGURE 1.27 Absolute Position values for `#sidebar1`

6. Click OK.

You will probably be surprised at the result that appears in Design view in the Dreamweaver document window. The `sidebar1` div now partially covers the content area. As we mentioned earlier, an element with absolute positioning is taken out of the natural flow of the document. The other content no longer "sees" it and thus can't react to it. We will fix this in the next part of the exercise.

Header

Sidebar1 Content

The background color on this div will only show for the length of the content. If you'd like a dividing line instead, place a border on the left side of the #mainContent div if it will always contain more content.

Donec eu mi sed turpis feugiat feugiat. Integer turpis arcu, pellentesque eget, cursus et, fermentum ut, sapien. Fusce metus mi, eleifend sollicitudin, molestie id, varius et, nibh. Donec nec libero

nsectetuer adipiscing elit. Praesent aliquam, justo convallis luct n. Maecenas urna purus, fermentum id, molestie in, commodo ligula. Phasellus tristique purus a augue condimentum adipisc ulputate at, odio. Donec et ipsum et sapien vehicula nonummy rius eget, tincidunt nec, suscipit id, libero. In eget purus. Vestil u, pellentesque eget, cursus et, fermentum ut, sapien. Fusce m ero.

nsectetuer adipiscing elit. Praesent aliquam, justo convallis luct n. Maecenas urna purus, fermentum id, molestie in, commodo ligula. Phasellus tristique purus a augue condimentum adipisc ulputate at, odio.

7. As in step 1, click the New CSS rule button. Use the same values as before but give this rule the name `#mainContent` in the Advanced field. Click OK.

8. In the CSS Rule definition, select the Box category on the left. Under Margin, deselect the "Same for all" checkbox so that it is empty.

   We want to apply a unique margin to the Left field.

9. Type 225 for the value, and make sure pixels, the default unit of measurement, is selected. Click OK.

   The result should look much better to you. We've now carved out a 225-pixel margin for the sidebar area to slip into.

This is a pretty good method for creating the look of side-by-side columns. There is, however, one potential problem. As long as the content column is longer than the sidebar column, the footer will appear below both columns and all will be well. If the sidebar column is longer—as it might be if there were navigation links above the sidebar text—then the footer will overlap the `sidebar1` div. Just as the `mainContent` div did not see the absolutely positioned `sidebar1` div, the `footer` div will be equally unaware of its existence.

Try removing a big chunk of text from the `mainContent` div to see this in action.

FIGURE 1.29 Carving a left margin for the `mainContent` div

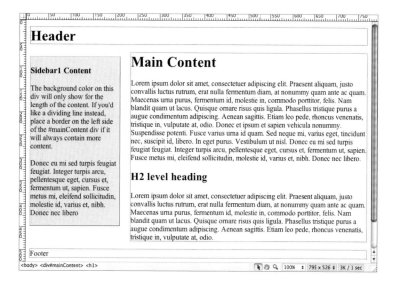

FIGURE 1.29 Carving a left margin for the `mainContent` div

The next method for creating side-by-side columns gives you the flexibility of either column being longest.

FLOATING COLUMNS

The page should still be open from the last exercise. If it is not, open it now. You can also use float.html from the Chapter 1 files.

1. Select the `#sidebar1` rule in the CSS Styles panel. (You may need to click the arrow next to the **style** element to expand the list of rules.)

2. Click the trashcan icon at the bottom of the panel to remove it.

FIGURE 1.30 Selecting the `#sidebar1` rule and clicking the trashcan to delete it

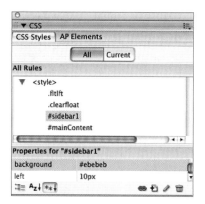

3. Select and delete the `#mainContent` rule as well. Your page will revert to non-positioned divs.

    When we want to float a div next to a non-floated element, we must place it in the source code before the element we want it to align with. Let's cut the `sidebar1` div and paste it before the `mainContent` div.

4. Put your cursor anywhere within the `sidebar1` div. Click `<div#sidebar1>` in the tag selector at the bottom of the document window to make sure the entire div is selected. Choose Edit > Cut.

5. Put your cursor anywhere in the `mainContent` div. Click `<div#mainContent>` in the tag selector at the bottom of the document window to make sure the entire div is selected, and press the left arrow key on your keyboard to place your cursor in front of the `mainContent` div. Choose Edit > Paste.

    Now your `sidebar1` div will be in front of the `mainContent` div.

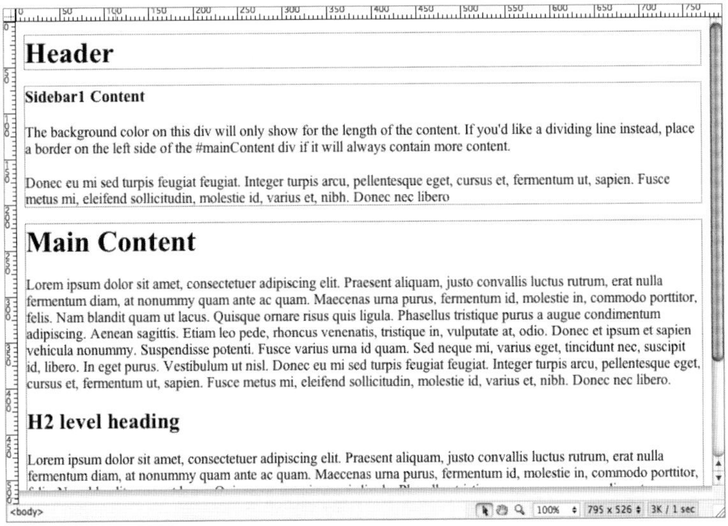

FIGURE 1.31 Moving the sidebar1 div before the `mainContent` div

Now we'll create a new Advanced rule for the `sidebar1` div.

6. Select the Background category, and next to the Background color field type `#ebebeb` as before. Select the Box category. In the width field, type 200 and set the measurement type to pixels.

    Remember, floats should have an explicit width, otherwise, the div will continue to fill 100% of its parent container.

7. Next to Float, select Left. Click OK.

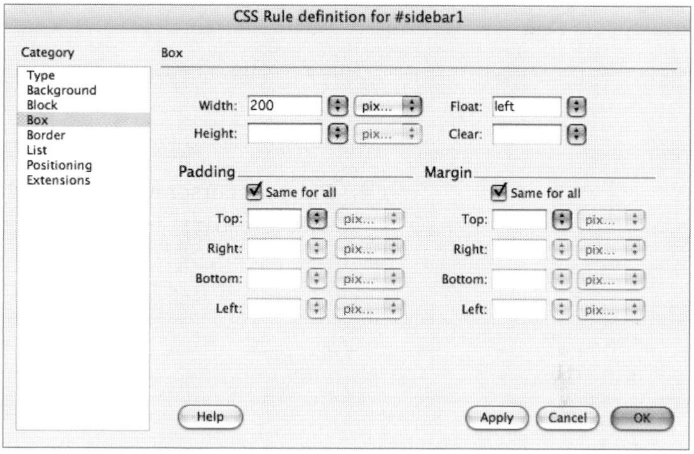

FIGURE 1.32 Adding the float property to the `sidebar1` div

FIGURE 1.32 Adding the float property to the `sidebar1` div

Now the `sidebar1` div is floated to the left of the `mainContent` div. However, you'll notice that once the content in `sidebar1` reaches its end, the `mainContent` div wraps around it. The default behavior for floats is that the elements that follow wrap around them. The `mainContent` div sees and makes space for the `sidebar1` div, but there is not really a true two-column look. We'll fix this by again carving out a left margin space on the `mainContent` div.

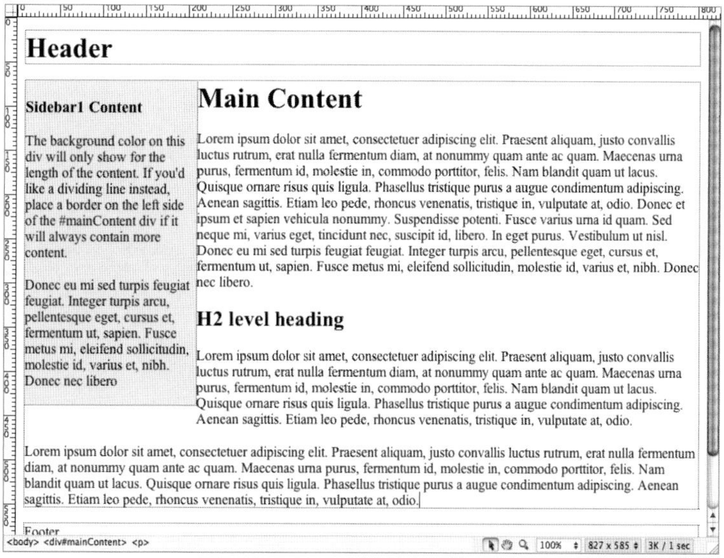

FIGURE 1.33 The float wrapping effect on columns

8. Create a `#mainContent` rule as you did in the floating images section. Select the Box category on the left. Deselect "Same for all" under Margin. Enter a value of 225 pixels for the Left property.

The look of two columns is now back.

As we look at the results, they look pretty similar to what we achieved using absolute positioning in the previous exercise. By floating our divs, however, we can allow either column to be longest without overlapping the footer div.

Clearing a Floated Column

The file from the previous exercise should still be open. Just as we discussed doing for the absolutely positioned exercise, let's make the two columns unequal with the `sidebar1` being the longest.

Copy the first paragraph or two in the `mainContent` div and paste the paragraph you just copied after the last paragraph in the `sidebar1` div.

FIGURE 1.34 The footer creeps up under the `mainContent` div.

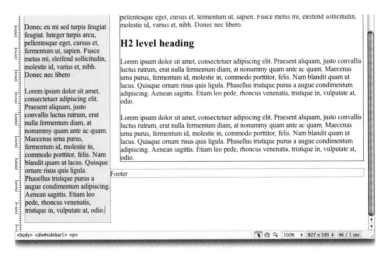

Hmm, that's strange. The extra text in the left column is still overlapping the `footer` div, though not the footer text. Think back to the image floating exercise. The image was taller than the paragraphs next to it, and the `h2` crept up to the space next to the image. Text stays next to a float until the float ends and then wraps below—unless the float is cleared.

Since the float is taken out of the flow of the document, elements following the float or containing the float, don't know exactly where it ends. But unlike the non-communicative absolutely positioned element, the shy float has a friend, the clearing element. When properly cleared, the other elements know where the float ends because of its relationship to the clearing element.

We haven't added a clearing element yet, so the `footer` div begins in the flow, right after the last element of which it's aware, the `mainContent` div. In fact, you can see that the footer will slide up under the floated div. However, a floated div will never overlap the content of a div/box; thus, the text stays out to the right of `sidebar1`. Let's solve this problem.

1. Put your cursor anywhere in the `mainContent` div, and select `<div#mainContent>` in the tag selector at the bottom of the document window to select the entire content area.

2. Press your right arrow key once.

3. In Code view, place a break element between the closing tag for the `mainContent` div and before the opening tag of the `footer` div and give it the class `clearfloat`.

```
</div>
<br class="clearfloat" />
<div id="footer">
    <p>Footer</p>
</div>
```

You already created the `clearfloat` class in the image floating exercise, so not only will Dreamweaver allow you to select it in the code hints as you type, but as soon as you return to Design view, the effect should be apparent. The footer now clears the `sidebar1` column!

Before you continue to the next exercise, delete the extra text that you pasted into the `sidebar1` column.

Centering a Layout

1. Click anywhere in the page and then click `<body>` in the tag selector at the bottom of the Document window.

    This will select everything on the page.

N *If you're not in Split view, click the Split button in the Document toolbar so that you see both code and design.*

N *In developing the CSS layouts for Adobe, one goal was to remain consistent across layouts and another was to keep the layouts solid and simple as starter points that users could develop more fully. In this example, we could apply a clear property to the footer div, but with further development by the user, the results could be unexpected. We chose a clearing method that's very solid and reliable in older browsers.*

2. Insert a Div Tag from the Insert bar. Give it an ID of `container` and click New CSS Style.

   The dialog shown will be auto-filled with `#container`.

3. Choose to define in this document. Click OK.

4. Select the Background category and for the Background color, select white.

5. Select the Box category. Set the Width to 780 pixels.

   This width allows users with a screen resolution of 800 by 600 to view the page without encountering horizontal scrollbars. Using 20px less than a full 800px width allows for the room taken up by the browser chrome, e.g., the scrollbar area, window borders, etc.

6. Deselect "Same for all" under Margin. Select auto from the drop-down lists next to Right and Left.

7. Click OK on both dialogs.

FIGURE 1.35 Setting auto margins on the container to center it

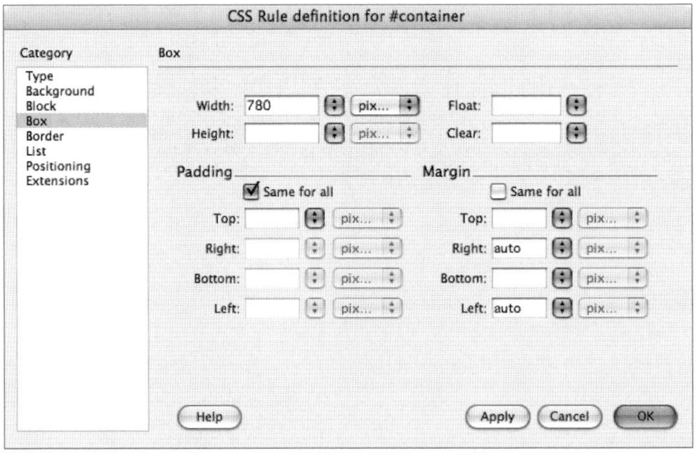

In a perfect world, that would be it. A width and the auto value for the right and left margins will center a div in modern browsers.

When we look at the page in Internet Explorer 4, 5, or 5.5 (6 and 7 when in quirks mode), we see a very different result: the auto margins are ignored. We'll have to use one simple line of wizardry to support these browsers.

Fortunately (we guess), these browsers get something else wrong: they center block elements as well as inline elements when you use `text-align: center;`. Therefore, if we add this declaration to the body rule of the page, these browsers will center everything on the page.

1. Create a new rule for the body.

2. Select the Background category and type #666666 in the Background color field.

3. Select the Block category. From the Text align drop-down list, select center. Click OK.

FIGURE 1.36 Setting text align to center on the body

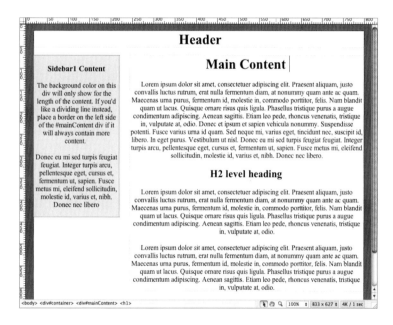

Of course, due to inheritance, everything is now centered, including all of the text. That's not exactly what we had in mind. We'll need to reopen the container rule (or simply type in Code view) to reset the text back to its default left alignment. The container will stay centered via the text-align property in the body rule, and all the divs nested in the container will align left via the text-align property for the container.

1. Double-click the `#container` rule in the CSS panel using the All view to reopen the `#container` rule. (Or, choose `<div#container>` on the tag selector and click the edit/pencil icon at the bottom of the CSS Styles panel.)

2. Select the Block category. Set the Text align property to left. Click OK.

FIGURE 1.37 The final result, centered in all browser versions— even early and quirks mode browsers

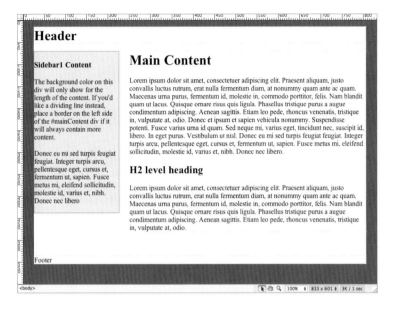

We now have a basic reconstruction of a CSS layout. To complete the layout, we would need to add the missing text formatting, margins, and padding that are in the two-column fixed CSS layout that comes with Dreamweaver CS3. But instead we'll dive into a real layout in the next chapter.

You should now have an understanding of using CSS to create layouts in general, as well as the specific CSS layout in Dreamweaver that represents a common web layout: two-column, fixed-width with header and footer. With this knowledge of essential CSS concepts behind us, let's delve into more complex methods for using Dreamweaver's CSS layouts.

To read more about the escaping margin effect that comes as a result of margin collapse, read The Practice of CSS Column Design: Boxes in Columns *by John Gallant and Holly Bergevin at* http://www.communitymx.com/ abstract.cfm?cid=CB7B3

Margin Collapse

The CSS layouts contain almost no styling for text elements. However, in the header and footer divs, you'll find that the top and bottom values have been "zeroed out." We establish the breathing room around the elements with padding instead. The reason for this is called **margin collapse**. The top and bottom margins for such elements often do not stay contained inside their parent div. Instead, they spill outside it holding the div away from the div above or below and causing a confusing gap if you don't understand what's going on.

This is not a bug but is actually the proper behavior, though in some cases it's undesirable. For example, if we have two paragraphs stacked one after the other, we wouldn't want the 10 pixels of margin space on the bottom and the 10 pixels of space on the top of the second paragraph to be added together, morphing the space into a height of 20 pixels. The W3C provides for this contingency by collapsing the 20 pixels into one 10-pixel value (if the margins that are touching have unequal values, the largest will be used). This collapsing effect influences how margins interact within divs. Of course, the effect works differently in Internet Explorer. Go figure!

In addition to removing margins by applying a 0 value, adding even one pixel of padding or a border at the top and/or bottom fixes the problem too. In the CSS layouts, an IECC was used to give IE more padding on the sidebars. Since IECCs do not appear in the CSS Styles panel, this can be nearly invisible to people who do not work in Code or Split view. This IECC requires us to change the padding value within IECC when we change the layout values from their defaults, possibly causing confusion.

A better solution might have been to remove the top margin from the first element in the sidebars (as was done in the header and footer). People wanting to add a margin back to their elements might have been confused by the margin collapse behavior, but it would have shown up in the CSS Styles panel. Apologies for any confusion or hair-pulling that may have ensued if you didn't find that immediately.

Our recommendation is to remove that rule from the IECC and either remove the top margin using a descendant selector, or create a class that removes the top margin from any element you place it on.

```
.noTop {
  margin-top: 0;
}
```

Using the Fixed, Centered Starter Pages

PROBABLY THE MOST COMMON layouts on the web, especially with blog-type sites becoming more popular, are fixed-width layouts. These layouts have an overall pixel width, side columns with specific pixel widths, and are usually displayed in the center of the browser window, though that's not required.

One reason this layout style is used so often is that when you have static sizes for most elements, interactions are more predictable. That makes the layout easier to design and code, because there are fewer unknowns.

For this chapter, we'll use a fictitious client, a horticulture site. We'll look at how to center your layout, create full-length columns, use and position background images, style and size fonts, and rearrange the pages and float the main content div to change your source order. We'll also see some good uses for absolute positioning. We've got a lot to cover, so let's dive in!

FIGURE 2.1 A screen shot of the final outcome shows what we'll be creating in this chapter.

Before proceeding, define a site within Dreamweaver CS3 and create a folder to contain your files. If you're unfamiliar with defining a site, go to Help > Dreamweaver Help > Working with Dreamweaver sites > Setting up a Dreamweaver site to learn more. If you're using our sliced images, place them into a directory called images within your site definition.

Beginning to Build

Let's begin by creating a new page using File > New. In the Blank Page section of the dialog, select Page Type of HTML and in the Layout area, choose the 2 column fixed, right sidebar, header and footer layout. Set the DocType to XHTML 1.0 Transitional and make sure that Create New File is selected. Click Create.

New Document
Page Type:
Layout:
Blank Page
Blank Template
Page from Template
Page from Sample
Other
HTML
HTML template
Library item
XSLT (Entire page)
XSLT (Fragment)
ActionScript
CSS
JavaScript
XML
ASP JavaScript
ASP VBScript
ASP.NET C#
ASP.NET VB
ColdFusion
ColdFusion component
JSP
PHP
<none>
1 column elastic, centered
1 column fixed, centered
1 column liquid, centered
2 column elastic, left sidebar
2 column elastic, right sidebar
2 column fixed, left sidebar
2 column fixed, right sidebar
2 column hybrid, left sidebar
2 column hybrid, right sidebar
2 column liquid, left sidebar
2 column liquid, right sidebar
Two columns, all widths in pixels, with right sidebar, header and footer.
DocType:
XHTML 1.0 Transitional
Layout CSS:
Create New File
Attach CSS file:
Help
Preferences...
Get more content...
Cancel
Create

FIGURE 2.2 Create a new page using the fixed-width CSS layout.

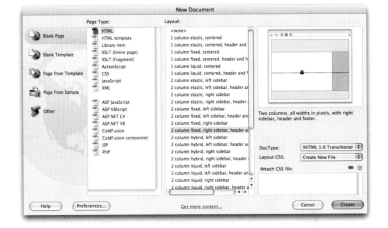

When prompted, save the CSS document with the default name (or any name) and save the HTML document as index.html. Dreamweaver has just created a solid, structure-only document so we can start creating our web site. Notice that all the divs are shades of gray. This lets us see where everything is, but isn't meant to stay: we'll be removing the gray as we change the various rules.

Header
Main Content
Lorem ipsum dolor sit amet, consectetuer adipiscing elit. Praesent aliquam, justo convallis luctus rutrum, erat nulla fermentum diam, at nonummy quam ante ac quam. Maecenas urna purus, fermentum id, molestie in, commodo porttitor, felis. Nam blandit quam ut lacus. Quisque ornare risus quis ligula. Phasellus tristique purus a augue condimentum adipiscing. Aenean sagittis. Etiam leo pede, rhoncus venenatis, tristique in, vulputate at, odio. Donec et ipsum et sapien vehicula nonummy. Suspendisse potenti. Fusce varius urna id quam. Sed neque mi, varius eget, tincidunt nec, suscipit id, libero. In eget purus. Vestibulum ut nisl. Donec eu mi sed turpis feugiat feugiat. Integer turpis arcu, pellentesque eget, cursus et, fermentum ut, sapien. Fusce metus mi, eleifend sollicitudin, molestie id, varius et, nibh. Donec nec libero.
H2 level heading
Lorem ipsum dolor sit amet, consectetuer adipiscing elit. Praesent aliquam, justo convallis luctus rutrum, erat nulla fermentum diam, at nonummy quam ante ac quam. Maecenas urna purus, fermentum id, molestie in, commodo porttitor, felis. Nam blandit quam ut lacus. Quisque ornare risus quis ligula. Phasellus tristique purus a augue condimentum adipiscing. Aenean sagittis. Etiam leo pede, rhoncus venenatis, tristique in, vulputate at, odio.
Sidebar1 Content
The background color on this div will only show for the length of the content. If you'd like a dividing line instead, place a border on the right side of the #mainContent div if it will always contain more content.
Donec eu mi sed turpis feugiat feugiat. Integer turpis arcu, pellentesque eget, cursus et, fermentum ut, sapien. Fusce metus mi, eleifend sollicitudin, molestie id, varius et, nibh. Donec nec libero.
Footer

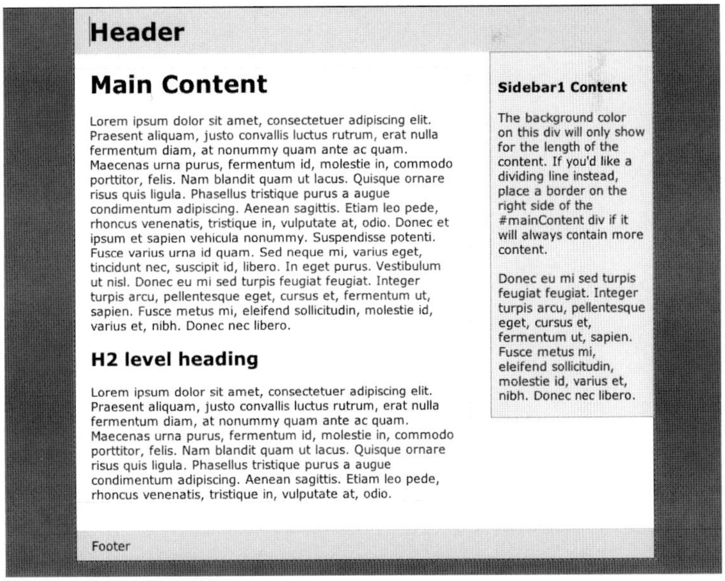

FIGURE 2.3 Dreamweaver CS3 gives us a totally gray palette to start.

Preparing the HTML Document

In Code view, we see the class `twoColFixRtHdr` on the body and preceding nearly every selector in our style sheet. Every CSS layout in Dreamweaver has a class on the body, with a similar pattern. It can be deciphered as follows:

- `twoCol`—two column

- `Fix`—fixed-width

- `Rt`—right column

- `Hdr`—header and footer

Following this pattern, a three column, elastic layout with header and footer would have the class `thrColElsHdr`. A three column, elastic layout without header and footer would be missing the `Hdr` at the end of the rule, leaving it as `thrColEls`.

These classes were created to keep the CSS code succinct while still letting us combine layout types (see Chapter 6). But when all pages of the site use the same layout, it becomes difficult to view all the information for descendant selectors in the Current view of the CSS Styles panel because the names are so long. Since the class isn't necessary unless you're combining layout types, we'll remove them at the outset using Find and Replace. For example, we'll turn `.twoColFixRtHdr #header h1` to just `#header h1`, which takes up considerably less room.

1. In your CSS document, select the text `.twoColFixRtHdr` (as well as the space that follows it) on any of the descendant selectors.

2. Select Edit > Find and Replace (Cmd+F).

    Dreamweaver automatically adds our selected class to the Find portion of the dialog.

3. Leave the Replace area blank (and be sure Ignore Whitespace is unchecked).

4. Click Replace All.

    All of the initial classes on your descendant selectors will be removed.

5. Do the same in your HTML document since the Internet Explorer Conditional Comments (IECC) are contained there.

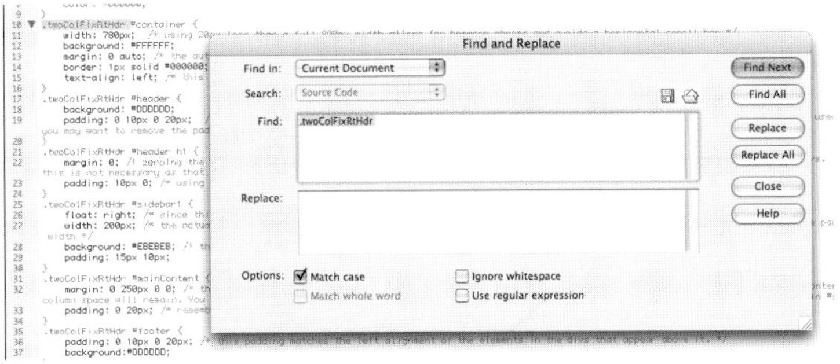

FIGURE 2.4 Use the Find and Replace dialog to strip the class names out of your pages.

N *Take a moment to look at the code in the CSS document. Within it are many, many comments that explain all the rules and declarations and describe what might be otherwise unexpected interactions between elements. Each type of CSS layout has comments specifically applicable to that layout.*

6. Finally, as shown in Figure 2.5, remove the class from the body element by right-clicking the body tag on the tag selector at the bottom of your document.

7. Choose Set Class > None.

FIGURE 2.5 Use the tag selector to remove the class from the body element.

Preparing the Comp

The point of this chapter is the techniques we teach and integrate into the CSS layout, not the look of the comp. To the graphic designers among you—make your layout more beautiful!

You don't have to use a graphics program to create page layouts using the CSS layouts. You could simply build the pages in Dreamweaver using a graphics program to create background glows and drop shadows, the rounded corners, and so on. We find, however, that either wire-framing and/or building the design in a graphics program is a much quicker and more efficient way to visualize our final outcome—before we get into the code at all. For this particular chapter, we created the overall look in Fireworks, although we didn't add the Latin text and headings.

N *You'll find this comp in the source directory of your download for this chapter (along with all the exported slices).*

The first step, before we begin to slice the comp, is to envision how it will be divided as HTML. Think in terms of vertical and horizontal lines. Though our page may not be all horizontal or vertical—it may be very curvy—we still have to break it up into square and rectangular areas to code. Don't ever feel limited by straight lines, however. There are creative ways to include portions of graphics into the tops and bottoms of other page divisions. We'll look at those as we progress through the chapter.

FIGURE 2.6 The page with divisions highlighted.

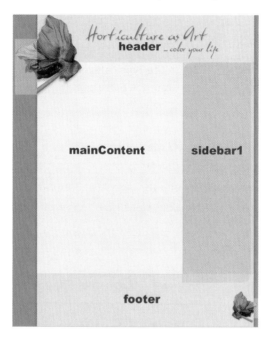

T   *You'll find that your slice's exported size, created from Fireworks, is substantially smaller than Photoshop. If you own Fireworks, we recommend that you do your web optimization there.*

For this chapter, we used Fireworks because we appreciate its vector and export abilities for the web. (We'll use Photoshop in Chapter 4). The slices we created are named within the comp. If you're following along in a classroom setting, or would like to practice slicing the comp as well, simply save the file under another name and delete the slices in the Web layer. You can also re-slice and Save for Web & Devices in Photoshop if that is your program of choice.

Styling the Body Element

Let's begin our work with the body selector. We often write and edit code within Code view, but in this chapter, we'll use the CSS Styles panel and CSS dialog. Feel free to work within your comfort zone and type directly in Code view using Dreamweaver's code hinting and code completion if you prefer.

1. With the body tag selected on the Tag selector at the bottom of the document, click the edit (pencil) icon on the CSS panel.

Dreamweaver will open the CSS Rules definition dialog.

T *There are a couple of different ways to find the color. You can choose the color in a graphics program, and copy and paste it into Dreamweaver. Or you can click and hold the Color Picker in the CSS Styles panel edit dialog next to Background color, and release the eyedropper over the background color in the graphics program: Dreamweaver will automatically fill the sampled background color into the Background color input.*

2. In the Background category > Background color, remove the default #666666 and replace it with the background color of the overall page in our comp, #7F98C3.

3. In the Type category, add a 1.5 value for line-height. In the drop-down list next to it, choose multiple as the unit of measure.

This will set the line height as a multiple of the size of the font of the element. It will appear in your CSS code with no unit of measurement.

4. Click the drop-down list next to the Font input. Choose Edit Font List at the bottom.

The Edit Font List dialog will appear. The fonts on our system will appear in the Available fonts list on the right. Instead of using one of the standard font lists Dreamweaver provides, we're going to create a new list. When we've completed it, the order will be Helvetica Neue, Helvetica, Arial, sans-serif.

5. Choose Helvetica Neue if it's shown in the list and click the left arrow key.

It will be moved to the Chosen fonts list on the left. If it doesn't exist on your system, no worries. You can still use it in your font list. Simply type the name into the input below the Available fonts list and then click the left arrow button to move it to the Chosen fonts list.

FIGURE 2.7 Creating a new font list using a font that doesn't exist on the system.

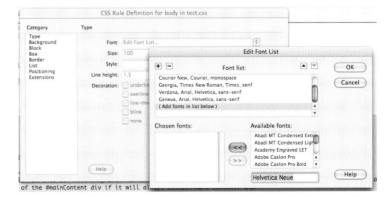

6. Create the complete list by continuing with Helvetica, Arial and the generic sans-serif. Click OK.

7. Choose the font list we just created from the drop-down list. Click OK on the CSS Rules definition dialog.

Styling with Font Cascades

We can create any font cascade we'd like. But here are a few things to keep in mind:

The order the fonts appear in matters. The browser attempts to render the text beginning with the first font on the list. But that only works if that font exists on the user's system! If it doesn't, the browser moves through each font in order finally ending with the generic font family (serif or sans-serif most commonly). For this reason, put your most desired font first in the list, followed by the next-most desired font and so on.

Sometimes we'd like to use a font for the Mac that doesn't exist for Windows, which means we need to also include a more common font for Windows users. If you do this, be sure that the Mac-only font comes first if the Windows font also exists for the Mac; otherwise the less-desirable font will be rendered on both platforms.

When creating new font cascades, test the default size of the fonts you choose. Make sure to create a font cascade that uses fonts in similar sizes in order to ensure that your user will see what you expect!

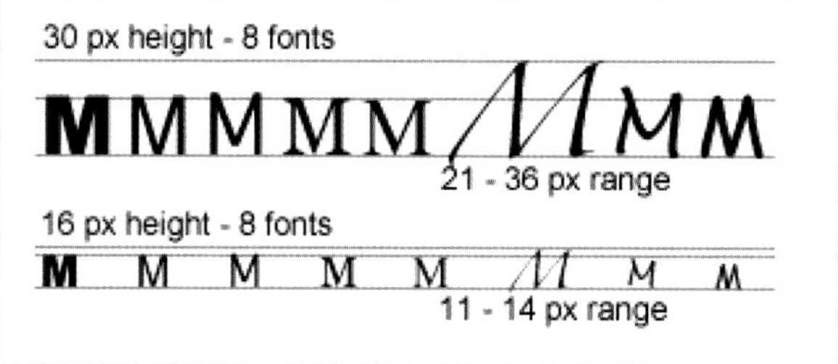

FIGURE 2.A Font sizes, even at the "same size" vary from family to family.

30 px height - 8 fonts

MMMMM/VIMM

21 - 36 px range

16 px height - 8 fonts

M M M M M /I M M

11 - 14 px range

Using Shorthand Properties in CSS

N *For the sake of space in the book, when we post code blocks, we don't include the comments. We do include them in our code, however, so the files will sometimes look slightly different.*

Your body rule should now look like this:

```
body {
    font: 100%/1.5 "Helvetica Neue", Helvetica, Arial, sans-serif;
    background: #7F98C3;
    margin: 0;
    padding: 0;
    text-align: center;
    color: #000000;
}
```

If you look at the font property, you may notice that your CSS may not look like ours. If you have individual font values on each line instead of all in one line, it is due to the way the CSS preferences are set in Dreamweaver: we keep our preferences set to write shorthand.

So what in the world is shorthand anyway? Simply put, shorthand lets you specify several values with a single property. It can be quite a space saver in CSS documents and once you get used to it, it makes it much easier to read your pages.

Order is generally quite important when using shorthand, because one property name may have several values following it.

Let's look quickly at a couple of shorthand examples, beginning with the font property. There are six possible values for font: font-style, font-variant, font-weight, font-size, line-height, and font-family. If one of these values is not declared, the default for the value is used.

In the case of our style sheet, you can see that we declared the font-size, line-height, and font-family. This means the other three properties are left at their default values. Our shorthand declaration equals this block of code:

```
font-style: normal;
font-variant: normal;
font-weight: normal;
font-size: 100%;
line-height: 1.5;
font-family: "Helvetica Neue", Helvetica, Arial, sans-serif;
```

The shorthand for applying background values is similar to font shorthand. The property is called **background** and it has five possible values: `background-color`, `background-image`, `background-repeat`, `background-attachment`, and `background-position`. Thus, `background: #7F98C3 url(images/body_back.jpg) repeat-y left top;` is equal to:

```
background-color: #7F98C3;
background-image: url(images/body_back.jpg);
background-repeat: repeat-y;
background-attachment: scroll;
background-position: left top;
```

Border is a similar property. It allows us to set the width, style and color of the borders of a box. It does not allow us to make one of the sides different than the other, however. To do that, we need to declare that value separately. So for instance, if we want to set the width of the left side border of our box to be 2px and the rest to be 1px, we could write it like this:

```
border: 1px solid #000;
border-left-width: 2px;
```

In the border example, you see the color defined as #000. This is equivalent to #000000. Some colors can be converted to shorthand and others can't. RGB color is written with a hash mark, immediately followed by either three or six characters—#RRGGBB or #RGB. That means a value like #006699 is equivalent to #069 and #FF9933 is the same as #F93.

The first line sets the entire box to have a 1px black border with a solid style. The second line overrides the width of the left border. Remember the cascade—to override the 1px border, the 2px border must come after it.

Font, background, and border are the most common mixed value shorthand properties.

Two other shorthand properties that we'll use throughout the book are margin and padding. The shorthand for these properties allows us to set all four sides of the box at once. Both properties are written in the same way: the specific order is top, right, bottom, left. People use different tricks to remember the order: you can think of the rule as trouble, from the acronym TRBL, or more simply, as clockwise (start at the top and moving around the box). After years of experience, we still find ourselves using our tricks of choice as we write our code.

For example, `margin: 0 20px 10px 15px;` is equal to:

```
margin-top: 0;
margin-right: 20px;
margin-bottom: 10px;
margin-left: 15px;
```

When the values of all four sides are the same, only one value needs to be used since it applies to all four sides: `margin: 0;`

Notice there is no unit of measurement after the 0. This is because, no matter what unit you place after zero—pixels, percent, em units—the value is still the same, zero.

If you're using equivalent top and bottom values as well as equal side values, you can use only two values: `margin: 10px 15px;`

This indicates that the top and bottom values are 10px and the right and left are 15px.

Finally, if your top and bottom sides have different values from each other, but the sides are the same, you can use three values in your shorthand: `margin: 0 20px 15px;`

This tells the browser to render 0 on the top margin, 20px on the right margin, 15px on the bottom and the lack of a fourth value indicates that the left side is equivalent to the right side. So it's 20px as well.

As you can see, shorthand is cool and it's absolutely the way we want to write our code. It's much too handy to not use, so throughout the rest of the book, we'll be using shorthand. Let's make sure you can do the same!

Dreamweaver CSS Preferences

The key to having Dreamweaver automatically write the shorthand for us, saving tons of time, is in the preferences. Dreamweaver actually gives you a lot of power within its preferences, but many people never venture in. Let's bravely enter!

1. Go to Edit > Preferences. (On the Mac, go to Dreamweaver > Preferences).

2. From the Category list, choose CSS Styles.

3. Make the following choices:

When creating CSS rules: Use shorthand for: (Check all properties)

When editing CSS rules: Use shorthand: According to settings above

When double-clicking in CSS panel: Edit using CSS dialog

While we're in the preferences window, let's look at one more thing.

4. From the Category list, choose Code Format. Notice there's a new setting there—Advanced Formatting. Click the button that says CSS.

FIGURE 2.8 CSS Code formatting preferences—Awesome!

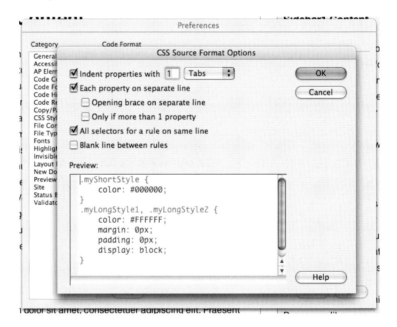

Dreamweaver opens the CSS Source Format Options dialog. This dialog allows us to set the way Dreamweaver, by default, writes our CSS. We're not going to change anything here now, but if you have a specific style you prefer to write your CSS in, it's likely you can set the indention, or the way Dreamweaver spaces your lines and other formatting preferences, to suit your personal style.

T   *The CSS formatting preferences can be handy in other situations as well. If you inherit a style sheet from someone else, formatted in an unusual way, you can choose Commands > Apply Source Formatting to the page and it will be reformatted according to your preferences. In addition, some people like to remove most of the white space before uploading their CSS by putting all declarations for a rule on one line. Though we find it difficult to work this way as we develop a site, it's quite simple to change your preferences to place the entire rule on one line, apply the new source formatting, and then upload the style sheet. Once that's complete, change the preferences back to your usual way to work. Voila! An instant removal of white space without all that tedious hand deletion we used to have to do.*

5.   Click OK to close and save your Preferences.

Using Background Images

Back to our layout!

This fixed-width comp is designed to be centered in the browser's viewport. Centering is a common technique since on today's larger monitors left-aligning the design can leave a lot of space to the right. Centering an element, like the container div, is accomplished by using the auto value for the left and right margin. Our design has an overall glow highlighting each side of the page, which wraps around the bottom, giving it the illusion of a three-dimensional object.

The design also contains a right column that needs to go all the way down to the footer, no matter how much content it contains. You may remember that in Chapter 1 we mentioned that the background color of a div ends when the content ends. There is no reliable way (outside of using JavaScript) to force columns to be equal in size and thus the color on one column will end shy of the other column. We'll create the illusion of equal height columns using a technique called faux columns.

Faux, in French, means false. During the faux painting craze of the 90's, many homes were painted using techniques that created the illusion of wood, stone, marble, or even a window, plant or animal in a room where there was none. That's the idea which is behind the faux column technique—we'll be creating the illusion of a column going to the footer of our page. It's almost as if we're painting with graphics.

Creating the "Faux" Right Column

Take a look at the current gray sidebar1 column for a good example of how a column ends when the content in it ends.

FIGURE 2.9 The gray column on the right ends when the content ends.

Adding a background image or color on the sidebar1 div doesn't fix the problem, because the background still ends where the content does, so instead we'll place the background image on the element containing sidebar1. In the case of the CSS layouts, that element is the container div that holds the entire layout.

You may use the column.gif slice created for you in your images directory. Or, in your graphics program of choice, export a slice from the white edge at the right of the comp to the left edge of the column. Make the slice about 10-15px high.

FIGURE 2.10 The columns slice, shown on the gray Fireworks canvas.

1. Click anywhere in your page and in the tag selector at the bottom, choose <div#container>. In the CSS Styles panel, click the Edit Style icon (pencil).

2. From the CSS Rule Definition dialog, choose the Background Category and set the following values:

Background image: (use the Browse button to create the correct path to the image) `column.gif` (in your images directory)

Repeat: repeat-y (this is the vertical axis)

Horizontal position: right

Vertical position: top

3. Click OK.

Since the default value of a background image is top left, and our column is on the right side of the content div, we must set our `column.gif` to begin on the right side of the element. The `repeat-y` property will allow the graphic to repeat from the top of the container div to the bottom. And yes, this includes behind both the header and the footer, so we'll make sure we have a background color or image in those divs to cover this faux technique.

The y axis is a vertical repeat and the x axis is a horizontal repeat. Setting your image with these values allows you to have a narrow slice that repeats over and over saving bandwidth.

```
#container {
    width: 780px;
    background: #FFFFFF url(images/column.gif) repeat-y
    right top;
    margin: 0 auto;
    border: 1px solid #000000;
    text-align: left;
}
```

4. Click into the `sidebar1` div, right-click the background property in the Properties pane of the CSS Styles panel and choose delete. This will get rid of Dreamweaver's default gray column.

Let's have a look at the page. There's a nice blue-gray column running all the way to the footer even though it's obvious the div stops well before it. If you want to peek under the header or footer, take its background color off and you'll see how obvious it is that this is a faux or false column.

Creating the Outer Glow

Our page didn't just have a column running the full length, did it? The technique we just used will work to create equal columns, but we've also got the outer glow or drop shadow appearance on our overall page. We can use the same technique with a different image. Create a slice (or use the one provided in your images directory) that goes from the outer edge of the left glow to the outer edge of the right glow. Ours is 10px tall and 700px wide (including the area outside the white page area on either side which is 9px). Include the right column we just applied in this image. We'll be replacing that right column now. Export it as a jpg (we named ours `body_back.jpg`) into the images directory of the site definition.

FIGURE 2.11 Overall page slice, including the column, shown on the gray Fireworks canvas.

N *No matter how wide you create your page graphic, be sure you have equal amounts of glow on both sides. Otherwise, you're going to have to tweak values to make it appear centered.*

1. Select the container div. Click the edit icon and in the Background category, remove the Background color and browse to the `body_back.jpg` image. Click Apply.

    We've removed the background color since it's no longer needed. The image contains the white page color as well as the column and outer page glow.

2. Remove the background placement values of vertical and horizontal.

    Since the graphic and the div will be the same width, there's no need to specify where the graphic should begin. It will begin at the top, left by default.

    We can see that the image from our comp is not the same width as the CSS layout. The image we're using is 700px wide. We need our container to match that width. Remember though, we've got the 9px on either side that isn't *really* part of our page. In the comp, it appears to be the outer edges, so we'll need to account for that.

3. In the Box Category, uncheck the "Same for all" box and set 9px of padding for both the left and right.

    Remember that padding is added to the overall width of the box in the proper box model.

4. Set the width to 682px.

    The width is 682px because 700px - 9px - 9px = 682px. This gives us the proper width for our container div.

5. In the Border Category, remove the border from all sides of the container and click OK.

N *All the CSS layouts come with a border to allow you to visualize the edges of the layout more easily. Many times you'll want to remove it.*

```
#container {
    background: url(images/body_back.jpg) repeat-y;
    margin: 0 auto;
    text-align: left;
    width: 682px;
    padding-right: 9px;
    padding-left: 9px;
}
```

Preview the page in a standards-compliant browser. Wow! It's really beginning to take shape, isn't it?

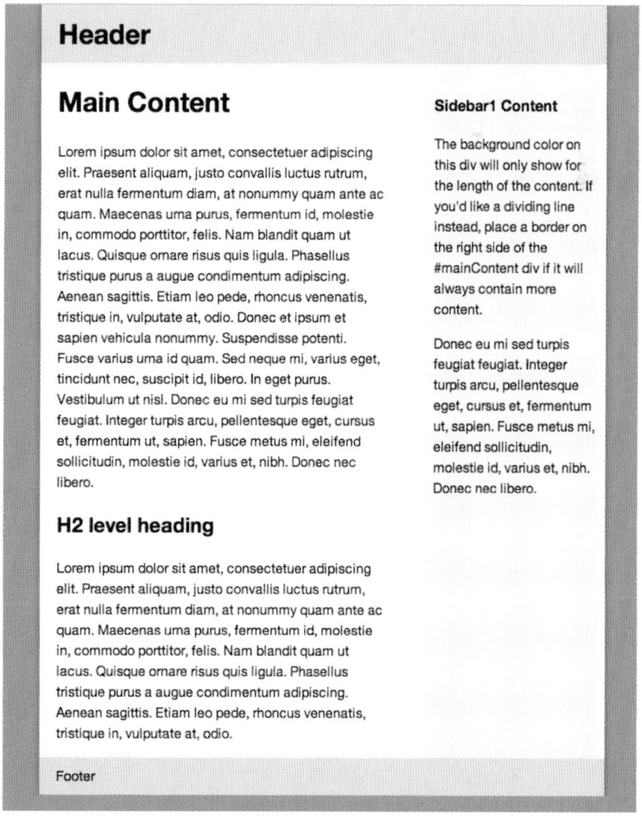

FIGURE 2.12 Our partially completed page—we've got the column and the glow!

Header

Main Content

Lorem ipsum dolor sit amet, consectetuer adipiscing elit. Praesent aliquam, justo convallis luctus rutrum, erat nulla fermentum diam, at nonummy quam ante ac quam. Maecenas urna purus, fermentum id, molestie in, commodo porttitor, felis. Nam blandit quam ut lacus. Quisque ornare risus quis ligula. Phasellus tristique purus a augue condimentum adipiscing. Aenean sagittis. Etiam leo pede, rhoncus venenatis, tristique in, vulputate at, odio. Donec et ipsum et sapien vehicula nonummy. Suspendisse potenti. Fusce varius urna id quam. Sed neque mi, varius eget, tincidunt nec, suscipit id, libero. In eget purus. Vestibulum ut nisl. Donec eu mi sed turpis feugiat feugiat. Integer turpis arcu, pellentesque eget, cursus et, fermentum ut, sapien. Fusce metus mi, eleifend sollicitudin, molestie id, varius et, nibh. Donec nec libero.

H2 level heading

Lorem ipsum dolor sit amet, consectetuer adipiscing elit. Praesent aliquam, justo convallis luctus rutrum, erat nulla fermentum diam, at nonummy quam ante ac quam. Maecenas urna purus, fermentum id, molestie in, commodo porttitor, felis. Nam blandit quam ut lacus. Quisque ornare risus quis ligula. Phasellus tristique purus a augue condimentum adipiscing. Aenean sagittis. Etiam leo pede, rhoncus venenatis, tristique in, vulputate at, odio.

Sidebar1 Content

The background color on this div will only show for the length of the content. If you'd like a dividing line instead, place a border on the right side of the #mainContent div if it will always contain more content.

Donec eu mi sed turpis feugiat feugiat. Integer turpis arcu, pellentesque eget, cursus et, fermentum ut, sapien. Fusce metus mi, eleifend sollicitudin, molestie id, varius et, nibh. Donec nec libero.

Footer

If our design didn't have the glow around the bottom of the page, we could actually put an image on the body element containing just the page side glow, leaving the single column on the container. In that case, the page side glow effect would run the full length of the browser viewport, regardless of the content within. With some designs, this may be desirable.

One issue to remember if you choose to put a background image of any kind on the body element is that Internet Explorer 7 has zoom capability. This can be lovely for people with low vision: they can simply scale the entire page up, not just the text. But Microsoft got one little thing wrong. Background images on the body element don't scale up with the rest of the page. Thus, text could end up on a background color you didn't anticipate, making it illegible. This can be especially problematic with the faux column technique.

Luckily, there's a simple fix. If we place a background color on the HTML element, IE7 will zoom the background on the body element. Why? Who knows, it's IE. But it works and it's valid. If you'd like to keep your CSS organized, you could place the fix into a style sheet that's fed only to IE7 using an Internet Explorer Conditional Comment (IECC) (see Chapter 1.) Otherwise, place the fix in your regular CSS, but leave a comment next to it so that you or any developer that comes after you know why it's there.

Creating the Header

Most of the time, we work on our pages in a specific order. First come backgrounds and faux columns. Then, we move from the top down, from the header to the footer. We'll turn our attention to the header area now.

This example may be fairly pedestrian, but let your creative brain think about the possibilities opened up by the techniques we're going to demonstrate.

The comp our designer handed us has a couple interesting design elements. The flower in the header overhangs the left side of the page and the small flower at the bottom right slightly overhangs the right side.

It's obvious from the comp that the client still wants to cater to the 800x600 resolution crowd. In order to keep the main area of the page centered in the browser window and not have the overhanging design elements go outside the viewport, the overall page (measured from the outside of each flower) is 770px.

FIGURE 2.13 The large flower overhanging the edge of the page glow.

Be sure to allow approximately 15px for browser chrome—the outer area of the browser—when choosing the width to create your comp. An 800px resolution target would have a maximum width of 785px. A 1024px target shouldn't exceed 1009px. In fact, many people choose a 980px resolution. If your client has statistics on who uses their site, use them to help decide on a target width. Resolution statistics can vary widely based on the audience of the web site.

The images directory contains an image called `lg_flower.jpg`. If slicing, leave the background in and slice from the top of the page to each edge of the flower. Make sure to include the drop shadow under the flower. (Our image measures 218px x 250px.)

Absolute Positioning—Not Always Evil

With CSS, there can be a variety of ways to create the same effect. We're going to use a positioning technique here. Remember in Chapter 1, we discussed the problems with absolute positioning since the element is taken out of the flow of the page and nothing on the page reacts to it. In most cases, we want to avoid absolute positioning an element that contains text and is given a height. In our case however, the image is a static height and width but contains no text that could cause the size to vary. This is a safe element on which to use absolute positioning.

Sometimes the fact that the absolutely positioned element is taken out of the flow of the page can be advantageous. We can place our image anywhere in the HTML of the container and set the positioning so it will appear at the top where we want it. In light of that, since this is a decorative page element we can move the code for it down to the bottom of our page. This keeps non-essential code out of the top area of our page, moving our text up, which is always a good thing for search engine spiders searching for tasty words.

1. Place your page in Split view (our favorite way to work) and place your cursor in the footer. Click `<div#footer>` on the tag selector and press the right arrow key on your keyboard.

   This will place your cursor between the end of the `#footer` and the end of the `#container`.

2. In the Common category of the Insert bar, click the image icon (sixth from the left). Navigate to `lg_flower.jpg` and select it. In the Image Tag Accessibility Attributes dialog, choose `<empty>` from the drop-down next to Alternate Text. Click OK.

N *There is some argument over whether a non-essential decorative element should be described to the non-sighted using the alt attribute. We would argue that most people (including those with sight) are coming to the web site for information, not to hear descriptions of the design. In this case, we chose to use an empty alt attribute. No matter your decision, the alt attribute should either be filled in with a brief description or given the alt="" (called empty) alt attribute to keep Assistive Technology (AT) from reading aloud the name of the image.*

In the Design view portion of your document, you'll see that the image is simply sitting down at the bottom of the page. We need to create a rule to position it up in our header area.

3. Select the flower image. On the bottom of the CSS Styles panel, click on New CSS Rule icon (document with +).

   Dreamweaver opens the New CSS Rule dialog with the Selector name pre-filled (#container img). Since it opens with the path to the image as the descendant selector name, we need to change it a bit.

4. Leave Selector Type: set to Advanced and Define in: to your external page. Change the Selector Name: to #container .overhang and click OK.

5. In the Category list, select the Positioning category. Choose the following values.

   Type: Absolute
   Top: 0
   Left: -65px
   Click OK

6. Right-click <img> on the tag selector. Choose Set Class > .overhang.

   Notice in the Design view the image has moved up to the top, but it's certainly not right where we want it. In fact, it's negatively margined off the left edge of the page!

   Remember that an absolutely positioned element positions itself off its last *positioned* ancestor. Since the container has been left with its default static positioning, it's not considered positioned at all. It takes at least relative positioning for an element to be considered positioned. So the image is calculating its negative left position off the body element, its last positioned ancestor.

T *An absolutely positioned element will continue up the document tree until it finds a positioned ancestor and will calculate its x and y coordinates from that point. If it doesn't find an element to position from along the way, it will position itself from the body element.*

```
#container .overhang {
   position: absolute;
   left: -65px;
   top: 0;
}
```

7. Select the **#container** and in the Properties pane of the CSS Styles panel, click Add Property. Type position (or choose it from the drop-down list) on the left column and choose relative from the drop-down list on the right column.

The flower is now in its proper position, but as you can see, the other page elements aren't aware it's there. We'll deal with that as we go.

Adding the Logo

Slice the logo from the comp or use the **logo.jpg** image in the site files.

1. Place your cursor into the header. Right-click the **<h1>** element on the tag selector and choose Remove tag.

   Dreamweaver will remove the **h1** that surrounds the word header leaving the word highlighted.

2. Press delete/backspace to remove the highlighted word and in the Common category of the Insert bar, insert the **logo.jpg** image. Type Horticulture as Art into the alt attribute. Click OK.

   You'll notice that the **logo.jpg** is inserted into the header, but it's sliding beneath the flower due to the absolute positioning. The header doesn't have as much space as in the comp either.

3. Select **<div#header>** in the tag selector. In the Properties pane of the CSS Styles panel, change the value of the background property (currently the default **#DDDDDD**) to the shorthand **#FFF**.

4. Change the padding values to be 40px on the top, 20px on the bottom, 0 on the right and 150px on the left.

The 150px on the left will keep the logo from sliding beneath the flower div. The padding on the top and bottom will create the needed space. The shorthand should look like this:

```
#header {
    background: #FFF;
    padding: 40px 0 20px 150px;
}
```

5. Save your page and preview in a standards-compliant browser.

FIGURE 2.15 The header and sides have really taken shape!

T *If you were linking to a real file, you would either type the name and path of that file into the input area or click the folder on the right of the input and navigate to the file you want to link to. Using a hashmark (#) causes Dreamweaver and browsers to style the element as a link for design purposes.*

Usability experts will tell you that users expect to have the site's logo link to the home page. We're going to give our users what they expect.

6. Click on the logo image. In the Property inspector, add the link by placing a # in the Link input below the Src input.

FIGURE 2.16 Ew! What's the ugly blue border?

We've suddenly found a bright blue outline around our logo. We're betting both the designer and the client will be unhappy with the mess we made! Don't worry, there's a quick fix: we'll create a simple rule to get rid of it. Since we've not yet defined our link colors, the default blue still applies. The border on our image is simply the default blue link color indicating that the image is linked.

7. Open your CSS document.

You'll notice the order of rules begins with the **body**, moves to **#container**, and then to each division on the page starting at the top with **#header**. In the header area, you'll see a rule called **#header h1** that is no longer in use (remember, we removed the **h1** element in the **#header**). Let's completely remove that as we create the rule needed for the blue border.

8. Find the **#header h1** rule, select the whole thing (including the ending curly bracket) and click delete.

Yes, we could have deleted it directly in the CSS styles panel before the element was removed from the page, smarty! Since we didn't, we're going to get our hands dirty in the code (our favorite place). Hey, it had to happen at some point!

9. Leaving our cursor in place, we'll create the new rule. Directly in your CSS code, type: **a img** (read by the browser as "any image that is a descendant of an anchor element)."

10. Type the opening curly bracket (**{**) and press return. Press tab. (The tab is just to keep the same styling as our other rules.)

Dreamweaver presents us with a helpful drop-down list of possible properties. As you start typing the selector name, the list continually gets more targeted.

11. When you see the **border** property highlighted, press return.

Dreamweaver adds the property name along with the colon separating it from the value.

12. Type **n** and the code hinting list will jump to **none**. Select **none** by pressing return. Add the semicolon, press return and add the closing curly bracket.

```
a img {
    border: none;
}
```

Though we love Dreamweaver's CSS Styles panel, sometimes it's just quicker to work directly in the code. Dreamweaver's code-hinting tools make it painless.

Our header is now complete with the blue border removed. We're really crankin' now!

T *When the CSS document is open, any changes you make using the CSS Styles panel will require you to save the CSS document before previewing the changes outside Dreamweaver.*

Rounding the Side Column

We're sure it didn't slip by your keen eye that our side column actually has a rounded corner at the top and the bottom. Like all CSS techniques, there's more than one way to skin the proverbial cat. In our case, the upper left and lower right corners are rounded. (With a fixed-width layout, however, the method would be similar even if the entire box were rounded since we can anticipate the exact width of the column.)

We want to keep presentation and structure separated as much as possible, so we're not going to place the image directly into the code for the top and bottom of the column. In fact, placing the bottom rounded graphic into the column itself would display that graphic where the right column content actually ends. Since our column background is actually "painted" on the container, the rounded corner could end up sitting somewhere in the middle. Yuck!

Let's Start at the Top

Let's think about our options. The top is simple, of course, because the top of the column will always be at the visual top of the column. The graphic we created for the top is a 28 x 28px slice containing only the left corner. We called it **corner_tl.gif** (tl stands for top, left in our shorthand).

FIGURE 2.17 The top left rounded corner of the side bar, in Fireworks.

Be sure, when you're slicing your own corners, to slice all the way to the area where the box becomes completely straight. This will ensure that you have perfect graphic/background color blends every time.

1. Place the **corner_tl.gif** image into **sidebar1** as a background image using the CSS Styles panel. (We know you can do this yourself by now—just click the edit icon on the bottom of the CSS Styles panel).

2. Set the Repeat property to **no-repeat**. Click OK and preview your page in a standards-compliant browser.

    We notice the border isn't sitting flush against the left side of our column graphic. That's because we haven't made any adjustments to our column size based on our designer's vision. We've still got our divs set to their defaults. In order to begin these adjustments, we'll first create a simple element selector for our **p** element. This will allow us to visualize more clearly the space available in the various divs.

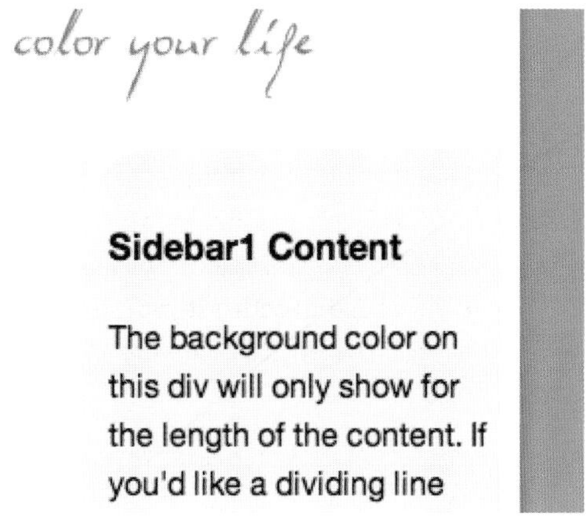

FIGURE 2.18 Hmmm...the corner doesn't meet up perfectly, does it?

color your life

Sidebar1 Content

The background color on this div will only show for the length of the content. If you'd like a dividing line

3. In the CSS code, or using the CSS Styles panel New CSS Rule icon, create a simple element selector for the **p** element. Set the font-size to 85%.

   If you allowed Dreamweaver to create the rule, it has placed it at the bottom of your list of rules. We like to stay organized as well as keep later cascading issues in mind, so we're going to move that up—just below the **a img** selector we created.

4. Change to the All mode of your CSS Styles panel.

   If all you see is your CSS page name, you need to click the little arrow button to its left to view all the rules within it.

5. Click-hold the **p** selector at the bottom and drag it up the list, dropping it directly below the **a img** rule.

   This is an awesome feature in Dreamweaver that allows you to manage and reorder your style sheets and rules right in the All mode window. Since CSS is a *cascading* language, this is a great timesaver!

   In our graphics program, we took some measurements. The width of the right column is 214px. It is sitting 10px away from the right edge of the page. 214 + 10 = 224. Our **sidebar1** div is currently 200px. Let's make the adjustments to our padding and width on **sidebar1** so the corner matches up.

6. Change your panel back to Current mode. Click into the **sidebar1** div.

Since we've added the **p** element selector, clicking into the **sidebar1** div shows us the properties for the **p** element first. Use the Rules pane to move up the cascade to the **#sidebar1** rules.

7. In the Properties pane, change the side padding to 20px on each side.

200px + 20 + 20 = 240px. This is too wide: we want that 224px width. Since we have to include the padding in this measurement, let's work backwards: 224 - 20 - 20 = 184.

8. Change the width value for **#sidebar1** to **184px**. Save and preview in your browser.

```
#sidebar1 {
    float: right;
    width: 184px;
    padding: 15px 20px;
    background: url(images/corner_tl.gif) no-repeat;
}
```

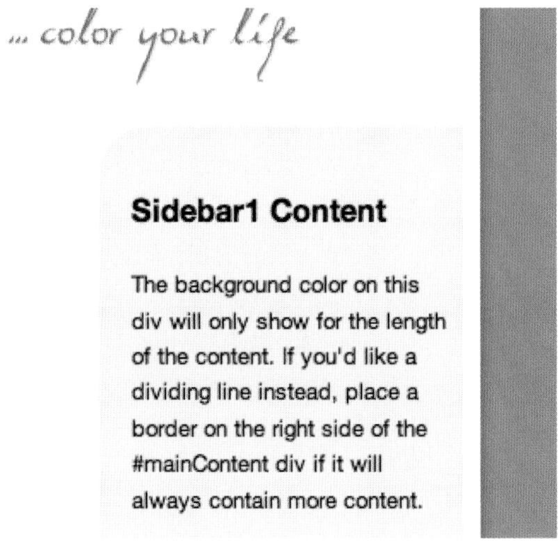

FIGURE 2.19 Ahhh—now this is more like it!

... color your life

Sidebar1 Content

The background color on this div will only show for the length of the content. If you'd like a dividing line instead, place a border on the right side of the #mainContent div if it will always contain more content.

Creating a Faux Bottom

We've recreated the top of our column, but now it's time to tackle the bottom. Whether we add the curved corner as a background image or into the sidebar1 div itself, unless the side column has more content than the main content area, we'll end up with an unsightly mess. The rounded bottom would end where the content ends and the column would continue. What other options do we have?

Let's think about what elements meet up with the side column—visually at least. On the bottom, we have the footer. What if we placed the bottom graphic of the column directly into the footer? No matter where the column ends, it would have a rounded bottom.

In your sliced graphics, you'll find our version of the sliced bottom graphic—called **corner_br.gif** (yes, br stands for bottom right). If you're slicing your own, slice from the right side of the white page area to the very left edge of the column. Make your slice as tall as the rounding of the corner—ours is 28px tall just like the top corner was.

Remember that, currently, only one background element can be placed on each element. If the footer requires its own background element, we could wrap a div around the mainContent *and* sidebar1 *divs, and place the column bottom on the bottom-right of that wrapper div instead. There's always another way!*

FIGURE 2.20 The bottom slice of the column, in Fireworks.

We tend to edit background images within the dialog since we can more easily navigate to the graphics. For simple property additions or value changes, we more often work directly in the Properties pane.

1. Place your cursor into the footer div and in the Rules pane, select **#footer**. Click the edit icon to change the properties.

2. In the Background Category, change the background color to white (#FFF or #FFFFFF). Add the Background image by navigating to the **corner_br.gif**. Set it to **no-repeat**. Click Apply.

   Your graphic is in the footer, but it's on the top left, not the top right.

Footer

FIGURE 2.21 Our image is in the footer, but in the default position.

By default, background images are applied beginning at the top left corner of an element.

3. Add Horizontal position: **right** and Vertical position: **top**. Click OK.

```
#footer {
    padding: 0 10px 0 20px;
    background:#FFFFFF url(images/corner_br.gif) no-repeat
right top;
}
```

FIGURE 2.22 We've got the entire column looking just like our comp!

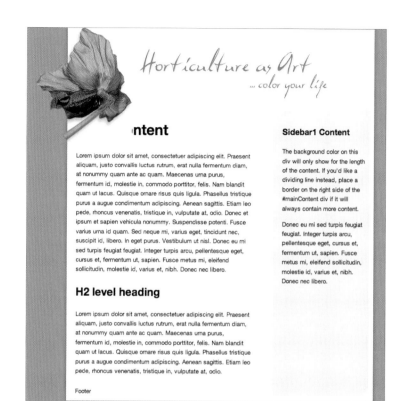

Adding the Bottom of the Page

Well, heck. While we're down here working in the bottom of the page, it might be a good time to add that page bottom graphic, the one that makes the edges look finished like a three-dimensional object.

But we don't seem to have an element on which to place the background image, do we? The page container has the background image of the column and the footer has the bottom of the right column. Since background images are one per customer, it would seem we're out of luck. Never fear, this sounds like a job for the multiple wrappers trick mentioned in the *Creating a Faux Bottom* exercise, and it's a handy CSS technique to have in your arsenal of tricks.

Adding an Outer Page Wrapper

The simple theory behind this technique is that by placing a second wrapper around our page, we can add a second background image. This can be handy for a variety of design challenges.

One important point to note is that a wrapper inside another wrapper, unless molded into shape using padding and margin, will be the same size as the outer, parent wrapper. So the precise technique depends on the design you're working with.

In our case, it's a simple bottom graphic. We sliced the graphic at exactly the same width as the `body_back.jpg` image that creates the page sides, as the two must precisely meet. We sliced the height from the white page area to just below the glow. Our image is 10px tall and we named it something really original: `page_bottom.jpg`.

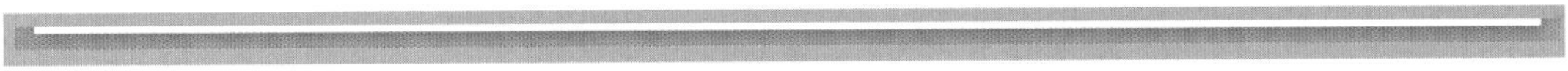

FIGURE 2.23 The page bottom graphic to be added to our new wrapper.

1. Click anywhere in the document and select `<div#container>` from the tag selector.

   Dreamweaver will highlight the whole page in Design view.

2. In the Common category of the Insert bar, select Insert Div Tag (the fifth icon from the left).

   Dreamweaver opens the Insert Div Tag dialog.

3. Make sure the drop-down list is set to "Wrap around selection." Leave the class field blank and in the ID field, type `wrapper`. This will be the name of the outer div we're adding. Click New CSS Style.

   Dreamweaver opens the New CSS Rule dialog with the name we typed pre-filled into the Selector field.

4. Make sure the rule will be created in your external style sheet and click OK.

5. From the Category list, go to Box. Set the width value to 700px (the same width as our graphic). Uncheck the "Same for all" box in the Margin property and set the Top field to zero. Use the drop-down list for the Left and Right fields and choose `auto`. Choose 15px for the bottom margin.

The bottom margin simply creates some space around the container so the page bottom, once applied, will be more apparent.

6. From the Background Category, browse to the page_bottom.jpg image. Set it to no-repeat, center, and bottom. Click OK.

   The dialog will close showing the Insert Div Tag dialog still open behind it.

7. Click OK in the Insert Div Tag dialog.

   It's possible we're a bit *too* organized about our CSS rules, but it's never hurt us any.

8. Change your CSS Styles panel view to the All mode. Drag the #wrapper rule from the bottom, where Dreamweaver just created it, to the space between the body and #container rules. Switch back to Current mode.

   We've got just a couple more tweaks to make before this works as expected.

9. Select your container div. In the Properties pane, right-click the margin property and choose delete. Do the same with the width property.

   The #container is now contained in the #wrapper. The #wrapper now has the auto centering properties, so we really don't need them on this selector anymore. The width is also unnecessary since the inner div will be as wide as its parent div unless otherwise constrained.

10. Right-click and delete the position: relative.

    We're going to move that to the containing div as well.

11. In the Rules pane, select #wrapper. In the Properties pane, click Add Property and type position. From the drop-down list, select the value relative as we had before on the #container. Save and preview in a browser.

    Oddly, our bottom graphic still isn't showing. We've created the surrounding div and given it the right width. We've placed the background image and positioned it at the bottom.

    As we mentioned earlier, the outer and inner divs will be the same size except where they are changed by padding and margin. Think of it as clay building blocks. Our wrapper is hugging up exactly around our container div. We need to create 10px of space at the bottom so that our page bottom graphic can show between them. That's easy enough!

12. With the wrapper selected, add the **padding-bottom** property. Give it a value of 10px.

We use 10px because that's the height of the graphic we're using. Too much padding and we'd be able to see the body background showing between the container and the bottom graphic in the wrapper causing an unsightly gap.

```
#wrapper {
    margin: 0 auto 15px;
    width: 700px;
    background: url(images/page_bottom.jpg) no-repeat center
bottom;
    position: relative;
    padding-bottom: 10px;
}
```

FIGURE 2.24 The footer with the nice, finished, bottom-page border.

quam ut lacus. Quisque ornare risus quis ligula. Phasellus tristique purus a augue condimentum adipiscing. Aenean sagittis. Etiam leo pede, rhoncus venenatis, tristique in, vulputate at, odio.

Footer

Positioning the Bottom Flower Graphic

We had to consider a few issues when we were envisioning how to handle the overhanging bottom flower graphic. First and foremost, it's sitting on three colors. Yes, we could actually create a slice as a jpg leaving all the background colors intact, and position the image (just as we did at the top). But right now, we'd like to demonstrate a technique that would be more flexible in a variety of layouts—especially if the color the graphic needs to sit on may vary from page to page.

True, clean transparency has always been elusive. We all know you can't create a transparent jpg. A jpg is best used when you have a photo-type image or an illustration with drop shadows, gradients or glows. The gif format *can* be transparent, but with irregular edges, it must be matted with one color in order to blend the edges smoothly. It's the best choice for flat, simple color but doesn't do well with the types of images the jpg format is best at. But those are the choices we've had for many years.

However, for the past few years, standards-compliant browsers like Safari and Firefox have offered support for a format called Portable Network Graphic, or png. The png format offers alpha transparency in a separate channel of information. This channel can be adjusted from opaque to fully transparent. It allows us to have beautiful jpg-quality images with better, halo-free transparency than a gif. So why haven't we all switched to the png format? Three guesses and the first two don't count. Yup, Internet Explorer, prior to version 7, did not support alpha transparency in pngs (yes, they did support non-transparent png images). Since IE was the dominant browser, most of us didn't bother.

To png or Not to png— That is the question

N *The png format online is not the same as the png files that Fireworks creates. Fireworks png files are not intended to be placed online and are simply Fireworks native file extension (like Photoshop's .psd). You must still export an image into the online png format for use on the web.*

FIGURE 2.25 Looking at the placement of the flower from our comp, we don't see a nearby element on which to place the background image.

With Microsoft moving to support pngs with alpha transparency in IE7, there's renewed interest in using this powerful format. But what to do about the older versions of IE? They're not going completely away anytime soon and a transparent png appears to have a light blue background in unsupported versions of IE. It can look pretty gross.

There are a variety of ways to use a png while still supporting all browsers, each with their own pros and cons. Many of them use JavaScript. But we're going to use a simple technique that uses no JavaScript and takes advantage of Internet Explorer Conditional Comments (IECC). This technique can *not* be used on an image sitting directly in the page, but it works quite well for background images.

There are two images in your images directory you'll need for this technique: `sm_flower.png` and `sm_flower.gif`.

If this image has to be placed into our page as a background, what element should we use? The overhang design challenge makes our choice a bit more complex due to the placement of the elements. However, we can put an empty div in our footer and give it height, width, and a background image. Then we can position it.

1. Place your cursor into the footer and select the **p** element on the tag selector. Press your right arrow key once to move outside the **p** element.

2. Select Insert Div Tag from the Insert bar. In the dialog, choose At insertion point and Class: overhang. Click New CSS Style.

   The New CSS Rule dialog will open with our class inserted—not the full path to the element. For reasons we'll discuss in a moment, we want to use a more complex descendant selector.

3. In the Selector name field, change to: **#container #footer .overhang**. Make sure the Advanced Selector Type is chosen, and set Define in to your external style sheet. Click OK. In the Background category, browse to the **sm_flower.png** image. Set it not to repeat.

   If you recall, we defined a rule for the **#container .overhang** selector. Unless changed, those same properties will cascade through to this selector. That means absolute positioning is already applied, so we just need to override the top and left values.

4. In the Positioning category, set the width to 84px and height to 100px to match our image. Set the top to 10px and left to 611px. Click OK in both dialogs.

   Notice that Dreamweaver allows you to set the width and height in both the box and positioning categories. The parent element in which this div is being positioned is the footer. So our top and left values will be relative to the footer div.

   ```
   #container #footer .overhang {
       background: url(images/sm_flower.png) no-repeat;
       height: 100px;
       width: 84px;
       top: 10px;
       left: 611px;
   }
   ```

5. Place your cursor in **#footer** and, making sure that's your selected element, add **position: relative**. Change the padding to **top: 70px**, **left** and **right: 0**, and **bottom: 30px**.

Obviously, the relative positioning is used to give the footer position, allowing us to position within it. Since absolute positioning is taken out of the flow of the document, we add the padding to provide space for the positioned div. Since there is no text within, we don't have to worry about resizing.

6. Remove the text that says, "Content for class "overhang" Goes Here."

FIGURE 2.26 The bottom looks great in most browsers, but in IE6—Ewwww!

We took a quick glance at IE6. From the image here, you can see that the light blue background that IE 6 and below gives to a png image is very unsightly indeed! (If you decided to have a look in IE6 for yourself, just ignore the rest of the issues there. Remember, right now we're coding for standards-compliant browsers. We'll fix the rest of the IE problems when we're all done.)

We do need to fix the png issue right now, though—using an IECC. But currently, our page has an IECC for version 5 browsers (`<!--[if IE 5]>`) and another for all versions of IE (`<!--[if IE]>`). We need this code to apply to IE6 and earlier, but not to IE7, which supports the transparent png format. We'll create a new IECC in our page to apply to IE6 and earlier. The syntax will be slightly different than those we have already, but along the same lines. Dreamweaver has no native way of adding an IECC to the page so we'll hand code this into our page.

As mentioned in Chapter 1, Community MX has an extension written by Paul Davis that will place the IECC into the document for you, saving you from remembering the syntax. For non-members, the extension costs $10.00. http://www.communitymx.com/abstract.cfm?cid=C433F

1. Place your cursor between the two IECCs already in the head of the document. Press return twice to create a space.

```
<![endif]-->(Place cursor here)<!--[if IE]>
```

2. Type the following block of text into your page:

```
<!--[if lte IE 6]>
<style type="text/css">
  #container #footer .overhang {
    background: url(images/sm_flower.gif) no-repeat;
  }
</style>
<![endif]-->
```

The syntax, `lte,` means that versions of IE that are less than or equal to the version shown should render the rule shown within the IECC.

Notice that the selector name is the same selector name we created in the main style sheet. The only difference is that we've specified a gif file to be shown for IE6 and earlier, instead of the png we showed the other browsers. We don't need to override any other properties in that selector so the rest will cascade through to IE6 as well.

You could also use a jpg as well as a gif but either way, exporting two files (either a png and gif or a png and jpg) is required to create this effect. The standards-compliant browsers will see a lovely, halo-free transparent image and IE6 and earlier may see something not quite as nice, but acceptable.

FIGURE 2.27 The bottom is nicely arranged now.

A Bit About Floating and Clearing

In Chapter 1, we discussed the basic principles of floating and clearing: now let's develop these principles a little more, and add containing floats, as well as clearing within a non-floated container. Many designs require a floated self-contained area of some sort, commonly referred to as a pod. A pod may contain an image floated within and some text. In this exercise, we'll add a bordered div to our page, float an image and text in it, and then look at various effects with floating and clearing.

Creating a Pod in the Page

1. First, to make the effect more apparent, copy one of the paragraphs in your side column and paste it below to make the column longer. Place your cursor about midway into the first paragraph of your `mainContent` div and hit return to create a new paragraph.

We'll be inserting our pod, or callout box, here.

2. Select the **p** element on the tag selector and arrow to the right (or, in code view, place a **div** element between the two **p** elements). From the Insert bar, place a **div** element with a class of **pod** into the page and click New CSS Style.

   Let Dreamweaver simply name the class **.pod** and place it in our external style sheet.

3. In the box category, set the padding to 10px on the top and 0 on the bottom. Set 15px on the right and 5px on the left. In the border category, create a border all the way around the box: 1px solid #628958. Click OK in both dialogs.

   ```
   .pod {
       padding: 10px 5px 0 15px;
       border: 1px solid #628958;
   }
   ```

   We've just created a nice little padded box to place our content in. If you haven't moved your cursor yet, Dreamweaver still has the text selected.

4. Choose Paragraph from the Property inspector. Add some text, so that you have about two lines of text. (Anything will do.) Place your cursor at the beginning of the paragraph and insert the **orangedaisy.jpg** image from your images directory.

5. With the image still selected, apply the **fltrt** class from the Property inspector.

   Using the float classes that come in the CSS layout's default style sheet, we can float our image to the right side of our pod. But what's up with the border? It's appearing beneath the flower image.

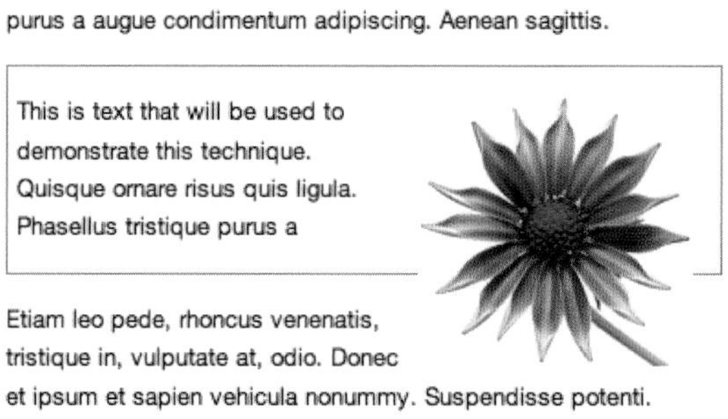

FIGURE 2.28 Our flower is falling out the bottom of our pod!

purus a augue condimentum adipiscing. Aenean sagittis.

This is text that will be used to demonstrate this technique. Quisque ornare risus quis ligula. Phasellus tristique purus a

Etiam leo pede, rhoncus venenatis, tristique in, vulputate at, odio. Donec et ipsum et sapien vehicula nonummy. Suspendisse potenti.

Avoiding Float Creep—or how to force a div to contain its floats

Remember how absolutely positioned elements are invisible to the other elements? The container won't enclose them and the other elements can run right underneath, because they're taken out of the flow of the page. Floats work in a similar way: they're taken out of the flow, since their containing element doesn't know where they end. But unlike absolutely positioned elements, other elements can still react to them and the float's container can be forced to see where the float ends if you use a clearing element.

In Chapter 1, we discussed the clearing element that comes with the CSS layouts: `clearfloat`. It is placed on a break element as the last item before the footer in all the CSS layouts. This clearing element lets the container div know where `mainContent` and side columns end and contain them properly. We're going to reuse `clearleft` here to force our pod container to see the image floated inside it.

1. Place your cursor in the **p** element inside the **.pod** div. Select it on the tag selector and press the right arrow. Press shift+return to insert a break element. In code view, add the **clearfloat** class to the break.

    Dreamweaver won't let you right-click to add the class directly to the break element. It will attempt to apply it to the parent element. Either type directly into code view or copy/paste the clearing element that precedes the footer div.

FIGURE 2.29 Whoa! What just happened to our pod?

Space, the Final Frontier

We've just run into the next "little issue" with floating and clearing. If you clear within a *non-floated div*, it will clear *all* floats. What we're witnessing here is not a train wreck: it's the browser obeying the specs. You'll notice that the bottom of our pod ends where the content in the right column ends. That's because the break element with the clear class is going all the way down to the end of the side content to clear it. If it were longer, the space in our pod would be bigger. What to do?

Since a float requires a width, and the hybrid layouts (discussed in Chapter 6) could not be given widths, none of the CSS layouts have a floated mainContent *div. This doesn't mean you can't change that!*

As we said above, this happens when clearing in a non-floated div. The `mainContent` div is margined away from the column next to it rather than floated itself. This was done so that all the CSS Layouts were consistent.

We have three choices. What you choose to do on your own will depend on your layout and the requirements of your client, but all of these choices will allow you to clear without clearing the side column as well.

- You can add a **float** property with a value of **left** to the `.pod` rule. This will allow you to clear within the pod, but will also require you to add some bottom margin to the `.pod` class since the **p** element following it will sit rather snugly up to it.

- You can float the `mainContent` div left. This will require some adaptation in the source order and CSS, but we'll use this method below.

- You can add a div right inside the `mainContent` div with no width—only a **float:left** declaration. You can do this by highlighting all the content within the `#mainContent` div and choosing Insert Div Tag from the Insert bar (choosing the "Wrap around selection" option). This will allow you to choose New CSS Style from the dialog and add the float declaration. Or, in code view, type `<div class="left">` right inside the opening of the `#main-Content` div with a closing tag right before the closing `#main-Content` tag (which is marked by a comment). You'll then need to create the `.left` rule, with the **float:left** declaration.

```
.left { float: left; }
```

The hybrid CSS layouts— percentage-based container with em-based columns—cannot be fully floated. That is, the width of the mainContent *cannot be dependably calculated in order to float it as needed. The div inside a div trick is a great way to get around the issue of clearing in the* mainContent *div of the hybrid layouts.*

FIGURE 2.30 Using any of the three methods, the pod will enclose its content without clearing the side column.

Though we didn't float the `#mainContent` div itself, placing a child div directly inside with no properties save `float:left` solves our clearing issue. The pod is now seen as sitting inside a floated div (so we can clear) and the div it's in is 100% of the width of the parent element (`#mainContent`). So for all practical purposes, we're clearing within `#mainContent`. Yes, it's cheating—or adding a non-semantic element which raises the ire of some—but there are times when this trick is handy and it really doesn't add any weight.

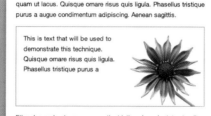

Let's look at our second option—floating the mainContent div—in more detail.

The Issue of Source Order

Search engines are a concern for many web sites. Everybody wants to feed the spiders properly so they'll come back for more yummy words. For search engines, words closer to the top of the page (and thus, higher in the source order) hold more "weight" than words *way* down the page. On a page the size of ours, it's likely not going to make a lot of difference, but on a page where the sidebar holds a lot of content, there can be advantages to putting the `mainContent` area first.

Changing the source order of our page requires a bit of copy-paste and the changing of a couple of rules. But for some sites, it's worth it to support search engines—and conveniently, it allows us to clear content within the `mainContent` div to boot!

1. Select the `sidebar1` element. Cut and paste it directly after the `mainContent` div.

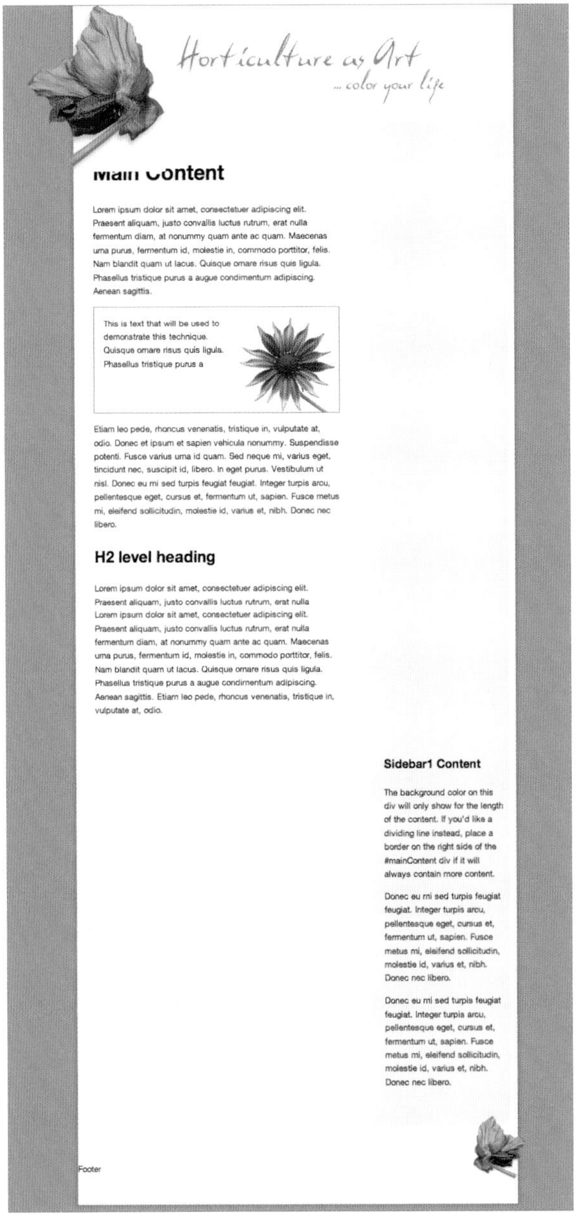

FIGURE 2.31 Whoa! Source order matters!

You'll see a comment right before the footer div that says: `<!-- This clearing element should immediately follow the #mainContent div in order to force the #container div to contain all child floats -->` *What that means is the clearing div should be the last thing in* `#container` *before the footer. So if you change the order, you'll still leave the clearing element where it is.*

2. In #mainContent, adjust the padding to 30px on the left to create the space and alignment we want down the page. Leave the 20px on the right.

To float the #mainContent, we'll need to give it a width. In the case of this layout, due to the fixed overall width, that's not too difficult. We're geeks—surely we all aced math class, right? Start with the overall width and begin subtracting anything that will affect the box model to see what we have left. 700 - 9 - 9 = 682px (That's the wrapper width minus the padding on the container that holds the rest of the page elements). Then we'll subtract the side column space (don't forget the padding and border), giving us 682 - 184 - 20 - 20 = 458px. Finally, we'll subtract the padding we're placing on #mainContent itself, 458 - 20 - 30 = 408px.

In the CSS code, a comment next to the margin declaration on the #mainContent div partially reads, "the right margin on this div element creates the column down the right side of the page—no matter how much content the sidebar1 div contains, the column space will remain." The comment is referring to creating the space *for* the right side column. But we won't need this space anymore when we float the column. We'll be giving the column a width instead of creating the space with a margin.

2. To the #mainContent div, alter or add these properties:

```
margin: 0
width: 408px
float: left
#mainContent {
    margin: 0;
    padding: 0 20px 0 30px;
    width: 408px;
    float: left;
}
```

The page looks just like it did before. But our source order is different. Sweet!

Fonts and Final Styling

N *For those of you that have been using CSS for styling only, this may be old hat. Consider this a review.*

Now that the markup, structure and background images are in order, it's time to turn our attention to the styling.

Anchors and Links

Anchors, commonly referred to as links, are likely the most commonly used CSS selectors. The big thing to remember with anchor styling is LVHA—or LoVe HAte—link, visited, hover, active. This is the order in which our selectors must come if they are to work as we expect.

- **Link:** Unvisited links

- **Visited:** Applies when a user has already visited the destination link

- **Hover:** Links are designated with a pointing device but not activated

- **Active:** Applies while activated by the user

- **Focus:** Applies while an element has focus (is able to accept keyboard events)

The above list includes one state that's not in our love-hate mnemonic. Focus is an often-neglected pseudo-class that's important for users who navigate with keyboards. As you know, a pointing device activates the hover state but keyboard navigators can't point: instead, the focus pseudo-class lets the keyboard navigator know where the keyboard focus resides so he or she can click to navigate to another page. Perhaps you don't think this is a common way to navigate—but for many people with carpal tunnel and other physical limitations, it's the only way.

Because hover and focus serve the same purpose, we like to group them when creating our link rules. We also group active in the same set (or compound selector). Wondering why, since active should be showing a different state when the link is clicked on? Well, for users who are navigating with the keyboard using Internet Explorer, `active` actually shows them the keyboard focus. Thus, by giving the `:hover`, `:active`, and `:focus` states the same properties, the majority of users get to see the styles we've chosen to let them know it's possible to activate a link. (And yes, we're sacrificing the ability to show a different state when the link is clicked, but that's the choice we have to make!)

1. Create a new rule for `a:link` by clicking the New CSS Rule icon. Notice when the CSS Rule Definition dialog opens that there's a drop-down list next to the Selector input. Choose `a:link` from the drop-down. Click OK.

FIGURE 2.32 The drop-down by the Selector input contains most pseudo-classes.

T *Many times, developers remove underlines from the links and style them using different colors and styles. If you're making your links very different from the other text, this may be fine, but studies have shown that users* ***expect*** *underlines on their links. This means you should never underline text that is not a link. Users will be annoyed when clicking the underlined text doesn't take them to another page.*

2. In the Type category, let's choose a dark green: #628958.

3. In the same way, create a new rule for the `a:visited` pseudo-class. This time, choose a more faded-out color. Perhaps #666.

4. Finally, create a compound selector for `a:hover, a:active, a:focus`. Set the text-decoration to none and change the color to the orange sampled from the daisy: #CE5441.

   Yes, the color could have been anything, but we find that using a highly contrasting color is best. Since orange is the complement to blue (the dominant color on our page), we used Dreamweaver's eyedropper to sample the color from the daisy. We removed the link underline so that if the user was color-blind or had difficulty seeing, the disappearing underline might make the link more apparent.

5. In the mainContent and sidebar1 divs, create a link to view the styles. Use a hash (#) as the Link to make it appear to be a link.

   We notice on previewing in the browser that the initial link state in the side column isn't quite as apparent due to the light gray/blue background. We can remedy that with a descendant selector.

6. Create a new rule called `#sidebar1 a`. In the Type category, give the weight property the value of **bold**.

   The **a** selector without a pseudo class will apply to and cascade to all the **a** pseudo-classes. The rest of the selectors will be inherited from the pseudo-classes we just created. Let's make sure they're in the right order.

7. Change your CSS Styles panel into All mode, select the rules we just created, and drag them up under the **a img** rule. Make sure they're in the proper order: LVHA.

```css
a img {
    border: none;
}
#sidebar1 a {
    font-weight: bold;
}
a:link {
    color: #628958;
}
a:visited {
    color: #666;
}
a:hover, a:active, a:focus {
    color: #CE5441;
    text-decoration: none;
}
```

FIGURE 2.33 Using a descendant selector for the side column gives it a heavier weight.

Nam blandit quam ut lacus. Quisque ornare risus quis ligula. Phasellus tristique purus a augue condimentum adipiscing. Aenean sagittis.

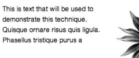

This is text that will be used to demonstrate this technique. Quisque ornare risus quis ligula. Phasellus tristique purus a

Etiam leo pede, rhoncus venenatis, tristique in, vulputate at, odio. Donec et ipsum et sapien vehicula nonummy.

instead, place a border on the right side of the #mainContent div if it will always contain more content.

Donec eu mi sed turpis feugiat feugiat. Integer turpis arcu, pellentesque eget, cursus et, fermentum ut, sapien. Fusce metus mi, eleifend sollicitudin, molestie id, varius et, nibh. Donec nec libero.

Styling the Headings

Headings, that is **h1, h2, h3, h4**, etc. elements, are important to search engine spiders. Many a developer or designer has made the mistake of using a **p** element, placing a class on it, and styling it *as if* it is a heading. But that's not *nearly* as yummy to a spider. They love those semantically marked headings. And after all, we really want to give them what they want!

Since all the headings on our site will use the same color, font and letter spacing, we'll set those values in one simple compound selector. (As you remember from Chapter 1, type selectors save a lot of weight in our CSS when properly used.)

1. Set headings 1 through 4 to use the **font-family** (pre-made in the Dreamweaver font drop-down list) that begins with Georgia. Set the weight to normal, the color to #628958 and the letter spacing to -.04em.

    ```
    h1, h2, h3, h4 {
        font-family: Georgia, "Times New Roman", Times, serif;
        font-weight: normal;
        color: #628958;
        letter-spacing: -0.04em;
    }
    ```

    All headings, whether in the **#mainContent** or **#sidebar1**, will get the font cascade starting with Georgia, and will be green with a close letter spacing, and a normal weight font.

If you look at the page, you'll see that although we've got our nice green styled headings, our first **mainContent** heading is hiding under the absolutely positioned flower at the top of our layout. This is obviously one of the treacheries of absolute positioning—the other elements are blind to the positioned element's placement. But we can easily work around this issue,

T *Be sure, as you create font cascades for headings, that the fonts look equally good in a normal or bold weight—whichever you've chosen to use. Also, be careful of using letter spacing since some fonts don't render it as well as others.*

FIGURE 2.34 The flower has overlapped the heading in the mainContent area.

ntent

Lorem ipsum dolor sit amet, consectetuer adipiscing elit. Praesent aliquam, justo convallis luctus rutrum, erat nulla fermentum diam, at nonummy quam ante ac quam. Maecenas urna purus, fermentum id,

Sidebar1 Content

The background color on this div will only show for the length of the content. If you'd like a

2. Click into the `#mainContent` div. Change the padding at the top to 32px.

   No, this isn't quite enough to force the heading out from under the flower. But we have another weapon as well. We can add bottom padding to the `#header`. That will shift the entire area below the header down, including the side column. If we shifted the side column itself down, the faux column would show above it and ruin the look of the rounded corner. So the side column must remain snug against the header—and be moved down using the header.

3. Click into the `header` div and change the bottom padding to match the top: 40px.

   Our designer has specified that headings in the `mainContent` div should be right aligned and matched up with the side column. We'll take care of that along with the sizing of the `h1,` `h2`, and `h3` selectors.

4. Create selectors for the `#mainContent` `h1` and `h2`. The `h1` should be set to a font-size of 180% and the `h2` should be 150%. The `h2` should have a top margin of 35px. Both should be aligned right with 20px of right margin.

   Since the element selectors have been created for `h1-h4` with color, font and style, it's not necessary to recreate those declarations.

5. Create an overall selector with a font-size of 130% for the `h3` element in any div.

   Your final outcome for the above selectors should appear as follows:

```
#mainContent h1 {
    font-size: 180%;
    text-align: right;
    margin-right: 20px;
}
#mainContent h2 {
    font-size: 150%;
    margin-top: 35px;
    text-align: right;
    margin-right: 20px;
```

```
}
h3 {
   font-size: 130%;
}
```

Evening the Side Column

One of the common issues many of us struggle with is margin collapse (or margin escape). We discussed it at the end of Chapter 1. In the IECC included in this, and several other, CSS layouts, padding is added at the top of `#sidebar1` or `#sidebar2` to force IE to render the same as the other browsers. But we're going to solve the problem using a different technique here: we will zero the top margin of any element that is the first element inside a div where there is *not* a border (if there is a border, it's unnecessary).

First, we'll create a class we can use to remove the margin at the top, then we'll remove the selector in the IECC that created the padding at the top of the div.

1. Create a class called `.first` and give it a top margin of 0.

```
.first {
   margin-top: 0;
}
```

2. Apply the class to both the h1 in `#mainContent` and the h3 in `#sidebar1`.

   You'll notice that the headings move up substantially. This evens browser defaults on the heading elements, avoids browser escape, and makes things work evenly across browsers. If you expect that you might have longer headings on the h1 in your `#mainContent` area, you may want to put more padding on the `#mainContent` to move it down a few pixels more. But remember to match whatever you do on the `#sidebar1` div.

3. Place your cursor into the `sidebar1` div and change the top padding to 40px so the top heading matches the top heading in the `mainContent` div. Give the bottom padding a value of 0 since it's not needed.

   With the bottom rounded corner graphic in the footer, there will always be a little bit of extra space.

T *With longer headings, you can see the value of having the alpha channel png we discussed earlier in the chapter. You wouldn't have to worry about the white portion of the flower overlapping the headings like we are right now.*

```
#sidebar1 {
  float: right;
  width: 184px;
  padding: 40px 20px 0;
  background: url(images/corner_tl.gif) no-repeat;
}
```

4. Find the IECC rule in the page head (within the if IE conditional comment) called `#sidebar1` and delete it.

`#sidebar1 { padding-top: 30px; }`

FIGURE 2.35 Nice, even top elements!

Drop Caps—Simple Page Interest

The print world has used drop caps, those large first letters that span 3-4 lines of text, to their advantage for years. But before CSS, it was difficult to pull drop caps off on the web unless you used images. And although the `first letter` pseudo-element was created for CSS 2, we still had to deal with rendering issues in older browsers. Now, with a small amount of markup, drop caps are a snap.

The secret is in the span element. Spans, which render inline by default, are handy elements for styling. In this case, we'll create a class called `.dropcap` and apply it to the first letter of any paragraph we want styled this way, using a span. We'll create the `.dropcap` class with the following properties:

1. Set `.dropcap` to `display:block` and float it to the left.

    This changes the rendering of the span so that we can float it, and allows the lines of text to appear next to it until they run out of space, then wrap around it.

2. In the text category, use the same font-family cascade as the headings: Georgia, Times New Roman, Times and serif. Set the font to 5em with .85em of line height.

    This gives us some continuity with the rest of the page, but uses a really large font. The line-height allows us to snug things up around the letter and remove some of the white space around it. It's better not to decrease it below .8em however, because if you do IE 6 will sometimes, cut part of the letter off.

3. Give the class padding on the top of .03em with .1em on the right.

    This simply allows a little breathing room around the letter.

4. Finally, give the class the blue color (#7F98C3) of the page background.

```
.dropcap {
    font: 5em/.85em Georgia, "Times New Roman", Times, serif;
    padding: .03em .1em 0 0;
    display: block;
    float: left;
    color: #7F98C3;
}
```

5. In your HTML document, highlight the first letter of the first paragraph under the **h1** element. Right-click and choose CSS Styles > **dropcap**. Remove the first few words of the first paragraph below the **h2** heading and apply the span again. (This is simply to avoid styling two Ls.)

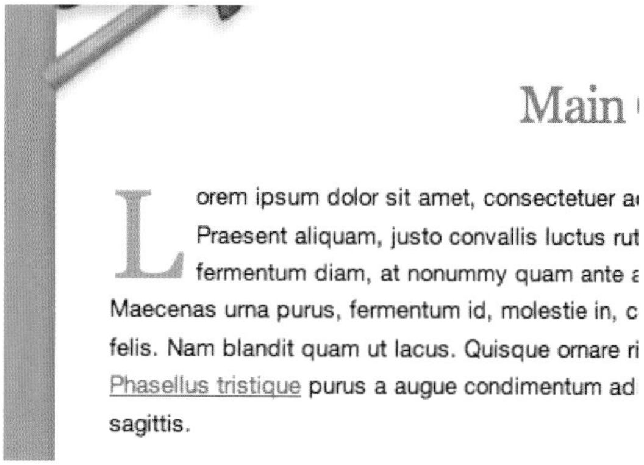

T   There are a variety of ways to style a drop cap. You can use a border and background color creating a box around the span. Fantasy and cursive fonts can also be used. Experiment!

FIGURE 2.36 A large drop cap for visual interest.

Completing the Footer

Typically, footers contain information that needs to be included on each page, such as copyrights. They tend to be a little less obvious with smaller font sizing.

1. Add some fake copyright text to the **p** element in the footer div.

2. Change the **#footer p** selector so that there's 70px of padding on the right and 20px on the left. Set the text to be centered.

   The padding on the right side allows the text to miss the flower that's absolutely positioned on the right.

3. Give the text a medium gray color (#666) and decrease the font size to 70%.

   ```
   #footer p {
     margin: 0;
     padding: 0 70px 0 20px;
     text-align: center;
     color: #666;
     font-size: 70%;
   }
   ```

Bust the Bugs

Now that our page is exactly as we'd like it in standards-compliant browsers, it's time to turn our attention to the browser with a mind of its own, Internet Exploder…errrr, Internet Explorer. If you're on a Mac, you'll need to access the page using your favorite way to view on the PC side so you can see what we're looking at here.

Adjusting Values for IE5—Quirks mode

First, in Internet Explorer 5-series browsers, we're dealing with the broken box model. This means that items that have width plus padding and/or border have to be recalculated and different values fed to IE using an IECC. Currently in our page, there's an IECC for IE5 which holds a different value for the **#sidebar1** width only.

We need to change the width of #sidebar1 to be 224px. This is the declared width (184px) plus the padding for the sides (20px + 20px). The quirks mode box model width is placed in the IECC.

We'll also change the source order and declare a width on the #mainContent div. In the IE5 IECC, add a selector for #mainContent with the width set to 458px. (That's 408px + 20px + 30px = 458px.)

Your code should look like this:

Place css box model fixes for IE 5 in this conditional comment*

```
<!--[if IE 5]>
<style type="text/css">
  #sidebar1 { width: 224px; }
  #mainContent { width 458px; }
</style>
<![endif]-->
```

hasLayout Issues Abound

If you don't have access to IE6, look at Figure 2.37 to see what is going on. The header isn't showing its background color. Since the header had a gray background color by default, and it showed just fine, we can be sure that the problem is caused by some interaction that we've created.

FIGURE 2.37 Business as usual. Internet Explorer 6 has issues in the header area.

By sleuthing and commenting out the **position:relative** on the #wrapper div, we find it's the typical IE **hasLayout** problem. (You can read more about this in Chapter 1.)

Since we can't remove the **position:relative** (it's needed to allow the top flower to be positioned properly), we can simply add the #header to the rule that gives the **zoom:1** declaration to the #mainContent in the IECC.

In fact, we can also remove the `#mainContent` from that rule since we've changed the source order and given it a width. (A width is one of the properties that triggers layout for an element.) We no longer need to include `maincontent` in the IECC.

We've got a small issue with the pod we placed on our page. It's not containing the float—and we've got a clearing element included. Rather than spend a lot of time on it, why don't we just try the hasLayout fix right off the bat?

FIGURE 2.38 Another issue with our pod.

This is text that will be used to demonstrate this technique. Quisque ornare risus quis ligula. Phasellus tristique purus a

Etiam leo pede, rhoncus venenatis, tristique in, vulputate at,

Adding the `.pod` class to the `zoom:1` rule in the IECC causes the `.pod` to contain its content.

Using Check Browser Compatibility

As far as we can tell, our page is peachy keen. But let's try one more thing. Dreamweaver has a new feature that will help you track down the most common bugs—and give you the fix for them as well. It's called Check Browser Compatibility and it's accessed through the Check Page icon in the Standard toolbar. We'll run it now to see if there are possible bugs we've not run into in our testing.

FIGURE 2.39 The Check Page icon in the Standard toolbar.

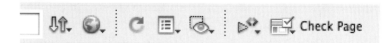

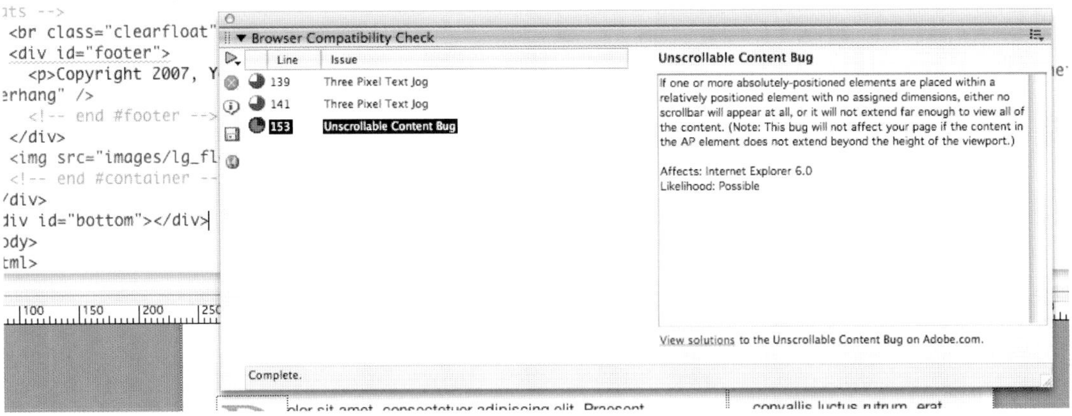

FIGURE 2.40 Check Browser Compatibility has reported three possible bugs.

T *When using IECC to fix bugs or override styles, it's best to have them as the last element, or at least the last CSS element, inside the head of your document to make sure that they are applied properly.*

Check Browser Compatibility has determined there are three possible bugs on our page. It gives us a description of them, which browser or browsers they affect and the likelihood of encountering them. It also gives you a View Solutions link at the bottom right so you can read more about the bug and its solutions at Adobe's CSS Advisor site. CSS Advisor is a moderated wiki where you can add issues and bugs you've found as well. Though it contains information on the most common bugs that Dreamweaver can spot and report, it also contains loads of details on many, many other bugs—and it grows all the time.

For our page, the first two in the report are related to the Three Pixel Text Jog. Double-clicking the line number takes us to our drop caps in both cases, so we're not too concerned about the issue. However, the Unscrollable Content Bug, though we don't necessarily see it with our large browser, could be a problem for some users. Fortunately, the fix is simple. Once again, apply zoom:1 to the affected element.

When double-clicking the problem line in the reporting window, Dreamweaver gives focus to the #footer as well as highlighting the possible trigger, position:relative, in the CSS Styles panel. We'll add the #footer div to our IECC containing the compound rule for zoom:1.

Looks like all our bugs are squashed flat!

Declaring Media Types

CSS gives us the ability to declare a media type in relation to a rule or an entire style sheet. Media types allow the author to specify how a document should be presented for a variety of media. From screen to print, from handheld to aural—it all sounds so useful. Sadly, the reality of the situation, at least at the printing of this book, is that many user agents don't support media types well, if at all.

The handheld media type may become more useful as pressure is placed on the industry to support it. Until then, the two basic media types of which to be aware are screen and print.

Be default, if no media type is specified, a style sheet is applied to all media. If you want it to only apply to one media type, you can declare that and you can also declare more than one media type by separating the media types with a comma.

FIGURE 2.41 Dreamweaver allows us to preview media types directly in Design view using the style rendering tool bar.

A typical linked style sheet with a media type of screen looks like this:

```
<link href="main.css" rel="stylesheet" type="text/css"
media="screen" />
```

Rules for Creating a Simple Print Style Sheet

There are two basic methods of creating a print style sheet. Using your browser's print preview will give you an idea of what your user will see, but not all browsers print the same way, so checking a variety of browsers is always a good idea.

- Give your main style sheet a media type of `all` (or leave it with no media type which will default to `all`). Then, override all the styles you need to with a second style sheet with the media type of `print`.

- Give your main style sheet a media type of `screen`. Then, create a second style sheet with the media type of `print` that gives basic styling to the flow of your page.

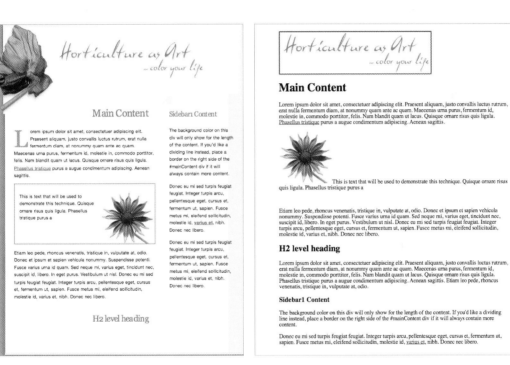

FIGURE 2.42 Our page in print preview mode with no print style sheet yet—but with our CSS being applied.

FIGURE 2.43 Our page in print preview mode with a screen style sheet (and still no print style sheet).

Both methods work: choosing which one to use basically depends on the way your site is coded. Often there are simply a few items to hide—such as unnecessary images—and some background, font and color changes. If your information is marked up semantically, you're 75% of the way there.

But let's face it, when someone prints a web page, it's rarely because they're in love with the design and want to remember it. Typically, it's because there's some information there that they want to keep. So giving them neatly formatted text, in black, white and gray (to save their color ink) is usually all you need.

We won't go through the entire creation process here, but we'll give you the principles to use as you create your own.

- When allowing the main style sheet to apply to `print` as well as `screen`, you'll likely want to hide some elements. Use `display:none`, not `visibility:hidden`. The former creates no box, or space, on the page. The latter *will* hide the element, but the space for the element will be reserved.

- Perhaps a client has a busy, colorful logo on their site, but for print, they have a black and white version. You can actually place both logos into the HTML. In the screen page, show the colorful one and set the print logo to `display:none`. In the print style sheet, set the print logo to `display:block` and set the screen logo to `display:none`.

- Use compound rules to hide elements using `display: none`. A list of selector names separated by commas may save a good deal of space.

- Hide unnecessary background colors and images in your print style sheet using the declaration `background: none`.

- Change your body fonts to serifs as they are more legible in print. Feel free to use points instead of pixels. This *is* print, after all.

- Change your headings and links to black or grays to save your user's color ink.

- Hide any unnecessary images. Obviously, you don't want to hide all images if you're dealing with a site selling homes. People may want to print the photo of the home and rooms. But for many sites decorative images are not necessary for print. If you choose to hide all images, you can add the `img` tag to the compound selector that you set to `display:none`, or alternatively, add a class that you can then place on any images that need to be hidden.

- You may want to allow the information to flow instead of keeping it floated. Floats are sometimes problematic in printing—edges can be cut off.

- Setting a width and margins on the body can sometimes be helpful.

Wrapping It Up

In this chapter, you've looked at some advantages and disadvantages of a fixed-width layout. You set your preferences in Dreamweaver and learned about using shorthand with CSS. We looked at a variety of ways to create faux columns, discovered source order, got some more detail on floating and clearing, and spent some time exploring when it's safe to use absolute positioning. Finally, we looked at print style sheets and media types.

Migrating a Table-based Layout to CSS

AS PROFESSIONAL web designers and developers, most of us dream of clients with no demands other than for us to unfold our creative talents for them and no constraints, just a blank canvas waiting for our artistic vision. Unfortunately, the reality of web design today is a different story; most clients have some kind of web presence already, which at best is reasonably coded but more often than not was "designed" by a 12-year-old nephew with a hacked copy of a WYSIWYG web design program. (Our apologies to those 12-year-olds who actually bought their software!)

In this chapter, we'll tackle that very situation. Our fictional client's nephew is busy with homework, but the client, owner of Acme Internet Machines, is ready to have his site updated. There are only a couple of caveats. First, he likes the current design and would simply like it streamlined. Second, his nephew can't seem to find any of the original graphics files. We'll have to make do with only the graphics and assets already on the web site.

Having received the login information from the nephew, we've successfully downloaded the site files and established a site in Dreamweaver. (Yes, this is truly a fictional story because clients can never find their login information, can they?!) Let's first take a look at the index page to see what we're dealing with from both a visual and code perspective.

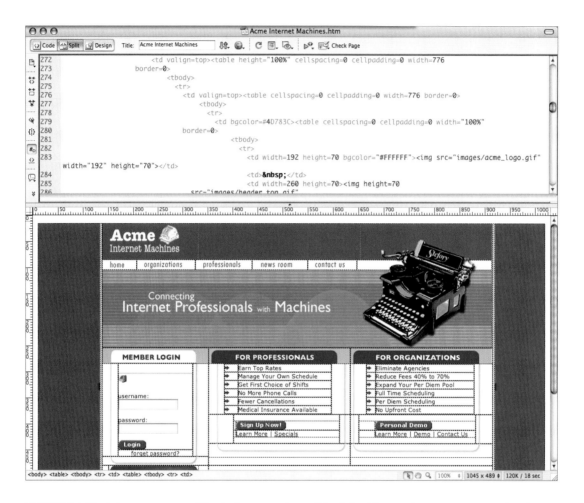

FIGURE 3.1 The index page looks pretty good, but the code is a nested mess.

The index page doesn't look bad from a browser perspective, but our glee quickly subsides when we get our first look at the code. What a mess!

There are two possible approaches to this project. On the one hand, it might be easier to throw the entire page out and rebuild it from scratch. While this definitely might be the best option for many designs, we'll work with the page exactly as it was given to us. Using some lesser-known Dreamweaver tricks and techniques, we'll quickly migrate this awful table-based nightmare into a well-formed, CSS-based page.

The CSS Issues

By looking at the code, we can see that the page contains numerous nested tables and inline image elements that we'll eventually have to deal with. Happily, we can also see that our intrepid 12-year-old took some baby steps toward CSS but not without falling victim to a couple of common issues. Most obvious is the fact that the CSS is local to this page instead of being placed in an external style sheet.

FIGURE 3.2 Anybody interested in some messy table soup?

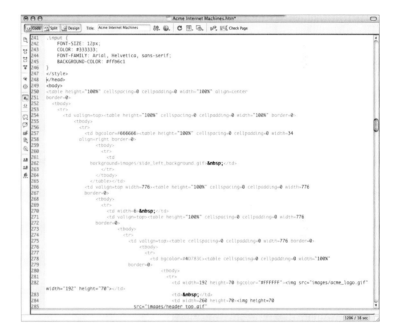

The CSS rules are also suffering from a severe case of "class-itis" and verbosity. This basic page has an overabundance of rules, along with redundant properties and values. Unfortunately, this is an all-too-common mistake among designers who are new to the use of CSS. Remember, the key to successfully implementing CSS is to use a minimalist approach when creating rules and using descendant selectors. We want to create as few rules as possible and use specificity to target specific page elements.

We'll begin our cleanup with the CSS. However, before undertaking any changes, let's save the index.htm file as index_css.htm. It's always good to have a backup!

With the page open in Dreamweaver, switch to either Code view or Split view and we'll begin cooking down some of the existing rules.

Using Find and Replace to Determine Existing Rules

A good starting point in a project like this is to first determine what rules are actually being used within the page. Though Dreamweaver doesn't have a feature that shows which rules are in use, we can figure it out with a little ingenuity.

From its very inception, Dreamweaver has had a command called Find and Replace. Now before you start rolling your eyes, let us point out that the majority of software users get into the habit of using a given feature or command in one particular way without considering other uses for the feature. Find and Replace is a perfect example. As you'll see, Find and Replace can be used several different ways, some of which may come as a surprise.

To determine which classes are used in the page, choose Edit > Find and Replace (or press Cmd+F). The dialog provides four search possibilities:

- Source Code
- Text
- Text (Advanced)
- Specific Tag

Choosing Source Code instructs Dreamweaver to search through the actual HTML code of the document (Code view), whereas the two text options limit the search to the text on the page as seen by the browser (Design view). The Specific Tag option searches the HTML code but provides the option of including parameters in the search. This is exactly what we need to find the classes used on this page.

1. Choose Specific Tag from the Search drop-down list.

2. Make sure that Current Document is chosen from the Find in drop-down list.

3. From the drop-down list to the right of the Specific Tag field, choose [any tag].

4. If a parameter line is not in the dialog, click the plus button under the Specific Tag option to create one.

5. In the parameter line, choose With Attribute from the drop-down list.

6. Type class into the field or choose it from the drop-down list to the right of the field.

7. Leave the Operator drop-down list set to "=" and type [any value] into the value field or choose it from the drop-down.

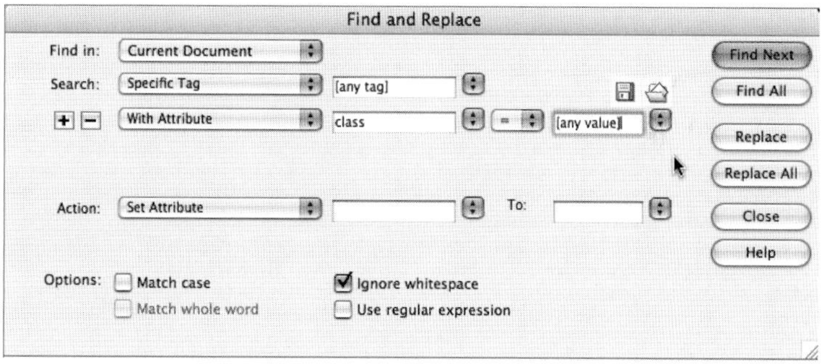

FIGURE 3.3 The Find and Replace dialog is one of the most powerful and flexible tools in Dreamweaver but should only be used under adult supervision.

8. With the search criteria defined, click Find All.

Dreamweaver opens the Results panel and displays a list of all elements that have a class attribute assigned.

For our page, it's a shocking result! Although there are numerous rules defined for the page, just a handful are in use. Only the basic, header, and purple rules have been applied to elements on the page.

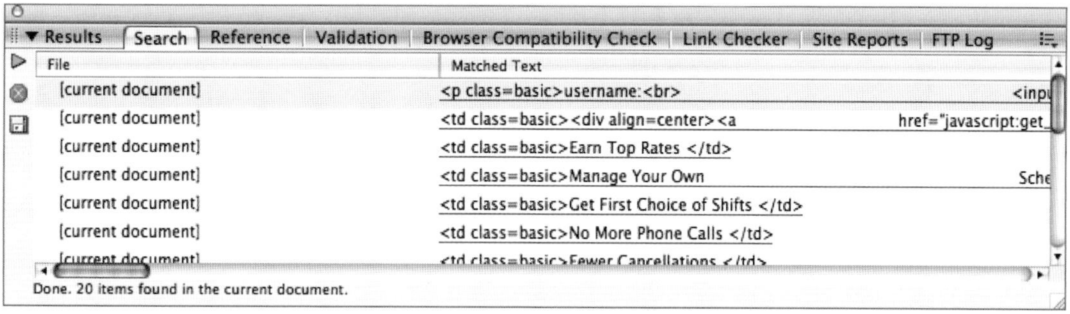

FIGURE 3.4 The Results panel displays each line of code corresponding to the search. Double-clicking on an entry highlights the element in the current view.

N *Regular expressions are powerful tools you can use within Dreamweaver. To learn more about how to utilize them more fully, read "Introduction to Regular Expressions in Dreamweaver" at Adobe's Developer Center http:// www.adobe.com/devnet/dreamweaver/articles/regular_expressions_02.html*

At first glance, you might think we don't need the rest of the defined rules for this page. But this isn't entirely true. Of the three basic types of selectors (type or tag, class, and id), we've only managed to locate the class selectors with our Find and Replace query. To compile a list of the IDs in use, repeat the same process used to find the class, but this time substitute "id" into the search criteria. (Of course, it is also possible to create a search to find the IDs and classes at the same time.)

We now know which IDs and classes are in use. To determine which elements have been redefined via the CSS rules (type selectors), we could write a regular expression and use the Find and Replace command. But honestly, this is simply too much work for the benefit it provides. Instead, we'll just deal with the type selectors as we come to them later.

Organizing the CSS Rules

At this point, we should make a decision about what to do with all the other rules that are not in use in the document. In most cases, we wouldn't want to delete them until we were sure that they were not in use anywhere in the site. But how would we know, you ask? Simple. Instead of running the Find and Replace query on the current page, we could choose Entire Current Local Site from the Find in option of the Find and Replace dialog.

N *To work efficiently with CSS, most of the time you'll establish your rules in an external CSS file, not in the page itself as is done here. As a general rule (no pun intended), even if you develop the rules locally, you should move them to an external style sheet. But, of course, the exception proves the rule (pun intended); on rare occasions, you'll have an instance of a rule designed to override a style on one single, solitary page in a site. In that case, it's perfectly acceptable to define the rule within the head of the page.*

In the case of our page, however, the CSS has been defined in the head of the document. Since rules in the head of the document only apply to that document, we can be sure that we no longer need the extraneous rules.

The traditional way to delete extra rules is to scroll endlessly through the rules in the `<style>` tag to locate and delete the unwanted ones. But Dreamweaver CS3 provides a welcome, far easier option.

Open the CSS Styles panel from the Window menu if it's not already open. As we've previously discussed, the panel reflects either all of the style sheets and rules attached to the page or defined within it, or only the rules and attributes assigned to the currently selected element in the document flow. Click the All button at the top of the CSS panel. We can see the `<style>` tag, and by toggling the tag open, all of the rule declarations defined locally in the page.

Click to select the rules that we have determined need to be kept. Hold Shift and click to make a contiguous selection; hold Cmd while clicking to make noncontiguous selections.

In our case, we've selected the following: `.header`, `.basic`, `td`, `#footer`, `.purple`, `input`, `body`, `a`.

Once all the rules have been selected, right-click one of them to display the contextual menu. Choose the new Move CSS Rules command.

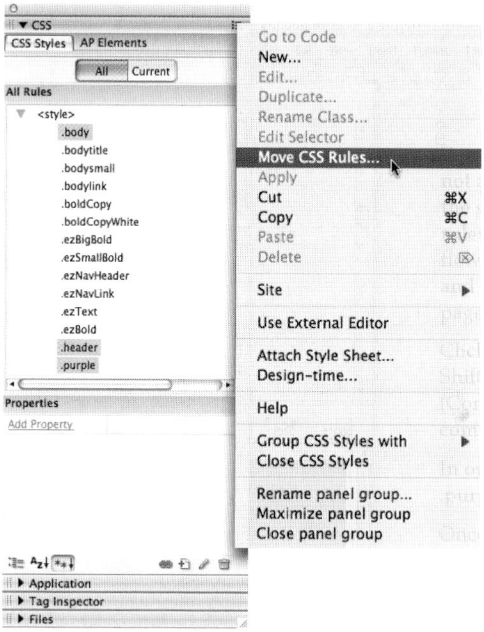

FIGURE 3.5 Pack up the boxes, we're moving out.

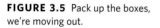 *In previous versions of Dreamweaver, exporting styles was an all-or-nothing proposition. It was impossible to export only selected rules from a page.*

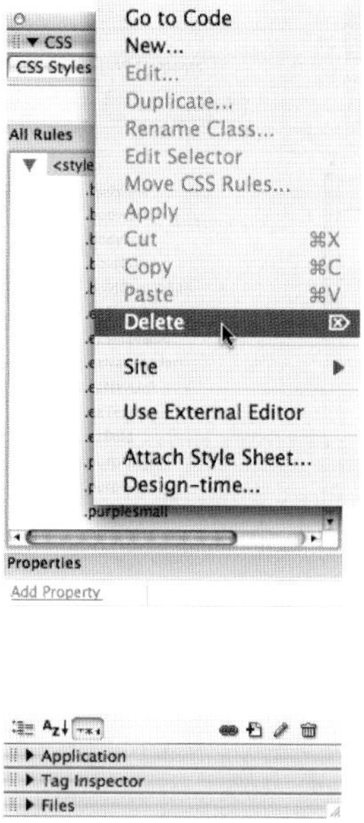

FIGURE 3.6 Say goodbye to the unwanted local rule definitions.

From the resulting dialog, choose a new style sheet file. Click OK. Dreamweaver prompts you for a new filename. For this site, we'll call the file acme.css and save it to the site root.

We have now created an external style sheet containing only the rules in use in the page. In addition, Dreamweaver has created a line of code in the header of our document linking the page to our newly created style sheet. In the CSS panel, we can see an entry for the acme.css file in the All view. As we continue to define rules for the page, we'll add them to this style sheet file. But before we can do that, we'll need to complete our housekeeping by removing the remaining local rules in the `<style>` tag.

T   *When moving rules to an already existing file using the Move CSS Rules command, it is important to remember that the rules being moved are appended to the end of the targeted style sheet file. They will be applied last, which can have undesired effects on page elements due to the cascade. It's always a good idea to examine the targeted style sheet file and perhaps rearrange the order of the rules manually if necessary.*

Click to select the `<style>` tag in the CSS panel. Delete the `<style>` tag and all of its contents by right-clicking and choosing Delete from the contextual menu or clicking the trashcan icon in the lower-right corner of the CSS panel.

Establishing Order

At this point, we've successfully eliminated the unwanted rules and moved the needed rules to an external style sheet. The final preparation before beginning work on the actual page contents is to eliminate the "class-itis" and verbosity in the remaining rules. We also need to establish a more logical flow or hierarchical order to the rules.

Open the acme.css file in Dreamweaver if it is not already open.

Take a quick look at the remaining rules. We can make a number of improvements to slim down the code.

```
.header {
  FONT-WEIGHT: bold;
  FONT-SIZE: 12px;
  COLOR: #ffffff;
  FONT-FAMILY: arial, helvetica, sans-serif
}
.purple {
  FONT-WEIGHT: bold;
  FONT-SIZE: 9pt;
  COLOR: #5b49b1;
  FONT-FAMILY: Arial, Helvetica, Sans-Serif;
  TEXT-DECORATION: none
}
td {
  FONT-SIZE: 12px;
  FONT-FAMILY:arial, helvetica, sans-serif;
  TEXT-DECORATION: none
}
.basic {
  FONT-SIZE: 11px;
  COLOR: #000000;
  FONT-FAMILY: Verdana;
  TEXT-DECORATION: none
}
```

```
#footer {
  background-color: #B6D4AA;
}
input {
  FONT-SIZE: 12px;
  COLOR: #333333;
  FONT-FAMILY: Arial, Helvetica, sans-serif;
  BACKGROUND-COLOR: #B6D4AA
}
body {
  background-color: #666666;
  margin-left: 0px;
  margin-top: 0px;
  margin-right: 0px;
  margin-bottom: 0px;
}
a {
  color: #4C2DA1;
  font-size: 12px;
  font-family:  Arial, Helvetica, sans-serif;
}
```

First and foremost, let's address the order or flow of the defined rules. We want to establish a logical flow on which we can build the rest of the CSS structure. In the style sheet, the **body** selector is near the end of the list of rules, but it will be the first element encountered by the browser agent. As such it should be at the top of the list of rules. As it stands now, with only margin and background declarations, the placement of the **body** selector is irrelevant. However, we'll soon be adding additional base definitions to the rule.

Again, we could scroll through the list of rules to find the **body** selector, select it, cut and paste it to the top of the file (or drag it to the top of the file). But another welcome addition to Dreamweaver CS3 is the ability to reorder rules directly in the CSS panel.

In the CSS panel's All view, click and drag the **body** selector to the top of the list. For cascade reasons, it's better to have basic type selectors at the top of the style sheet, so repeat this procedure for the **td** and **a** selectors, placing them directly under the **body** selector.

Consolidating Attributes

Now take a closer look at these three selectors. Does anything jump out at you?

```
body {
  background-color: #666666;
  margin-left: 0px;
  margin-top: 0px;
  margin-right: 0px;
  margin-bottom: 0px;
}
td {
  FONT-SIZE: 12px;
  FONT-FAMILY:arial, helvetica, sans-serif;
  TEXT-DECORATION: none
}
a {
  color: #4C2DA1;
  font-size: 12px;
  font-family:  Arial, Helvetica, sans-serif;
}
```

If you said, "yes, the `td` and `a` definitions have the same `font-size` and `font-family` defined," give yourself a pat on the back. You have just identified another common mistake—creating (multiple or verbose) duplicate declarations. In fact, we can see that almost every defined rule has `font-family: Arial, Helvetica, sans-serif;` defined.

If the majority of our text will use the same font group, we can remove this attribute from the individual rules and instead define it for all instances of text on the page. We'll allow a couple of the rules to override the behavior by leaving the `font-family` definition intact for them. With Find and Replace, Dreamweaver can quickly make the change.

1. Select `FONT-FAMILY:arial, helvetica, sans-serif;` from the `td` rule and then select Edit > Find and Replace.

    Notice that Dreamweaver has already added the highlighted text to the search field.

2. Ensure that the Find in option is set to Current Document.

3. Paste `FONT-FAMILY:arial, helvetica, sans-serif;` into the Search field if it is not already filled out.

4. Click Find Next.

Did something happen? No? Why is Dreamweaver indicating that there is only one instance of the string in the document? We know for a fact that five of the defined rules have this definition. But if we look closer, we can see that our 12-year-old has struck again! When writing the CSS, he wasn't consistent. In this instance there is no space between the colon and the start of the value. In other instances there is a space separating the colon and value, and in one instance, there are two spaces.

Additionally, the **font-family** rule for **header** doesn't end with a semicolon, so we'll have to work around that as well. And finally, you may have noticed that the capitalization varies, but that isn't an issue here because we didn't select the Match case option.

A regular expression can solve the problem of finding the definition regardless of the way in which it was written.

1. In the Search field, add \s* to the statement between the colon and the beginning of the value and * at the very end, so that you have the following:

   `FONT-FAMILY:\s*arial, helvetica, sans-serif;*`

   This instructs Dreamweaver to look for any instance of the string with or without spaces and with or without a semicolon at the end.

2. Check the Use regular expression check box.

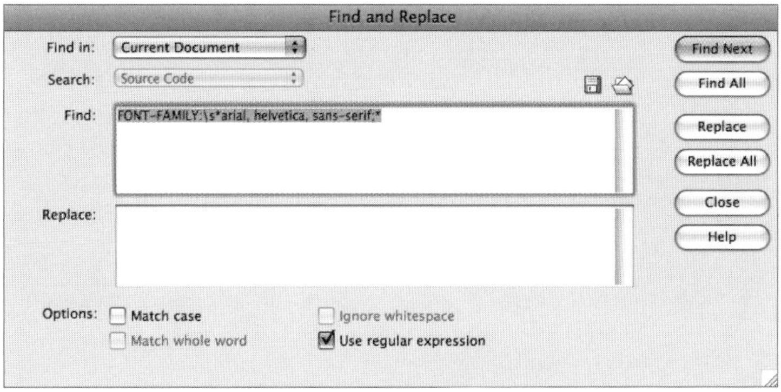

N *The Find and Replace dialog has a check box titled Ignore Whitespace when using the Search in Source Code option. You might think that in the current example of searching for an entry that has a few spaces as its only variance, we could use this check box to find all of the instances. Unfortunately, when searching source code, Dreamweaver only checks to see if there are one or more spaces—zero spaces, as in this example, doesn't match. Mark that one down as a bug—yikes!*

FIGURE 3.7 Using a regular expression to find all occurrences of the property/value pair.

3. Click Find Next to loop over the individual instances of the search criteria in the document to ensure that your query is working properly. Be sure to leave the Replace field empty.

4. Click Replace All to remove all the definitions that meet the search criteria from the document.

    Notice that Dreamweaver has left a blank line in the CSS code where the deleted lines were. We like nice and tidy code, and we're sure that you do as well.

5. Select Commands > Apply Source Formatting menu.

    Text attributes applied to the **body** will be inherited by all page elements. Therefore, let's add the **font-family** definition to the rule for the body element.

FIGURE 3.8 Dreamweaver displays a list of standard CSS properties when working in a CSS file.

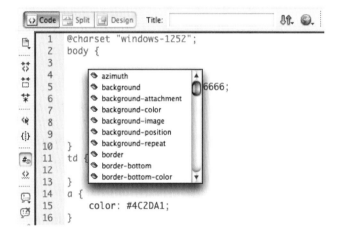

6. Click in the **body** element rule within the acme.css file, placing the cursor immediately following the opening curly bracket and press Return to add a new line.

    Dreamweaver displays a list of CSS properties.

7. Begin to type **font-family**.

    Dreamweaver's tag completion function moves to the entries corresponding to the letters typed. (You can also use the arrow keys to move up and down through the list.)

8. With **font-family** selected, press Return.

    Dreamweaver adds the corresponding property and displays a list of possible values.

When working with CSS in Code view, Dreamweaver does not add a semicolon to complete the property/value pair. Though you can omit the semicolon from the last property/value pair in a given rule, we recommend that you properly complete each line. That way you'll never accidentally forget the semicolon when adding additional properties by hand.

9. Select `Arial, Helvetica, sans-serif` from the Font list, and press Return. Type ; to complete the entry.

We can now repeat the process for the `font-size`. Unfortunately, not all of the rules use the same `font-size` definition. In fact, they don't even use the same unit of measure! Obviously, this is not good. Looking through the rules, it appears that **12px** is the most common size, so let's use that as the base size for our text. Remember, it's a best practice to assign a relative unit of measure to any text elements.

Add a new line in the rule for the body element and type `font-size: .8em;` since, at browser defaults, this will be close to the original `font-size`. Remove the `font-size: 12px;` property/value pairs from the respective rules using either Find and Replace or by selecting them manually.

We're now left with two rules that also define a `font-size`. The `.basic` class uses a slightly smaller font size of **11px**. Therefore, change its value to **.75em**.

Finally, change the `.purple` class `font-size` to **1em**. Though the current size appeared to be set smaller than the rest, it was actually rendering larger in a browser. And without access to the original developer, we'll assume that the browser rendering was actually what was wanted, so we'll keep that `font-size` as it was rendered.

Wrapping Up the Consolidation

There are a few more consolidation possibilities. Three of the rules define a `text-decoration` property. The `text-decoration` property is generally associated with links and used to add or remove the underline from `a` elements. But since text elements by default do not have a `text-decoration`, declaring the property within a rule is redundant. You can remove the `text-decoration` from each of the respective rules.

With no `text-decoration` property, the `td` element rule is now empty; it should be removed as well.

Finally, let's look at the `color` property defined in the `.basic` class. The `color` definition is for black text. A quick glance through the rest of the rules doesn't seem to indicate that black overrides another text color, so moving the `color` property to the `body` rule declares a default color for the page and is more efficient CSS.

The following are our optimized rules:

```
body {
  font-family: Arial, Helvetica, sans-serif;
  font-size: .8em;
  background-color: #666666;
  COLOR: #000000;
  margin-left: 0px;
  margin-top: 0px;
  margin-right: 0px;
  margin-bottom: 0px;
}
a {
  color: #4C2DA1;
}
.header {
  FONT-WEIGHT: bold;
  COLOR: #ffffff;
}
.purple {
  FONT-WEIGHT: bold;
  FONT-SIZE: 1em;
  COLOR: #5b49b1;
}
.basic {
  FONT-SIZE: .75em;
  FONT-FAMILY: Verdana;
}
#footer {
  background-color: #B6D4AA;
}
input {
  COLOR: #333333;
  BACKGROUND-COLOR: #B6D4AA
}
```

Cleaning Up the <table> Mess

With the style sheet file cleaned up, it's time to start working on the page structure. Like a majority of pages on the web even today, this page consists of a number of nested tables. When migrating a table-based design to CSS, it's usually best to find the most deeply nested table and work your way out from there.

The two areas shown in **Figure 3.9** each consist of three tables— one functioning as the main container with two tables nested within. One table holds what appears to be a list (although it is not semantically marked up as a list) and the other contains a button and a couple of links.

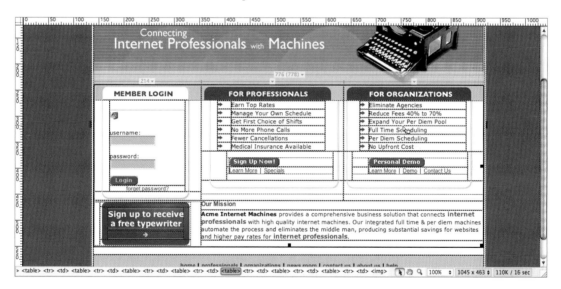

FIGURE 3.9 Two areas that are similar and nested deep within the page structure are in the center of the layout, and are identified by the For Professionals and For Organizations graphics.

Let's begin by eliminating the table containing what appears to be the list in one of the areas. For no particular reason, we'll start on the right, in the area headed For Organizations.

Click on a cell containing text that appears to be a list. As you can see, it's really just text in a table cell. Using the tag selector at the bottom of the document window, click to select the <table> tag containing the table cell into which you placed the cursor. 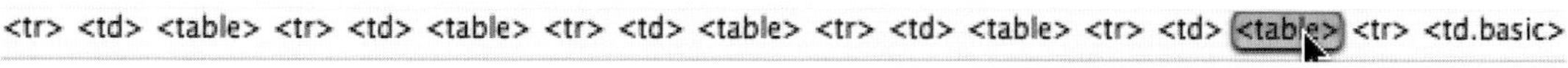

<tr> <td> <table> <tr> <td> <table> <tr> <td> <table> <tr> <td> <table> <tr> <td> <table> <tr> <td.basic>

FIGURE 3.10 The tag selector can really drive home the point of just how messy this table-based layout really is!

Using Find and Replace to Eliminate Table Code

We'll use the Find and Replace command to strip the table cells and rows from the document, leaving only their content in the form of an unordered list.

1. With the <table> tag selected, select Edit > Find and Replace. Choose Selected Text from the Find in drop-down list and choose Specific Tag from the Search drop-down list.

   The `<tr>` tag in this table is a perfect candidate to turn into a list item because it contains the table cells with the data we are interested in.

2. Type `tr` into the Specific Tag search field or select it from the drop-down list. Remove the parameters, such as With Attribute, by clicking the minus button. Select Change Tag from the Action drop-down list and type `li` into the criteria field or select it from the drop-down list. Click Replace All.

   The Dreamweaver Results panel now shows us a list of the items that were removed. Leave this panel open.

3. Click to select the `<table>` tag from the code line at the bottom of the document once again. Click the little green triangle in the top-left corner of the Results panel.

   This reopens the dialog with the same selection you used before.

4. Type `td` into the search field or choose it from the drop-down list. Choose Strip Tag from the Action drop-down list. Click Replace All.

   We've now eliminated all of the `<tr>` and `<td>` tags, leaving us with only the final `<table>` tag to remove.

5. Select the `<td>` tag that contains the `<table>` that we've been modifying. Click the green find and replace triangle to retain the same settings as before, but of course change the search criteria to `table`.

6. From the Action drop-down list, choose Change Tag and in the Action field type `ul` or select it from the drop-down list. Click Replace All.

As we go about this process, you'll notice at times that the Design view of Dreamweaver no longer displays the page contents properly. That's to be expected, since there will be moments when the code is a complete train wreck. Don't worry about it!

You may not need to remove the parameters if you have recently used the Specific Tag option in the Find and Replace dialog, because Dreamweaver remembers the way in which you left the dialog the last time you used it.

When choosing the Change Tag action in the Find and Replace dialog, Dreamweaver will replace the searched for tag with the tag selected. But if the tag being replaced has any attributes, the attributes will be left intact on the new tag. In some instances, this can mean that you have attributes applied to the tag that do not belong there. In this case, you'll need to strip these attributes by hand or use a regular expression to strip them all at once.

You can use Dreamweaver's Split view to ensure that you have the proper code selected.

The Replace Tag action has replaced the `<table>` tag with the `<ul>` tag, but the attributes of the `<table>` tag have been left intact.

```
<ul height="100%" cellspacing=0 cellpadding=0 width="100%"
border=0>
```

We could write a regular expression in the Find and Replace dialog to remove these attributes, but it is just as easy to switch to Code view or Split view, select them, and delete them manually. Do that now.

Styling Lists with CSS

In Design view, you can now see that the table is gone and a list is left in its place. You can also see a few problems with the list. Remember, we're trying to replicate the original design using CSS. To do that, we need to change the bullets to arrows, get rid of the arrow images in the list items, and properly position the list. 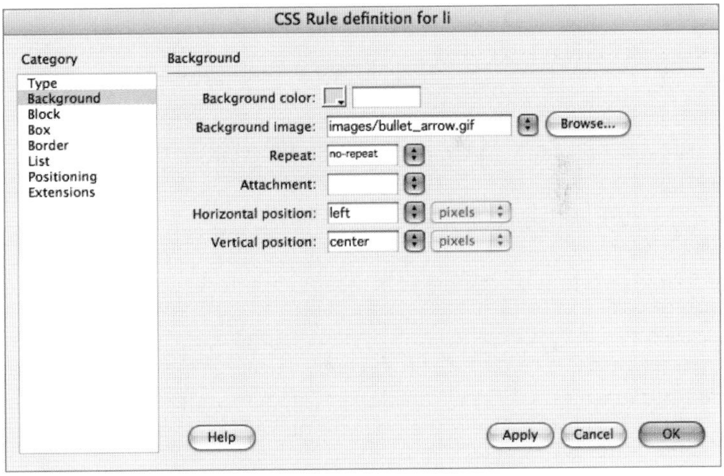

FIGURE 3.11 Comparing the two lists we can see that we still have work to do to override the default appearance.

Let's start with the bullets. By default, a list item is displayed with a bullet. The original table used an arrow image for a bullet, but the arrow image is now part of the list item. We'll fix this by deleting the arrow image using our hard-working Find and Replace command. Do the following:

1. Place the cursor in one of the list items and select the `<ul>` tag from the tag line at the bottom of the document.

2. Choose Edit > Find and Replace.

3. Ensure that Selected Text and Specific Tag are selected from their respective drop-down lists.

4. In the search field type img or select it from the drop-down list.

5. In the Action drop-down list, choose Remove Tag.

6. Click Replace All.

With the images now gone, we'll create a rule to modify the look of the list items. Do the following:

1. Click the New CSS Rule button at the bottom of the CSS panel.

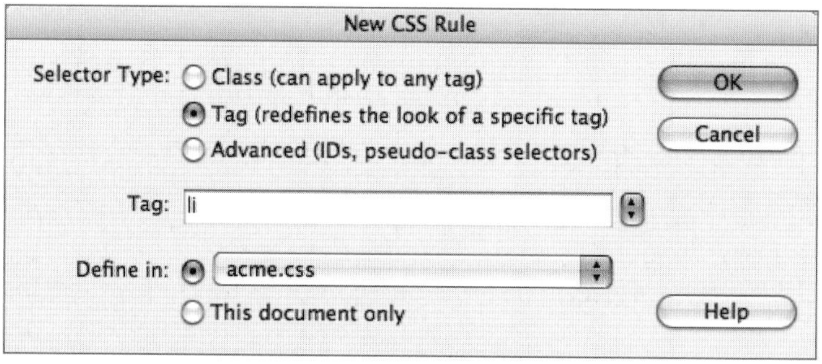

FIGURE 3.12 Defining a list item selector.

> New CSS Rule
>
> Selector Type: ○ Class (can apply to any tag)
> ● Tag (redefines the look of a specific tag)
> ○ Advanced (IDs, pseudo–class selectors)
>
> Tag: li
>
> Define in: ● acme.css
> ○ This document only
>
> OK
> Cancel
> Help

2. Choose Tag as the selector type and type li in the tag field or choose it from the drop-down list.

3. Select the acme.css file as the location for the new rule. Click OK.

4. The CSS Rule definition dialog appears. Select List from the category listing on the left side of the dialog.

There are three options for defining the appearance of the list. One option lets us use an image for the bullet, so we could select the arrow image to use as a bullet image. And in some circumstances that might actually work. However, the arrow images in the original are placed some distance from the actual pseudo list entry. Unfortunately, when using a bullet image for list items, you can't specify a distance or offset for the images. To space the image properly, we'll need to use a background image to create our bullets. But before leaving this area of the dialog, we need to remove the bullet completely.

5. Type none in the Type field or select it from the drop-down list. Select Background from the category listing.

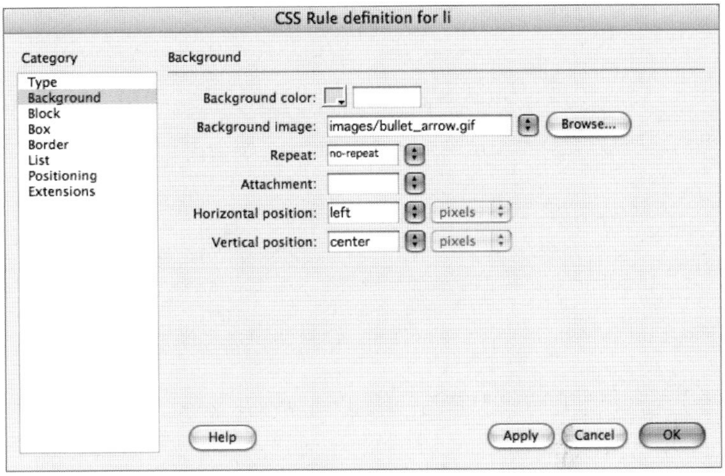

FIGURE 3.13 Styling a list using a background image is more flexible than using bulleted list items.

FIGURE 3.13 Styling a list using a background image is more flexible than using bulleted list items.

6. Click the Browse button and locate the bullet_arrow.gif image to use as a background image.

   By default, the browser tiles and repeats the image both horizontally and vertically behind the selected page element, in this case the list entry. But we only want a single instance of the image.

7. Type **no-repeat** in the Repeat field or select it from the drop-down list.

   We also want to make sure that the image is placed vertically in the middle of the list item and to the left of the entry.

8. Type **left** in the Horizontal position field or select it from the drop-down list. Type **center** in the Vertical position field or select it from the drop-down list.

9. Click Apply and take a look at the list.

   We can see that the background image has been applied; however, it is directly underneath the text. By default, a background will simply fill the defined space of the element. In this case, since we chose to left align the background image, the image went to the left side of the actual text of the list item. To render this properly, we need to create space to the left and increase the "size" of the list element.

10. Select the Box category in the dialog.

The Box category provides all of the physical dimensions of the selector. But since we are working with a text element that may increase or decrease in size due to the amount of text, we don't want to define a width or height for the element. Instead, we'll simply add some padding.

Padding and margins can both be defined uniformly around the element or can be applied with different values on all four sides of the element.

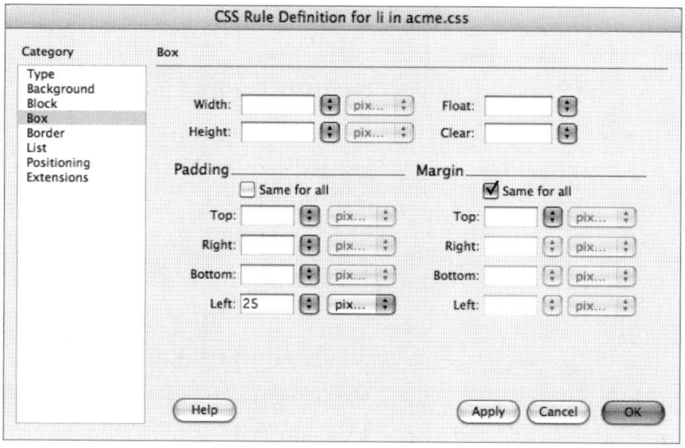

FIGURE 3.14 Padding and Margin attributes can be applied to all sides of an element or any combination of sides.

11. Uncheck the "Same for all" check box in the Padding section and enter **25** in the Left field. Leave the unit of measure set to pixels. Click OK.

The list is coming along nicely, but you might have noticed that the list items are placed farther to the right than they should be when compared to the original table-based design. To move the entire list to the left, we'll need to redefine the `<ul>` selector.

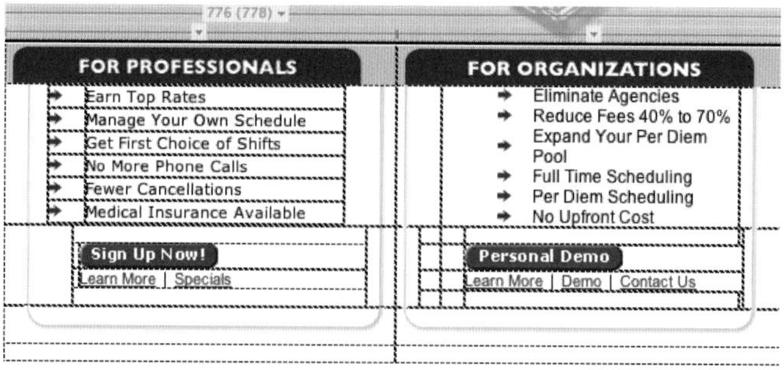

FIGURE 3.15 Looking better, but there are still some problems to be addressed.

Browser defaults for margin and padding on lists vary wildly. For consistency, it's best to give definite values, even if that means simply zeroing those values to start at a level playing field.

12. Click the New CSS Rule button at the bottom of the CSS panel. In the dialog, choose Tag as the selector, type ul in the Tag field or select it from the drop-down list, and ensure that we are adding the rule to the acme.css style sheet. Select the Box category.

13. Uncheck the "Same for all" check box in the Padding section and type **10** in the Left field, leaving the unit of measure set to pixels. Leave the "Same for all" check box checked in the Margin section and type **0** in the Top field. Click OK.

Pulling Tables Out of Their Nest

Check the Design view again. Looks like this section of the page is coming along nicely. But now we have a bigger issue to deal with. Two more nested tables contain a button graphic and some links. Why multiple nested tables were used we'll never know, but we need to remove them. To save some work, let's use a little known feature of Dreamweaver that allows us to collapse one table into another.

This feature is known as Layout Mode. Originally, Layout Mode was designed to allow web designers to simply draw table cells in Design view. Dreamweaver would subsequently write the table code around the drawn table cell. Unfortunately, the resulting table code was bloated since Dreamweaver didn't optimize it.

We don't recommend using Layout Mode for creating tables, but its ability to remove table nesting comes in quite handy.

1. Select View > Table Mode > Layout Mode to enable Layout Mode.

With Layout Mode enabled, we can easily see all of the tables on the page; each is indicated by a small green Layout Table identifier.

FIGURE 3.16 Layout Mode can help identify the individual nested tables on the page.

2. Place the cursor inside the table cell in the table containing the button and select the `<table>` tag from the tag selector at the bottom of the document.

3. Find and click the Remove Nesting icon on the right of the Property inspector.

```
<body> <table> <tr> <td> <table> <tr> <td> <table> <tr> <td> <table> <tr> <td> <table> <tr> <td> <table> <tr> <td>
```

| Layout table | Width | ● Fixed | 282 | Height | 211 | | CellPad | 0 | | Class | None | |
| | | ○ Autostretch | | Bg | | | CellSpace | 0 | | | | |

FIGURE 3.17 The Remove Nesting icon removes the `<table>` tag from a table, allowing the table contents to become part of the containing table.

The table has now "collapsed," becoming rows and columns in the parent table. But we don't need the parent table either.

4. Select the `<table>` tag from the tag selector at the bottom of the document (formerly the parent table) and once again click the Remove Nesting icon. Place the cursor in the list we created earlier.

5. Select the `<table>` tag from the code line and click the Remove Nesting icon from the Property inspector.

We're now left with only a single table to deal with in this area of the page. Before proceeding, turn off Layout Mode by selecting View > Table Mode > Standard Mode.

Modifying Graphics with Adobe Fireworks CS3

As with any image, using an alt attribute so that nonvisual user agents know what this graphic indicates makes our page more accessible.

Before we continue replacing this table with the CSS-based design, we need to decide what to do about the images that are forming the visual border of the table. The purple header graphic conveys information and, as such, needs to remain an actual image on the page rather than a background image.

However, the gray line graphics used to form the box are simply decoration. In other words, it is ridiculous to have them inline in the HTML. It would be much simpler to use a single background image to serve the same purpose. Unfortunately, we don't have the original images (the 12-year-old designer lost them, remember?), so we can't simply reslice and reexport the graphic, and merging the images in a new file of the right size would be guesswork. But Fireworks can solve this problem for us!

1. Select the table once again by placing the cursor into the table and selecting the `<table>` tag from the code line at the bottom of the document window.

If you're unable to copy/ paste and use keyboard shortcuts, check to be sure your page rendering is in Standard Mode. It's not possible to do those things in Layout Mode.

2. Select Edit > Copy. Create a new HTML document by selecting File > New. Select HTML as the document type and <none> from the Layout column. In the new document, select Edit > Paste.

   If Dreamweaver prompts you to assign an Alt text to the images, simply click Cancel because we'll only be using this file temporarily.

3. Save the file as "temp.htm" in the site structure. Open Adobe Fireworks CS3.

   If you do not own Fireworks CS3, you can download a fully functional 30-day trial from the Adobe web site.

4. Select File > Reconstitute Table. Browse to the temp.htm file we just created and click Open.

   Fireworks creates a PNG file based upon the table structure complete with slices for each table cell.

FIGURE 3.18 Fireworks rebuilt the HTML table containing graphics and text as a single image.

5. In the Layers panel, select the Web Layer and click the trashcan icon at the bottom of the panel.

You're deleting all of the slices in the document, so we can create our own slices.

6. Select the Slice tool from the Tools palette and draw a narrow slice across the middle of the graphic. A good height is 10–15 pixels.

7. Right-click on the slice and choose Export Selected. Name the graphic box_background.gif and browse to the images folder of the site. Click Save.

We now have an image that we can use as a background image for the box, and Fireworks made the whole process simple!

FIGURE 3.19 Slicing gets us just the piece of the graphic that we need for the background image.

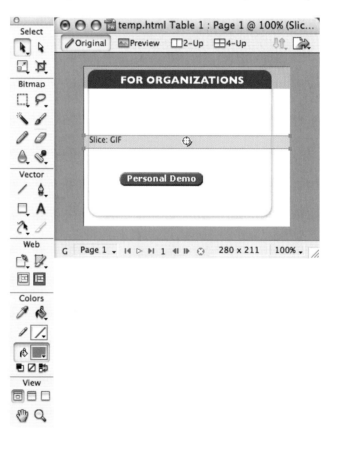

Wrapping Things Up with Divs

It's time to start implementing the CSS-based framework for this section of the page. The first step is to remove the images that form the box border on the left and right sides, and establish a container `<div>` for the table that we'll be removing.

1. Select each of the four images of the box border and delete them, leaving the purple header graphic and the bottom box graphic.

2. Select the table and switch to the Layout tab of the Insert bar. Click the Insert Div Tag icon.

3. From the Insert Div Tag dialog, ensure that the Insert drop-down list is set to "Wrap around selection", and then click the New CSS Style button.

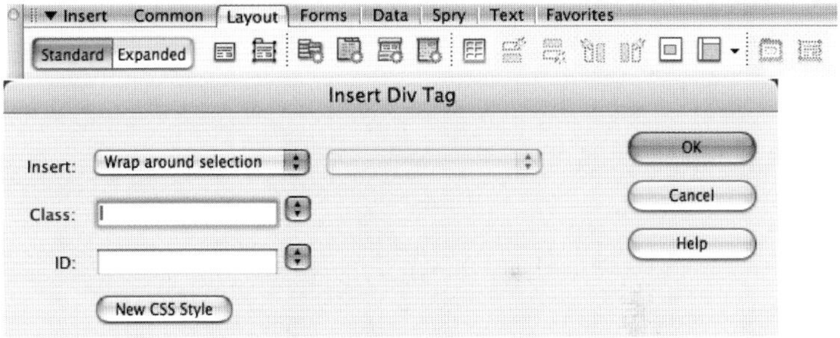

FIGURE 3.20 The Insert Div Tag dialog specifies how the `<div>` tag will be inserted and provides the opportunity to assign existing rules or create new rules.

The Insert Div Tag dialog allows us to create the rule for the element or div that will enclose the page elements that will be left over after we delete the table markup.

Before proceeding, we need to establish the type of selector that we'll define. Because we'll want to use this rule multiple times on the page, we need to create a class selector.

T *Remember, the names you assign to the rule should be descriptive but not limiting. In other words, avoid names like "leftcolumn" since modifications could easily be made to the rule that might place the element on the right.*

4. Choose Class as the selector type. In the Selector field for Class, type `.contentBox`. Click OK.

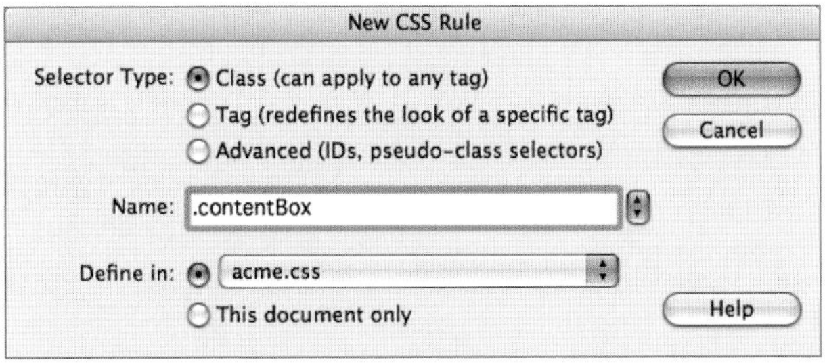

FIGURE 3.21 The new rule is created and automatically assigned to the new `<div>` tag.

5. Select the Background category in the dialog. Click the Browse button. Navigate to the images folder where we exported the image slice from Fireworks. Select box_background.gif. Click OK.

    We want this background image to tile or repeat vertically within the defined space.

6. From the Repeat drop-down list, select **repeat-y**. Click OK. Click OK in the Insert Div Tag dialog.

We now have a **<div>** tag wrapping the table that will hold all of the content in place. This means that we can easily remove the rest of the table markup from this page element. Using the techniques you've already learned, strip the remaining **<table>**, **<tr>**, and **<td>** tags from the table. (Remember to place the cursor anywhere within the table and select the **<div>** tag from the tag selector to begin.)

Upon completing the process, the area of the page should look something like Figure 3.22.

FIGURE 3.22 Pared down but still slightly messy.

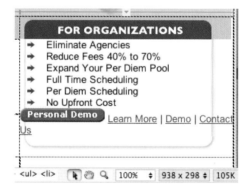

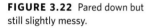

Fine-tuning the List

Without the table markup, it's clear that we need to fine-tune the list. Let's start by moving the list to the right.

1. Place the cursor anywhere in the list and select **<ul>** from the tag selector at the bottom of the document window.

2. In the CSS panel, select the Current view. Ensure that the CSS Properties section is only displaying properties that have a

value assigned by clicking on the Show only set properties icon at the bottom of the panel.

FIGURE 3.23 The third icon selects only properties that have a value assigned.

Since we've removed the inline images that separated the list from the box, we'll need to replace that space.

3. From the Properties section of the CSS panel, click on the value for **padding-left** that is currently set to 10px.

4. Change the value to 40 and leave pixels selected as the unit of measure.

The list should now be positioned properly, but we still need to correct the button image and links at the bottom of the box. What we need is a container for the button image and the three links to which we can attach a class. We have three options:

• Wrap the links in a **<p>** element.

• Wrap the links in a **<span>** element.

• Wrap the links in a **<div>** element.

All three options would work, but when you have to make this kind of decision, you should always try to think semantically. The purpose of the links and the button image is best represented as a paragraph, so let's use a **<p>** element.

1. In Design view, click and drag to select the three links and image. Choose Modify > Quick Tag Editor or use the keyboard shortcut Cmd+T/Ctrl+T.

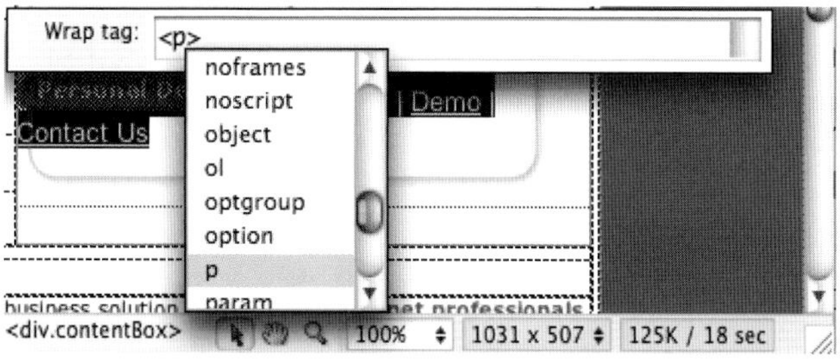

FIGURE 3.24 The Quick Tag Editor allows us to either wrap a selection in a tag or insert a tag at the current cursor location when nothing is selected in Design or Code view.

2. In the Quick Tag Editor, type **p**. Press Return twice.

   The automatic code hinting scrolled to the tags beginning with "p." Since we actually wanted a `<p>` tag, it landed right on our choice.

3. In the CSS panel, click the New CSS Rule button at the bottom of the panel to create a new descendent selector. Select Advanced as the Selector type.

   If you have the `<p>` element selected when you open the CSS Editing dialog, Dreamweaver autofills the selector input with `.contentBox p`. We'll use that.

4. Choose to add the new rule to the acme.css file. Click OK. Select the Box category. Uncheck the "Same for all" check box in the Padding section. In the Left field, type 40 and select pixels as the unit of measure. Click OK.

   Looking at the area in Design view, the button image has moved to the right, but the three links still need to be moved to the line below the button. We can accomplish this by modifying the display of the button image.

5. Select the button image and then click the New CSS Rule button at the bottom of the CSS panel.

   Dreamweaver will suggest a descendent selector of `.contentBox img` in the Selector field and will likely have the acme.css file preselected since we have added our previous rule to it.

6. Click OK. Select the Block category. From the Display drop-down list, select block (Figure 3.25). Click OK.

The block display property has now formatted the image vertically and thus, has forced the links to the next line.

FIGURE 3.25 Selecting block display formats the element vertically starting at the top of its parent container.

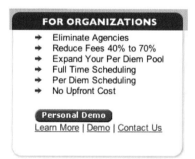

With that, we've completed this section of the page. To ensure that everything is, in fact, as we expect, preview the page in the browser of your choice.

FIGURE 3.26 The completed section of the page.

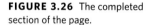

While we've only completed the transformation of a small part of the page, we are actually much further along than it might appear. We've now mastered all of the basic techniques needed to complete the transformation.

Picking Up Speed

To illustrate this process more clearly, we'll move to the box area in the center of the page. This box uses the same structure as the area that we just completed. Therefore, it will be even easier to transform. In fact, because we've already established the necessary rules, we can streamline the process even further using a slightly different workflow.

FIGURE 3.27 The next set of nested tables will be even easier to format.

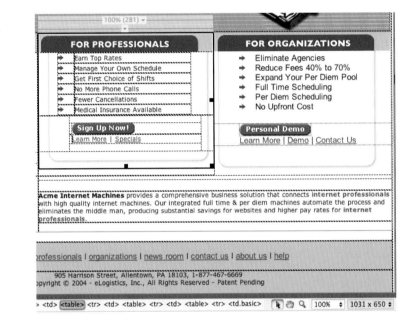

1. In Design view, place the cursor into the list in the middle of the box.

2. From the tag selector, click on the `<table>` tags sequentially from the right to locate the `<table>` tag that represents the parent table for this section of the page. Depending on where you placed the cursor, it will probably be the third table tag from the right.

3. Click the Insert Div Tag icon in the Layout section of the Insert bar. From the class drop-down list, choose the class `.contentBox` that you created earlier. Click OK.

With the entire `<table>` tag and all of its contents wrapped in a `<div>`, you can easily clean out the table markup. Using Find and Replace, strip all of the `<table>`, `<tr>,` and `<td>` tags from the `<div.contentBox>` tag. Remember to ensure that you have chosen Selected Text from the Find in drop-down list. Also be sure to reselect the `<div.contentBox>` tag in the tag selector after each successful Find and Replace.

FIGURE 3.28 After removing the table markup, we're left with a bit of a mess.

We're left with just the contents of the formerly nested tables. Time to clean up!

1. Click to select the images that were representing the right and left sides of the box and delete them.

2. Select each arrow image and press Return to replace the `<img>` tag with a `<p>` tag.

3. Place the cursor in front of the purple button image and press Return to enclose it in a `<p>` tag, separating it from the list entries.

4. Place the cursor at the end of the links and press Return to enclose the image used as the bottom of the box in a `<p>` tag, separating the graphic from the button and links.

5. Click and drag to select all of the entries that we want to turn into a list. In the Property inspector, click the Unordered List button.

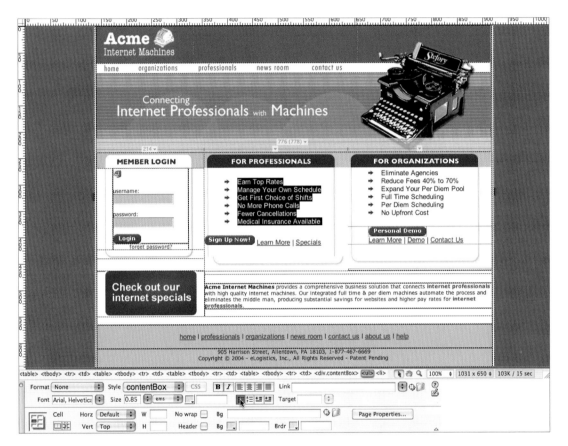

FIGURE 3.29 The unordered list takes on the properties assigned, but other elements still need to be styled to match the area on the right.

The bottom images of the boxes would be better as background images. Applying the faux column principles to these boxes is a best practice because it keeps noninformational graphics out of the HTML.

The For Professionals graphic needs to sit flush with the top of the `<div>`, so click to select the image. You can see in the tag selector that the image is wrapped in a `<p>` tag. Right-click on the `<p>` tag in the tag selector and choose Remove Tag.

Repeat the process for the `<p>` tag that contains the image representing the bottom of the box.

And with that, another piece of the page is complete.

Practicing What You've Learned

To test what you've learned so far, rebuild the Member Login area on your own. Here are a few hints:

- **Fireworks CS3:** You'll need to use Fireworks CS3 to create a background image for the box. Unfortunately, you can't just use the image that we've already created for the other boxes, because you can't define a width for a background image in CSS. Since the Member Login area is a different width then the other boxes, you'll need a new image.

- **Layout Mode:** Use Layout Mode to flatten the table structure of the area before using Fireworks to attempt to reconstitute the table.

- **Styling forms:** We'll discuss styling forms in-depth in a subsequent chapter but for now, redefine the `<form>` element using a descendant selector in case there are forms on subsequent pages. Give it a `padding-left` value of 30 pixels.

FIGURE 3.30 If you've completed the Member Login area, you're making great progress.

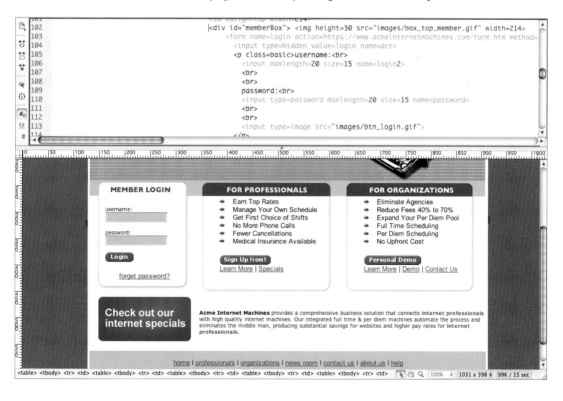

Rebuilding the Page Header

It's time to address a more difficult situation. In the header of the page, we can identify a number of navigational images, a logo, and some furniture graphics—meaning graphics that are purely cosmetic.

The problem once again is that the graphics are in a number of slices to accommodate design elements, such as the typewriter bleeding into the white and green areas above it.

T *Before proceeding, let's make a quick list of the actual links on the navigational elements so that we can reassign them later.*

You've probably already guessed where we're going with this. Yep, it's back to Fireworks.

Using Layout Mode, flatten the nested tables in the header area into one table. Save the flattened table as an HTML document and reconstitute it in Fireworks as we did previously. You'll notice an odd white space appear to the right of the logo. Don't worry, we'll attend to that later.

FIGURE 3.31 The header area as it appears in Fireworks CS3 with the individual slices showing.

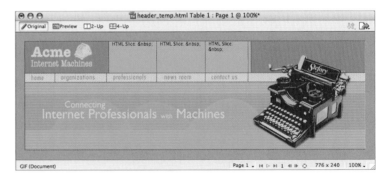

As you can immediately see, Fireworks has almost done the job correctly. But the "almost" is apparent if we turn off the slices. (To turn off slices from the keyboard, press 2.)

Without the slices, there is a large, white rectangular area between the Acme logo and the top of the typewriter. That particular area of the table was composed of empty table cells with a background color applied. Since we'll use this entire image as a single background image, changing the canvas color of the Fireworks graphic will solve this problem.

1. Select the solid arrow tool and click outside of the canvas area in the Fireworks image to ensure that nothing is selected.

With nothing on the graphic selected, the Property inspector provides a color swatch to define the canvas color.

2. Click the color swatch and move the eyedropper over the dark green area of the Acme logo. Click again to select the color. Now our white box area has been filled with color to match the rest of the graphic.

The navigational elements are next up for removal. We don't need to export them as part of the image. So, using the solid Arrow selection tool, select the buttons and press Delete or backspace to get rid of them. (Hold down Shift while you click to select all five buttons at once.)

We'll need to reexport the image as one large background image, so we won't need any slices. Open the Layers panel and click to select the Web Layer. Click the trashcan icon at the bottom of the panel to delete all of the slices.

After removing the buttons, there's an area that's blank. We'll need to fill that in.

1. Select the rectangle vector tool. Select white as the Fill color from the Property inspector or at the bottom of the toolbar.

2. Draw a rectangle in the space underneath the logo graphic ending at the white rectangle of the typewriter graphic.

    You'll want the rectangle to be the same height as the other white band. If your hands aren't steady enough, simply draw a square anywhere on the canvas and use the Property inspector to give the object a width of 509 and a height of 20. Place the object at X:0 and Y:70.

Our image should be perfect now, so it's ready to export.

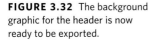

FIGURE 3.32 The background graphic for the header is now ready to be exported.

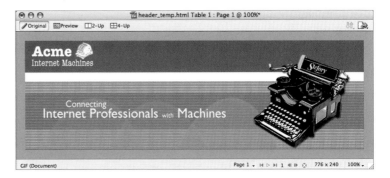

1. Open the Optimize and Align panel.

2. Select JPG as the format, and then select File > Export.

3. In the Export dialog, name the graphic "header_background.
   jpg" and choose the site's images folder. Ensure that the Export
   drop-down list is set to Images Only. Click OK.

Feel free to save the graphic as a Fireworks PNG if you think you
might want to reedit it. Before leaving Fireworks, make a mental
note of the dimensions of the graphic we've just created—776 x
240 pixels.

Adding the Background Graphic in the Header

Back in Dreamweaver, we can quickly complete the page header
and navigation.

1. If it is not already selected, select the table on the index page
   that we just used to reconstitute the header graphic.

2. Wrap the table in a `<div>` using the Insert Div Tag icon in the
   Layout section of the Insert bar.

3. Give the div an ID of **header** and create a new rule in the acme.
   css style sheet.

4. Switch to the Background category and click the Background
   image field's Browse button. Browse to the JPG file that you just
   exported from Fireworks: header_background.jpg.

5. Change to the Box category and define a width of 776 pixels
   with a height of 240 pixels. Click OK twice.

We can't yet see the background image that we just inserted,
because the table markup and all of the graphics are still there.
We'll solve this problem by simply deleting the table markup.

Dreamweaver should still be highlighting or selecting the header
graphics on the page. Make sure that this is the case by looking at
the tag selector. It should be selecting the `<table>` tag for the header
graphics. Press Delete to remove the entire table and its graphics.

And there's our header graphic—now properly appearing as a
background image.

Positioning the Navigation

All that's left is to place the navigational images back on the page.

As you know from our earlier review, CSS has different methods of positioning. So far, we've only used static positioning on this page, because we've been positioning <div> elements within a basic table structure that holds the elements in place. We'll eventually remove this table markup—but first, we still have work to do.

Absolute positioning can create problems when textual content is resized, so generally it's good to avoid it, but when dealing with image content, absolute positioning can be quite effective.

Over the years, many professionals have ridiculed Dreamweaver's Draw AP Div tool (previously called the Layer tool). The criticism was deserved because the tool wrote CSS code inline in the HTML (a serious no-no!). But since Dreamweaver 8, the Draw AP Div tool writes its CSS code in the head of the document. We'll still have to remember to move it to the external style sheet when finished, but it's a fast and easy way to create an absolutely positioned (AP) <div>.

N *When using the Draw AP Div tool, the element is assigned a width and a height. Generally, we don't want to assign a height attribute to a page element. The primary exception is when the background image used is larger than the actual content of the element. Under most circumstances, you should manually remove the height attribute that the Draw AP Div tool automatically assigns to the div.*

1. Switch to the Layout section of the Insert bar.

2. Select the Draw AP Div tool.

3. Click and drag to draw a div covering the white area where the navigational images will be placed.

4. Click to select the newly created absolutely positioned (AP) div.

5. Assign the div an ID of **nav** by typing it into the name field of the Property inspector.

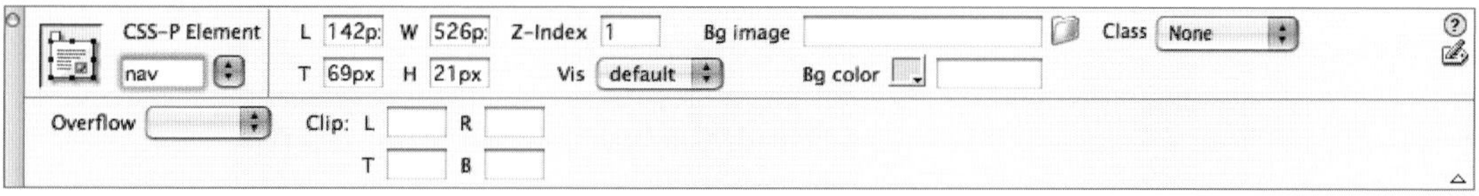

FIGURE 3.33 The Property inspector for absolutely positioned div elements.

By default, when an AP element is created using the Draw AP Div tool, Dreamweaver adds the `<div>` immediately following the opening `<body>` tag. If we were to add additional AP elements, Dreamweaver would simply add them sequentially.

Because an AP div is out of the flow of the document (absolutely positioned, in other words), having this div as the first element in the source order causes its only parent container to be the body. Since our layout has a fixed dimension, centered within the browser window, this is a problem. To see the problem, make the document window wider or narrower. The AP `<div>` remains stationary, even though the rest of the elements on the page move. Let's fix that.

1. With the `<div>` still selected on the page, select Edit > Cut to temporarily remove it from the page. Click on the header graphic.

    Because the header graphic is a background image of the `#header` `<div>`, it will not be selected; however, the cursor has now been properly placed.

2. Choose Edit > Paste to place the `#nav` `<div>` inside the header.

    If we experiment with the window width again, we can see that the `#nav` `<div>` is still misbehaving.

3. Open the CSS panel in the Current view. Select the `#nav` `<div>` on the page if it is not already selected. In the Properties section of the CSS panel, change the value for Position from absolute to relative.

    On the page, we can see that the element has moved to the right. Since the relative value tells the browser agent to render the element relative to its parent container, which is now the `#header` `<div>`, we need to change the positioning values of the `#nav` `<div>`.

4. In the CSS panel, change the Left value to 0 pixels and the Top value to 70 pixels. Set the width to 509 pixels. (We'll delete the height later when it's easier to select the space within the `#nav` `<div>`.)

5. Switch to the Files panel and open the images folder. Drag the image menu_home.gif into the **#nav** **<div>**, followed by the menu_professionals.gif, menu_organizations.gif, menu_news-room.gif, and menu_contactus.gif.

After dragging each image onto the page, Dreamweaver prompts us for an alternative text attribute for each image to make them more accessible to nonvisual user agents. Enter a meaningful but concise description of the image.

6. With each image selected on the page, click in the Link field of the Property inspector and establish the respective links for the navigational elements.

You're done! Well, almost. As soon as you add your first link, the last image drops to the next line because you now have a blue outline around each image, which takes up space not accounted for in the width of the **#nav** **<div>.**

Let's add a new rule that eliminates the outline from all linked images.

1. Create a rule called **img**. Give it a property of border with a value of 0.

FIGURE 3.34 The navigation bar has been added to the page using relative positioning.

2. Switch back to the All view in the CSS panel.

Notice that the rule for the **#nav** selector has been added locally to the page in the **<style>** tag. We obviously want this in the acme.css file.

3. Click and drag the **#nav** rule from the **<style>** tag and drop it in the acme.css section.

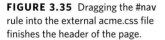

FIGURE 3.35 Dragging the #nav rule into the external acme.css file finishes the header of the page.

Dreamweaver will leave the empty `<style>` element in the head of the page. For the sake of neatness, once the rule is moved, simply right-click the `<style>` tags in the All pane of the CSS Styles panel and delete it.

It's now safe to delete the height attribute for the `#nav <div>`. Click to select the `#nav <div>` and open the CSS panel in the Current view. In the Properties section, delete the value for the height attribute.

Continuing the Cleanup Process

Our next task will be a bit easier since our 12-year-old actually used some limited CSS to style a bit of the text on the page. All we need to do is remove the table markup and adjust the rules slightly.

1. Select the `<table>` tag that contains the text from the Our Mission area of the page.

2. Insert a `<div>` with an ID of `mission` and click OK twice.

   This assigns the ID identifier to the `<div>` tag and creates the rule in the CSS file but doesn't set any properties for the rule. We'll add them a little later, using the Properties pane of the CSS Styles panel.

3. Remove the table markup from within the newly created `#mission <div>` element.

If you're in Design view, switch to Split view to take a peek at the code for this section of the page. As you can see, the paragraph of text is within a `<p>` element. The Our Mission heading, however, is a span, styled with the class `.header`. To mark up our document semantically and to make it tastier for search engine spiders, this should be a proper `<h1>` heading.

1. Go to the All pane of the CSS Styles panel, double-click on the `.header` rule, and rename it `h1`.

   We're keeping the declarations already created for the `.header`. Notice, in Design view, that the styling is lost from the Our Mission heading. That's because it is not an `h1` element.

2. Place your cursor into the words Our Mission and right-click on the `<span.header>` in the tag selector. Choose Remove Tag. In the Property inspector, choose Heading 1 from the Format drop-down list.

Our text is now too large, but we'll quickly remedy that.

3. With the CSS Styles panel set to Current, add a `font-size` property of `1em` to your `h1` rule. Add a `margin-top` and `margin-bottom` with a value of 0 pixels.

Look at the page in Design view. The space didn't decrease, did it? This is because the **p** element still has a top margin of its own. We'll change the amount of space by modifying the behavior of `<p>` elements within the `#mission <div>` element using a descendent selector.

4. Create a new CSS rule called `#mission p` in the Selector field. Select the Box category and uncheck the "Same for all" check box for the Margin section. Assign a margin-top of 5 pixels and margin-bottom of 6 pixels. Click OK.

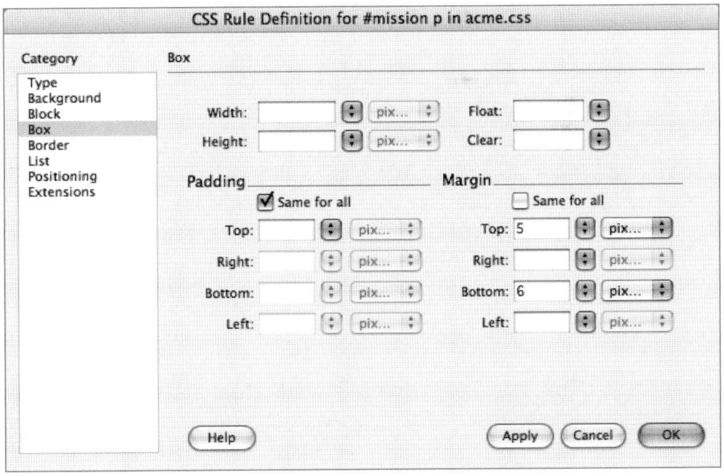

FIGURE 3.36 A top margin of a few pixels will keep the paragraph nicely separated from the title.

Moving on, a quick look at the tag selector reveals that the image to the left has for some reason already been wrapped in a `<div>`. Peeking behind the scenes at the code reveals another beginner's mistake.

```
<div align="center"><img src="images/badge.gif" alt=""
width="181" height="84" /> </div>
```

As we can see, the align attribute has been applied directly to the `<div>` tag within the HTML. This is a typical beginner's mistake and is easy to fix.

In this case, however, go ahead and remove the `<div>` tag entirely. There's no logical reason to have wrapped the image in it—it's just a bad case of "div-itis."

We'll create a new rule to add alignment that mirrors the Member Login box above.

1. Create a class selector called `specialImage`.

2. Give it a `padding-left` of `15px`.

3. Be sure the image is selected and, using the Property inspector, select `specialImage` from the Class drop-down list (or right-click the img in the tag selector and choose Set Class > `specialImage`).

Organizing the Footer

The next to last stop on this page is the footer area. The footer consists of a nested table containing two rows. This area will be easy to style, given that once again our intrepid 12-year-old has used a couple of `<div>` tags to help establish some basic formatting within the table cells.

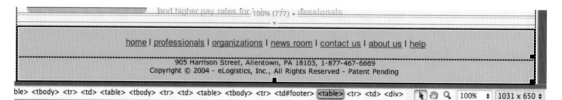

FIGURE 3.37 Entering the homestretch; only the footer is left to clean up before removing the final table markup on the page.

The background color of the footer has been applied to the `<td>` tag containing the nested table directly in the HTML. It has also been applied using an ID. We can see this by placing the cursor anywhere in the footer and using the tag selector to select the `<td>` tag containing the table. Notice that the tag selector for the `<td>` is `<td#footer>`. In the Current view of the CSS Styles panel, with the table cell selected, we can see a background color property of #B6D4AA.

Since the #footer selector has already been created, we simply need to establish a <div> to apply it to.

1. Place the cursor into one of the table cells in the footer and use the tag selector to select the nested table.

2. In the Layout section of the Insert bar, click the Insert Div Tag icon.

    If you select the Class drop-down list, you'll find a list of the available classes. However, clicking the ID drop-down list does not provide a list of IDs to choose from. Dreamweaver only shows ID selectors that can actually be applied and, as you know, an ID can only be applied once within a given page. Because the #footer selector has already been applied to the <td>, it doesn't show up in the list. No worries, we'll cheat, since we know that we'll be deleting the <td> shortly.

3. Type footer into the ID field. Click OK.

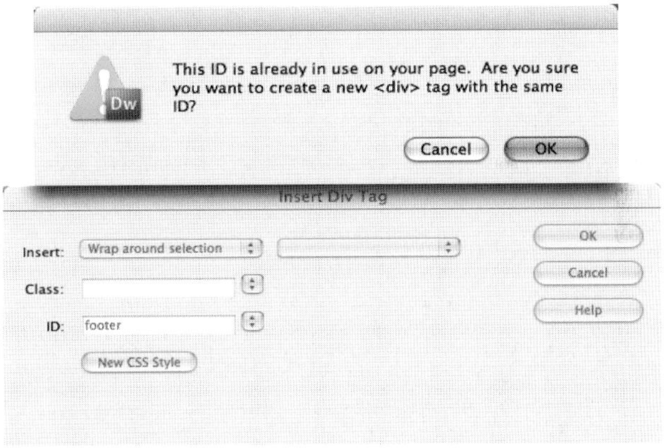

FIGURE 3.38 Dreamweaver warns us that an ID selector should only be applied once in the page.

Dreamweaver warns us that the ID selector is already in use. Click OK to confirm that we do, in fact, know what we're doing and Dreamweaver should write the code for us anyway.

4. Select the newly created #footer <div> using the tag selector and remove the table markup using the Find and Replace method.

    The #footer <div> still contains two additional <div> tags that were used to center its content. Semantically, we should replace the two <div> tags with <p> tags.

5. Select the first of the nested `<div>` elements using the tag selector.

   We need to wrap this selection in a `<p>` tag. Previously, we used the Quick Tag Editor to do this, but we'll use a different method to wrap the selection this time.

6. On the Insert bar, select Common. Click the last icon in the row titled Tag Chooser.

   The Tag Chooser allows us to insert a given tag at the current cursor position or wrap any selection in the chosen tag.

FIGURE 3.39 Use the Tag Chooser to insert a tag or wrap elements in a given tag.

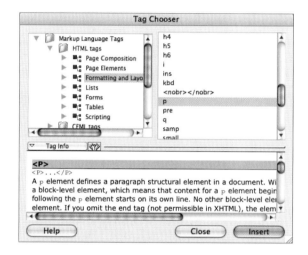

The Tag Chooser lists folders containing all of the tags recognized by Dreamweaver CS3.

7. Open the HTML tags folder and choose the Formatting and Layout section. Scroll through the list on the right and select the `<p>` tag.

8. Click Insert and then click OK. Close the Tag Chooser. Remove the `<div>` tag we wrapped with the `<p>` tag using the tag selector. Repeat the process for the second nested `<div>` tag.

There seems to be a lot more space than we would have expected in the footer. Switch to Split view and the reason quickly becomes clear. To establish space, `<br>` tags were used. Since style and structure should be separated, this is a no-no in CSS. A `<br>` tag should only be used to break a line, not for spacing. Select the `#footer` `<div>` and use Find and Replace to strip the `<br>` tags from the selection. You'll then notice that the second section of text is now all on one line. Oops. Quickly add a `<br>` by placing the cursor in front of the word Copyright and pressing Shift+Return.

We now need to override the behavior of the `<p>` elements within the footer to achieve the proper spacing from our original layout.

1. Create a new descendent selector called `#footer p`. In the Block category of the dialog, select center from the Text Align drop-down list.

    We also don't want the standard full line between the paragraphs.

2. In the Box category, assign a `margin-bottom` of 10 pixels.

    Finally, we'll add back the space above and below the content of the `#footer <div>` by modifying the `#footer` rule.

3. Select the `#footer <div>` using the tag selector and add a `padding-top` and `padding-bottom` property, each with the value set to 5 pixels.

    The Design view still shows a bit too much spacing around the footer, because we have the `#footer` selector still applied to the surrounding `<td>` tag.

4. Select the `<td#footer>` tag from the tag selector. Right-click on the tag and choose None from the Set ID menu.

Removing the Final Table Markup

The last of the table markup includes four nested tables. While that might have struck fear in your heart at the beginning of the chapter, by now you know how easy it is to clean up. Ready? Here we go:

1. Select the outermost table using the tag selector and wrap it in a `<div>`. Give it an ID of `main`. In the Background category, choose a white (`#FFFFFF`) background for the selector. Assign a width of 776 pixels in the Box category and add `padding-left` and `padding-right` of 2 pixels.

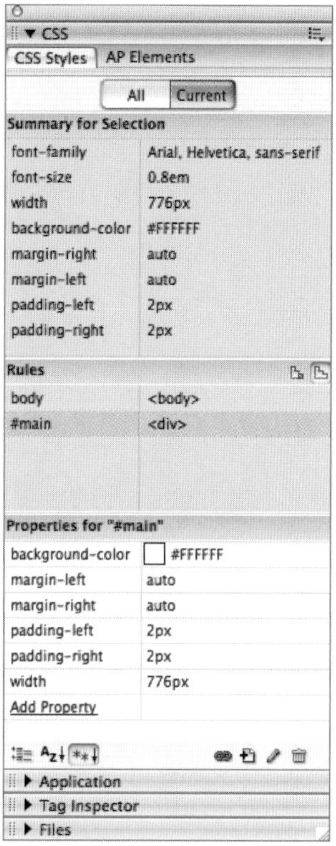

FIGURE 3.40 The settings for the #main selector that will hold all of the page contents.

T   When using the auto value for the left and right margins of a container to center it, we must also assign a fixed width to the element.

Without any other declarations, the content would begin in the upper-left corner of the browser window. However, the original table-positioned page centered itself horizontally within the browser viewport. This can be easily achieved using CSS.

2. Uncheck the "Same for all" check box in the Margin section. Assign a value of auto to the left and right margins. Click OK. Using your Find and Replace skills, remove all of the remaining `<table>`, `<tr>`, and `<td>` tags from the page.

FIGURE 3.41 Yikes!!! I thought we were finished, but the page looks even worse now!

Right now, you're probably screaming at the way your page looks, thinking that you've done something wrong. Calm down. Because we've removed all of the table markup that our `<div>` elements were nested in, they have reverted to their default behavior. Remember, a `<div>` will assume 100 percent of the width of its parent container. As a result, each of the `<div>` elements on the page have lined up vertically within the parent div, according to the document flow. A few quick adjustments and we'll be back in business.

The #header `<div>` is displaying properly, so we'll begin with the Member Login area.

1. Use the tag selector to select the `<div>` containing the login form.

2. In the Current view of the CSS panel, add a width value of 214px to the rule.

This is the same width as the Member Login graphic at the top of the box. As you'll recall from the previous chapter, to allow other elements to exist next to the `<div>`, we also need to add a float property to the rule with a value of left.

3. Add `float:left` to the rule.

4. Repeat the process for the Professionals area. Select the `<div#contentBox>` from the tag selector and assign a width of 281px and a float of left.

5. Select the badge image and add the following properties to the `.specialImage` rule:

```
.specialImage {
    padding-left: 15px;
    float: left;
    margin-top: 7px;
    margin-bottom: 12px;
}
```

6. Select the `<div#mission>` selector and add the following properties:

```
float: left;
width: 563px;
padding-left: 15px;
```

With all the page elements floated, in order for the footer to remain below the other page elements and not sneak up into some little space somewhere, we'll need to add a clearing element. This should be added between the `#mission` `<div>` and the `#footer` `<div>`.

1. Place your cursor into the `#footer`, select the `#footer` on the tag selector and click your left arrow key once.

2. On the Insert bar, click the Insert Div Tag icon, but don't wrap the element.

3. Give the `<div>` the class `clearfloat` and define the rule as follows:

```
.clearfloat {
    clear: both;
    height: 0;
    font-size: 1px;
    line-height: 0;

}
```

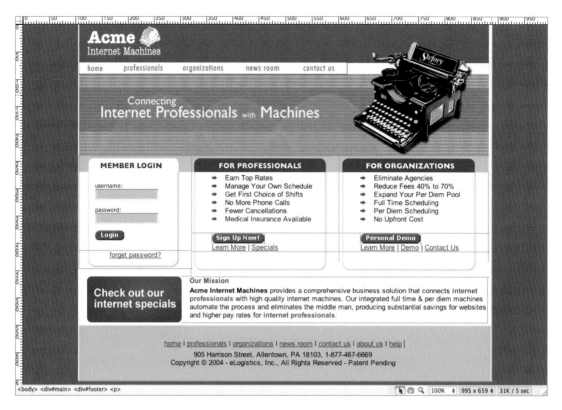

FIGURE 3.42 The completed page is now entirely table-less!

There's one more little detail we'll attend to now that everything's in place. If you kept your original file intact to compare with the final file, notice that our list items seem a bit crowded. One simple declaration will take care of that.

1. Place your cursor into one of the lists and, in the CSS Styles panel, add the `line-height` property.

2. Give it a value of 1.25.

   Notice the default that appears as the unit of measure is "multiple." Leave that unit of measure. It will be calculated as a multiple of the element's font. Since our font is set to .8em, the 1.25 multiple will make it one and a quarter of that size, or 1em. This allows a bit more breathing room and will more closely match the original spacing created by the table cells.

A Final Review

In this chapter you learned how to move a traditional table-based layout to a modern table-less layout. In so doing, not only have you dramatically reduced the amount of code in the page, allowing the page to load faster, you've also established a set of CSS rules to be used when adding additional pages to the site. This will make future updates to the site very easy to maintain.

Along the way, you optimized tables using Dreamweaver's Layout Mode, stripped and replaced tags using Find and Replace, and added `<div>` elements to organize page content. You also learned the basics of styling list elements and background images. As an additional bonus, you explored the use of Fireworks CS3 to help modify graphics, even when the original file is missing.

Using the Liquid CSS Layouts

WITH THE PROLIFERATION of large monitors, creating a layout that serves the same fixed width (typically either 800 x 600 or 1024 x 768) to all browsers may leave a good deal of empty space on some screens. Clients often question this unused space, since using more of the viewer's screen *must* give the client more bang for their buck, right? Liquid layouts, based on a percentage of the size of the browser's window, are one way to create flexible sites that work for a variety of users.

In this chapter, we will look at the pros and cons of creating a liquid layout using our fictional client, the Pleasantville Regional Chamber of Commerce. Their in-house designer has sent us a Photoshop comp and has requested that the blue portion of the design fill the browser window. They want no space on the sides.

FIGURE 4.1 The design comp from their in-house designers shows their vision of the site.

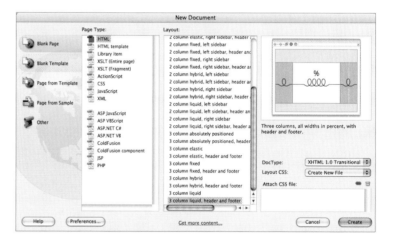

Before proceeding, define a site within Dreamweaver CS3 and create a folder called Pleasantville to contain your files.

The easiest way to fill the browser window and remain flexible is to use one of Dreamweaver's three-column liquid layouts with header and footer. The liquid layouts are composed of percentage-based columns contained within a percentage-based container. We'll need to make a few modifications to achieve the desired effect, but we'll discuss that as we go.

1. Create a new page using File > New.

2. In the Blank Page section of the dialog, select the 3 column liquid, header and footer layout.

3. Set the DocType to XHTML 1.0 Transitional and make sure that Create New File is selected in the Layout CSS drop-down list.

4. Click Create.

FIGURE 4.2 Choose the 3 column liquid, header and footer layout.

Dreamweaver allows you to name the CSS file as well as determine where it will reside in your site structure. If you use the defaults, your file will be called thrColLiqHdr.css and will reside in the root folder of your site.

Simplifying the CSS Selectors

Since our pages will all contain three columns in this site, we won't need to mix layouts and create descendent selectors. As we discussed in Chapter 2, if you don't need to mix layouts, you don't need to keep the class on the body that precedes the selectors. For simplicity's sake, and to make the selectors more readable in the CSS panel, let's strip out all the `.thrColLiqHdr` classes.

1. Open your thrColLiqHdr.css document.

2. Highlight a class that begins with `.thrColLiqHdr` in the CSS of your document (as well as the space behind it) and use Cmd+F/ Ctrl+F to open the Find and Replace dialog.

   It opens with the class you highlighted in the Find portion of the window. Make sure Find in is set to Current Document and leave the Replace area blank.

3. Click Replace All.

   Dreamweaver quickly strips those classes right out of the CSS document.

4. Moving back to the actual XHTML document, place your cursor anywhere in the page and right-click on `<body.thrColLiqHdr>` in the tag selector. Choose Set Class > None from the drop-down list.

   This removes the class applied to the body selector.

5. Save both documents.

We're ready to begin the process of modifying the page for our intended layout.

Since our design uses 100% of the browser window, the background color on the body element will no longer be visible on the sides. But if you were working in a short page (which might happen if a user's browser window was set to be large), the space below the footer will show the background color, or lack of color, if none is defined. A white space below the footer will be visible, and with this design that could be quite jarring. Sampling the footer color and using it for our overall background color allows us to leave the footer background transparent and ensure we have a seamless transition when our page ends.

1. Open the CSS Styles panel in the Current view and select `<body>` on the tag selector and click the edit (pencil) icon at the bottom of the CSS Styles panel.

T   *In order to determine the color value of a given element in a Photoshop or Fireworks comp, you'll need to arrange your screen so that both documents are visible. Then click on Dreamweaver's color picker in the CSS Rule dialog or in the CSS Styles panel's Properties section for any property which uses color. On the Mac, simply move the eyedropper over the section of the comp you are interested in sampling and click to confirm the choice. On the PC, hold the mouse button down as you drag out of the color picker and release the mouse when you are over the desired section of the comp.*

2. In the Background pane, change the background color to #1B1A52.

   Notice that in the comp from our designer, all the fonts except those in the main body are rendered in Georgia.

3. While you're in the CSS Rule dialog, change the font property to the preset font set of Georgia, Times New Roman, Times, serif and click OK.

   Viewing the CSS document, you'll notice the body selector is now changed to:

```
body {
    font: 100% Georgia, "Times New Roman", Times, serif;
    background: #1B1A52;
    margin: 0;
    padding: 0;
    text-align: center;
    color: #000000;
}
```

For some designs, we'd want the container (the div that contains all other divs) to be a percentage of the total browser width, and centered. In this case, we want the design to fill the entire window, so we'll adjust the width.

4. Click anywhere in the main layout and select `<div#container>` from the tag selector.

   In the Properties section of the CSS panel, you'll notice that this layout, by default, is 80% of the browser window (based on the body rule which is left at its default 100%).

5. Change the width to 100%.

   We also won't need the border, nor will we need to center the div using the value of auto assigned to the side margins since it will completely fill the browser window. Later, we will be bringing our colors and images in through other divs, so the background can go as well.

T   *Many times, when you're dealing with a layout that is predominantly white (or any other color), it's simplest to define that color in the overall* `#container` *rule.*

6. Delete the border, margin and background properties by right-clicking each property in the Properties pane and choosing delete or by selecting the property and clicking the trashcan icon at the bottom of the panel.

Finally, let's scale all our fonts down to a size that is closer to the 12-pixel size most people are used to seeing when their browser is left at its default sizing.

7. With `<div#container>` still selected in the tag selector, click the Add Property link in the Properties pane of the CSS Styles panel and type (or choose from the drop-down list) `font-size`. Tab to the next input field and type 80%.

Our `#container` rule is now:

```
#container {
  width: 100%;
  text-align: left;
  font-size: 80%;
}
```

We've now completed the preliminaries and we're ready to move on to creating our client's actual page.

Creating the Header

During this chapter, we will be using Photoshop as the basis for our comp. If you prefer to use Adobe Fireworks CS3, that's fine—simply substitute Fireworks for each of our references to Photoshop. We're also not going to give true step-by-step instructions for the tasks you need to complete in your graphics program, since we can't know what software you're using, and it's beyond the scope of the book. If you prefer not to complete the graphics-related tasks, you can always use the files you've downloaded from the book's Web site.

Open the comp from the source folder in either Photoshop or Fireworks. Since the logo is created using the Minion Pro font, and this is not a common font, we'll slice and export the entire logo area. Create a slice around the little box image and the words in the logo. Export it into the images directory of your site as a transparent gif (or png if you prefer) matted to white. We named ours logo.gif, but feel free to use any naming convention you commonly use.

We also need to slice the triangles on the right side of the header in the comp. Slice them as close as you can to the left side and export as a transparent gif (or png) matted to white. Name the file logo_background.gif.

Inserting the Background Image

N   *Though there are many ways to edit CSS within Dreamweaver, we find that using the CSS dialog is simplest when dealing with background images.*

1. In Dreamweaver, select the XHTML file and click in the **header** div. Click **<div#header>** in the tag selector so that the CSS panel shows the properties of the header and not the header **h1**, and click the pencil icon at the bottom of the CSS styles panel to edit the header.

   If you look at the Box category, you'll notice that there is 10px of padding on the right and left sides of the header in this starter layout. We're not going to need this padding.

2. Delete the values in the padding fields. In the Background pane, change the Background color: to #FFFFFF.

3. Click Browse and navigate to the logo_background graphic you just exported. Click Choose.

N   *If you prefer to use short-hand, as we do, the white background can be written as #FFF. Color shorthand uses the first, third and fifth digit of the color, as long as they're identical to the second, fourth and sixth. So, for instance, #FF0066 would be written as #F06. #CC3333 would be written as #C33, and #000000 is written as #000.*

We also keep our preferences set to write shorthand for all other properties as well. This means that rather than having four property/value pairs for the background, we have one declaration as seen in step 4.

4. Select **no-repeat** in the Repeat drop-down list. We want the graphic to be positioned on the right, so choose top and right for the positioning. Our code looks like this:

   ```
   #header {
       background: #FFFFFF url(images/logo_background.gif)
   no-repeat right top;
   }
   ```

   Back in Design view, notice that the word Header (as an **h1** element) is sitting boldly on the left, with only a tiny bit of the background image we just placed within apparent on the right. Don't worry—the header simply has no idea that graphic is there, or how large it is, since it's a background image. The amount of graphic showing depends on the amount of content in the header, and we're about to replace that content as well. Though it's going to get ugly for a minute, we'll be fixed up in no time.

5. With your cursor in the header div, right-click the **<h1>** on the tag selector and choose Remove Tag. The word Header will become highlighted, so simply hit the delete or backspace key to remove it completely.

   With no content in the header div, this should remove all but the smallest trace of the background image for the moment.

   Since we won't be using any **h1**s in the header within our site, go ahead and delete the **h1** rule.

6. Right-click the selector name in the All pane of the CSS Styles panel and choose delete.

Inserting the Logo

Making graphics as small as possible keeps the page weight light, so we sliced right around the logo. In the original Photoshop comp, the logo sits 20px from the top and 40px from the left so we'll position it in the same place in Dreamweaver. (If you sliced your logo differently, you'll need to adjust your values so that the alignment of the logo matches the navigation and sidebar below it).

The alt attribute is not only an important accessibility resource for screen readers and those navigating with images turned off, but it is also a required attribute when writing your document in XHTML.

1. Place your cursor into the header and, on the Common tab of the Insert bar, click the image icon. Navigate to your logo.gif and click Choose.

   The Image Tag Accessibility Attributes dialog will appear where you can give your image an alt attribute and, if necessary, a long description.

2. Fill in the descriptive text for your image and click OK.

   Most users expect to click the logo to link back to the home page. This is a good reason *not* to place the logo into the header as a background image. A CSS background image has no alt attribute, so a non-visual user agent would not even know it existed; background images are best left for decorative, non-important graphics.

3. Select the logo image and, using the Property inspector, link it to your site's index page (or the URL where your index page will eventually reside).

   Viewing in Design view with the image deselected, you'll see we now have a lovely blue border around the image. Dreamweaver (and some browsers) use this border to indicate a link. But it spoils our design. We can quickly remove that blue indicator, as well as the blue around any images we may link later, by using code similar to that we used in Chapter 3.

4. Add the following code to the end of your CSS document:

```
a img {
border: 0;
}
```

In Chapter 3, we used img { border: 0; } *because we knew that the site we were recreating wouldn't be using any borders on the images. In this comp, however, we're only going to remove the border from images that are linked.*

Our image is 114 pixels tall—yours may vary based upon how you sliced it. The header area as designed is 175 pixels tall. Go ahead and give some thought to how we should best make up for that discrepancy so that the header is held open the full height to show the entire background image. And you can't use a height on the div, that's cheating. We'll wait for a moment till you decide…

If your idea was to use a top margin to position the image properly, give yourself a gold star. If you developed the thought a little more and decided you could use a descendent selector as opposed to a class on the image itself, you get even more credit. Kudos to you! That's exactly what we decided.

Since there are no other images directly in the XHTML in our header **div** we can write a selector that targets *only* the logo image within that header.

1. Click the New CSS Rule icon at the bottom of the CSS Styles panel, or type directly into the CSS document, and create a rule called **#header img**.

If you type directly into the CSS document, you'll see Dreamweaver begin to auto-complete quite quickly after you start typing the first couple of letters of each property. Simply hitting return will then complete the property so that you can type the value.

2. In the box section of the CSS styles dialog, use these values for the margins:

top: 30px
right: 0
bottom: 31px
left: 40px

The 114 pixel height of the image, plus the 30 pixel top and 31 pixel bottom margins equals the full 175 pixel height. This holds the header div open and shows the whole background image as designed.

FIGURE 4.3 The header now looks just like the comp we were given.

Creating the Horizontal Navigation Bar

Back in the old days, a horizontal navigation bar like the one in our comp would be created entirely with images as we did in Chapter 3. If we wanted to add functionality to show a hover state or which page a user was currently on, we'd use JavaScript. Using CSS, however, is much more lightweight and accessible. You can simply use text within a list to get the same image-like look.

The horizontal navigation is composed of a gradated orange horizontal bar. The designer used two single lines at the top and bottom of the bar to make it appear to have more depth. We'll discuss in a moment how the look will be recreated with CSS, but first, we'll build the semantic, XHTML structure for our navigation.

FIGURE 4.4 The horizontal navigation at 400%—notice the top and bottom lines

Our header **div** visually matches the comp. Since we used margins on the image for proper spacing, we can add an unordered list of links after the image. The list doesn't need a class or ID or even to be housed within a separate div. Keeping it within the header lets us use a descendent selector to target *only* the unordered list we'll be styling as our horizontal navigation. We won't affect any of the other lists within the document as long as all our rules that pertain to the horizontal navigation begin with **#header**.

1. Place your cursor immediately after the logo image and tap the Return key.

2. Type:

    Regional Living
    Regional Business
    Regional Chamber

3. Select all three entries and click the Unordered List button in the Properties inspector.

    We are not yet sure what page our navigation will actually go to, but we want to style them as links now; using a pound sign or hash mark (#) in the link field will make them display as if they were links.

Our list looks like this in Code view:

```
<ul>
  <li><a href="#">Regional Living</a></li>
  <li><a href="#">Regional Business</a></li>
  <li><a href="#">Regional Chamber</a></li>
</ul>
```

When we added the Return after the image, Dreamweaver wrapped the image in a `<p>` element. Since the `<p>` element is unnecessary in our semantic markup, we'll need to remove it.

4. Click to select the logo on the page, and on the tag selector, right-click on the `<p>` tag surrounding it and choose Remove Tag.

Clean, simple and straightforward, right?

Creating the CSS for the Horizontal Navigation

In the world of menus, or any element for that matter, it's always better to allow an increase or decrease in size to happen organically. This allows a user with his or her browser's default set to a different font size to comfortably view the element. In the case of the menu, we could slice the orange bar from top to bottom and assign a height. But if the user's text was larger, the links within the menu could spread outside the orange bar creating an unsightly mess. There is a creative way to get around this by including the top two lines with the overall image slice and using an orange background color for the rest. This creates a seamless transition between the image and the color. The bottom two lines are then created with CSS.

Always remember, there are a myriad of ways to get the same results using CSS. There's no "right way" for everything. Learning the principles and then making a decision based on the requirements of your design is always the best approach.

In your comp, slice from the very top edge of the orange bar down to the area where the gradation ends. We sliced nearly down to, but didn't include, the bottom two lines. Due to the gradient, this should be exported as a jpg. Name it nav_bar_back.jpg.

As we mentioned before, we like to keep our code clean, semantic and as small as possible. For this reason, the container for our menu is actually the ul element itself. Why add an extra container when

N Since we've already covered a variety of ways to edit your CSS, including directly in code, in the properties pane, or using the CSS dialog, choose the method you prefer and use it to modify your properties.

you don't have to? The `ul` will have two other descendents contained within it: the `li` element and the `a` element. Each of these will be given declarations that will, in the end, duplicate the look the designer wanted with no JavaScript or images within the XHTML.

1. Zero out the list defaults.

   Browsers have varying default values for lists, so for consistency, a best practice is to zero the padding and margin.

2. Set the list-style value to none, to get rid of the bullets that unordered lists generally include.

   This gives us the following rule:

```
#header ul {
   margin: 0;
   padding: 0;
   list-style: none;
}
```

Previewing this in the browser will show you that we have a nice, unordered, bullet-less list. Not quite what we wanted yet, but a good start. Let's start the transition to a navbar look. This will require the background image we sliced and a couple of new rules for the `li` and `a` elements.

First, let's add a property to the `#header ul` rule. As we mentioned before, the principle behind creating this navigation bar so that it can adjust to the user's font size is to *not* limit the height. Remember we only sliced the image with the top two lines included? We'll set that background image to repeat on the x axis (across the page) and we'll use the orange color our graphic ends with as the background color. Wherever the repeating graphic ends, the orange that matches will show through seamlessly. We sampled the color using the techniques we discussed earlier and came up with `#FFAD00`. Our rule now looks like this:

```
#header ul {
   margin: 0;
   padding: 0;
   list-style: none;
   background: #FFAD00 url(images/nav_bar_back.jpg) repeat-x;
}
```

Regional Living
Regional Business
Regional Chamber

FIGURE 4.5 The color runs all the way across, but it's too tall!

The color is now completely enveloping the li elements. But they're still stacked up like a regular list. Just as we did in Chapter 3, let's add a rule to float the list elements to the left. We'll also adjust the font size to match the comp we were given.

```
#header li {
  float: left;
  font-size: 110%;
}
```

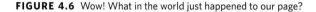
Regional LivingRegional BusinessRegional Chamber

Sidebar1   **Main Content**   Sidebar2

FIGURE 4.6 Wow! What in the world just happened to our page?

This is one of those little float gotchas we talked about in Chapter 2. Now that the list elements are floated, the ul doesn't "see" them, and so it's not containing them. The list elements interact with each other, so they're not taken completely out of the flow of the document as they would be if they were absolutely positioned, but the container is unaware of their presence. You'll also notice that the floats (the columns below) that follow them in the flow of the document have moved up to the same line where the floated list items end. They believe there's room for them there and quite frankly, there is, but that's not where we want them.

We could use a clearing element (as we discussed in Chapter 2) to force the container to "see" the floated elements within, but in this case, a quick little remedy is to float the ul. A floated element will contain other floated elements. So let's add a float and width property to the ul rule and see what effect it has.

```
#header ul {
  margin: 0;
  padding: 0;
  list-style: none;
  background: #FFAD00 url(images/nav_bar_back.jpg) repeat-x;
  float: left;
  width: 100%;
}
```

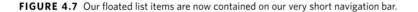

Regional LivingRegional BusinessRegional Chamber

FIGURE 4.7 Our floated list items are now contained on our very short navigation bar.

Styling the Anchors as Buttons

Now that the navigation bar runs the full length of the page, we can complete the look our designer created. There are a few things to be aware of to make your links act like buttons and to avoid creepy, crawling bugs.

First, if you want the link to act like a button in Internet Explorer—activated by the mouse for its entire height and width, not only on the text as a link is—you'll need to add the `display:block` declaration into the rule for the **a** elements:

Next, in some circumstances, IE (of course) stacks the links like a list. To avoid this, in addition to floating the list items, you'll also need to float the **a** elements within them.

Add the following rule to the **header** menu area:

```
#header li a {
   float: left;
   display: block;
}
```

Another common design mistake is to use a margin on the first element of a floated element on the same side as the float (for example, a left margin on a left floated element). You can avoid the dreaded IE doubled margin bug by using padding instead. If you must use a margin due to design constraints, adding `display: inline` to the element will zap this bug. To learn more about the doubled margin bug, read up on it at Adobe's CSS Advisor site: http://www.adobe.com/cfusion/communityengine/index.cfm?event=showDetails&postId=785&productId=1

Now that we've circumvented a couple of bugs, we'll move on to creating the space around those navigation items. Right now, they're all running together and that's certainly not the plan. There's yet another possible bug in IE that, with a little wise planning, we can completely avoid. It's called the doubled margin bug and is caused by using a margin on the same side the element floats toward. We'll avoid using a margin by using padding instead.

Now, the amount of padding required is where the rocket science enters in. How do we determine the padding values to use for our **a** element? We could get out our ruler and measure the exact spacing, making allowances for font sizing and such—and if you have an advanced mathematics degree from Stanford or MIT this might be a choice. But we find that guessing at it works just as well. Our first guess is 10px, which, of course adds 10 pixels of padding to all sides of the element. In previewing our page in the browser and then comparing it to the comp, 10px seems to be slightly too tall, but doesn't add enough space between each link. Using 8px for the top and bottom and 12px for the left and right sides does the trick in our eyes.

Finally, let's get rid of those nasty default blue, underlined links. We'll change their color to white and use none as the value for the `text-decoration` property. The selector now looks like this:

```
#header li a {

    float: left;
    display: block;
    padding: 8px 12px;
    color: #FFF;
    text-decoration: none;
}
```

Using Design-Time Style Sheets

It's starting to look pretty good in the browser, huh? You may have noticed a little issue within Dreamweaver though. When the **a** element is floated within the list item, Dreamweaver stacks the words up on top of each other, each word on a new line.

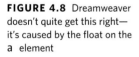

FIGURE 4.8 Dreamweaver doesn't quite get this right— it's caused by the float on the **a** element

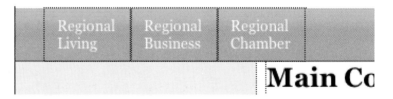

You have two choices. Either use a non-breaking space ( ) instead of a regular space, or use a **Design-Time Style Sheet** within Dreamweaver. For those unfamiliar with Design-Time Style Sheets (DTSS), they're a separate CSS document, attached within DW, and *only* rendered within DW. They affect nothing on the server or in a browser. Though Dreamweaver's rendering has gotten substantially better with each release, it still occasionally has odd rendering. Attaching a DTSS allows you to correct the rendering of your page, within the DW design environment, without affecting your browser view. Let's do it:

The specs from the W3C say that an author's style sheet always overrides a user's style sheet. However, the !important declaration takes precedence over a normal declaration. If both style sheets contain an !important declaration, then the user's declaration wins out. This is a change from CSS1 where the author's won.

1. Create a new CSS document using File > New > CSS or by right-clicking inside the files panel and choosing New File.

   We've named our document dtss.css so we don't forget what it is later. Inside this document, we simply need to give our anchor element a **float: none** declaration. Here's what we have:

   ```
   #header li a {
   float: none !important;
   }
   ```

   The !important declaration tells DW to always render this rule within DW: otherwise, because the rule has the same specificity as the one in your regular style sheet, the styles will conflict.

2. To attach this style sheet, click on the contextual menu in the top right-hand corner of the CSS Styles panel and choose Design-time.

3. Select the + sign in the "Show only at design time" drop-down list and navigate to dtss.css.

   You'll notice that you can also hide an entire style sheet in this same dialog—though this is usually only necessary with extremely complex pages that DW just can't handle.

4. Click OK.

   The words are now displaying in a line, instead of stacked on top of each other. This keeps your navigation area, within Dreamweaver, more like the final browser version.

Putting the Final Tweaks on the Horizontal Navigation

Let's move to the final details of our navigation. The alignment in our navigation should match the logo above. You may remember that was 40px from the left. We'll need to subtract the 12px of padding on the left of our links from the total amount needed. Grabbing a wandering fourth grader, we quickly figure out that 28px of left padding on the ul will be needed to hold the links away from the edge of our document.

You'll also remember from the comp that we need two subtle lines on the bottom of the navigation bar. You can't put two borders on an element. However, we have two elements at our disposal—the ul and the **header** div it is within—so we'll get creative and use both. The first border, the darker purple (#575691) will go on the inner element—the ul. The second border, the light purple (#9290BF) will be placed as a bottom border on the header. Our adjusted code looks like this:

```
#header {
   background: #FFF url(images/logo_background.gif) no-repeat
right;
   border-bottom: #9290BF 1px solid;
}
#header ul {
   margin: 0;
   padding: 0 0 0 28px;
   list-style: none;
   background: #FFAD00 url(images/nav_bar_back.jpg) repeat-x;
   float: left;
   width: 100%;
   border-bottom: #575691 1px solid;
}
```

N *If you're following along with these exercises, make sure these rules end up in the thrColLiqHdr.css file, not the dtss.css file.*

Preview your page in a browser. You'll notice that you see the dark purple bottom border on the ul, but the one on the header is missing. Let's see if we can force the issue. Change the bottom border of the header to 10px to be sure we're not just missing it and preview it again. Dang. Still not working. What's going on now?

Dreamweaver has a great feature called CSS Layout Backgrounds that will help you see why a problem like this is happening. This tool puts a different, random background color on every block level element. If there is already a background color or image, the tool temporarily hide it so that you can fully visualize the interaction between the various elements in your layout.

If you have the Document Toolbar open at the top of your document, select Visual Aids > CSS Layout Backgrounds or, from the menu, choose View > Visual Aids > CSS Layout Backgrounds.

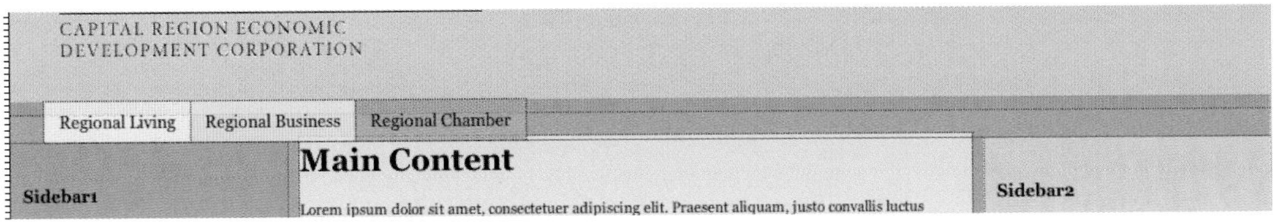

FIGURE 4.9 My eyes! My eyes! CSS Layout Backgrounds at work.

Although we'll admit that most layout background combinations are hideous, they can certainly be useful. Notice that the 10px lavender border we added is sitting right at the top of the ul?

What in the world? Isn't the ul sitting *inside* the header?

Well, yes. You remember correctly. However, remember that in order to get our ul to render its background (due to the floated li and a elements inside), we floated it. That means that the header div that contains it doesn't really know its there, so the header is closing before the floated ul.

The two ways to force a container to contain other elements are to float the container or to use a clearing method. Though we used the floating method to force the ul to contain the elements within and could float the header with the same effect, we've found that too much floating can become buggy. Thus, we chose to use the clearing method and not float yet another element.

This little issue is easy to solve with a clearing element. We'll use the same method we used with the overall container div (discussed in Chapter 2). As a reminder, in your XHTML document, you'll see the clearing element as the last element within the container—<br class="clearfloat" />.

Copy and paste that line so that it's also the last element before the close of the header div.

```
<div id="header"><a href="index.html"><img src="images/logo.
gif" alt="Pleasantville Regional Chamber logo" width="330"
height="114" /></a>
<ul>
  <li><a href="#">Regional Living</a></li>
  <li><a href="#">Regional Business</a></li>
  <li><a href="#">Regional Chamber</a></li>
  </ul>
  <br class="clearfloat" />
  <!-- end #header -->
  </div>
```

In Design view, we see that the 10px border is now sitting below the **ul** as desired. Unless you're enjoying the bright colors, select Visual Aids > CSS Layout Backgrounds, and turn off the backgrounds. Don't forget to change your **border-bottom** on the header back to the desired 1px height.

Fixing the Horizontal Scroll

You may have noticed that a horizontal scrollbar has appeared on our page. That scroll is because the **ul** was set to a 100% width, but then we added 28px of left padding. Remember with the box model, the padding is added to the width to get the *actual* width. Our current width, then, is 100% plus 28px!

Unfortunately, since we're working in percentages, we can't really change the overall width of the **ul**. But we really need to keep that padding for the proper alignment. What to do?

One possibility is to move that spacing to another element. What about the list items within the **ul**? Currently, each list item has the same 12px of side padding. Changing the padding on all the list items to 40px on the left would be too much for our designer to stomach: remember we're trying to match his design as exactly as we can. That means we have a choice of using a class or an id to target only that first list item.

In a moment, we're going to look at creating an indicator that shows what page the user is on. For that, we'll need unique ids on each list item as well. So let's add those now.

We discussed earlier that it was a best practice *not* to use class and id names that were specific to the placement or look of the element they're placed on. Well, rules are made to be broken. Since it will actually help us track the proper page later, now is the time to break this rule.

1. Click into the first link—Regional Living.

2. On the tag selector, right-click the `<li>` and select Quick Tag Editor.

   A dialog appears that lets you set the id and name. (You could, of course, also do this directly in the code if you prefer.) The Quick Tag Editor works very much like Code view in that it uses code completion.

Since all of the links here begin with the word Regional, we'll drop the word Regional on each and simply use the second word to identify the link.

3. In the id field, type `living`.

4. Continue in the same way with the next two list items, naming them business and chamber respectively.

```
<ul>
   <li id="living"><a href="#">Regional Living</a></li>
   <li id="business"><a href="#">Regional Business</a></li>
   <li id="chamber"><a href="#">Regional Chamber</a></li>
</ul>
```

We can now target only the first link in the `ul`.

5. Change the padding on the `ul` to 0. Now, add that padding to the first `li`, using a descendent selector. The descendent selector looks like this:

```
#header li#living {
   padding-left: 28px;
}
```

Refresh the page in a browser and you'll see that the horizontal scrollbar has magically disappeared.

Creating the Hover and Current Page Indicator State

Now that our menu is all set, let's create a hover state. Since the navigation bar is orange with white text, a good hover indication color would be the deep blue we used for our page background. It's dark enough to give good contrast, but still blend with the page.

Since we want to include people that navigate in a variety of different ways, we'll use more than just the typical `:hover` pseudo class. The `:hover` pseudo class works for a user navigating with a mouse. But what about the person using keyboard navigation? For them to see the same change in color when a link has focus, we'll need to use the `:focus` pseudo class. But wait, using those two would be too simple. For some reason, Microsoft decided to use the `:active` pseudo class for keyboard navigation instead (most other browsers use `:active` as you're activating or clicking the link). So you'll need to set up a compound list of selectors for this rule. It looks like this:

```
#header li a:hover, #header li a:active, #header li a:focus {
  color: #1B1A52;
}
```

The above rule selects a link with focus that is a child of a `list` element that is within the header div. All three selectors are there, separated by commas, so the same color is applied and indicates focus with any method of surfing.

FIGURE 4.10 The middle button shows the `hover/focus` state for our button

A common way to show a user what page or section of a site he or she is on is by placing a class on the link you want to indicate. In that scenario, each XHTML page has a different menu. But what if we're using server-side includes or Dreamweaver templates where the navigation menu is in a locked region? We couldn't put a different class on at a different time (unless we did it programmatically).

CSS saves us. (Of course!) With a unique ID on each list item, we can easily create a descendent selector that controls our page indicator and never touch the actual menu again. We'll add a class to the body element that matches the id on the menu.

Any method can be used, but using the same name keeps us from getting confused later and makes it easy to write the selectors needed. For the Regional Living page—since the list item has the ID of `living`—we'll add a class of the same name on the body element. There's no problem having a class and ID of the same name—as long as it doesn't confuse *you*.

The descendent selector to control the page indicator and the XHTML code for the body element look like this:

```
.living #living a {
  color: #1B1A52;
  font-weight: bold;
}
<body class="living">
```

T *In order to work properly, the* hover, active, focus *order must be honored. Be sure not to put a comma after the last selector in a list since that will cause the rule to fail.*

N *This rule will select any link that descends from an element with an ID of* #living *(our list item) that is a descendent of an element with the class of* living *(our body element). It could also be written as* body.living li#living a*, if you think you might forget what the selector controls. Once you get used to the CSS, though, you probably don't need the extra code.*

We'll create a compound list of selectors for each page, or section, for which we'll need an indicator. In the case of our horizontal navigation, we'll create three.

```
.living #living a, .business #business a, .chamber #chamber a {
  color: #1B1A52;
  font-weight: bold;

}
```

FIGURE 4.11 Users of the site will have a visual indication of which page or section they're in

Laying Out the Main Content Area

It's time to get down to the real meat of our page—the content area. We need to recreate the overall gradient and shadowed side columns. The background gradient needs to begin where the horizontal navigation ends—no matter where on the vertical axis that happens. That means we need to another wrapper div around the three columns.

Before you do the following steps, delete the background colors from both `sidebar1` and `sidebar2` so that they are transparent.

In your graphics editor, slice from, but not including, the light lavender single pixel line—remember we placed that line on the header—to the area where the gradient ends and becomes a solid color. Once again, you're saving page weight by using CSS to place the overall background color and putting the gradient on a background image. Since it's so subtle, how do we know where that line of demarcation is? More super scientific methods!

Our method is to eyeball it, put a guide where we think the transition is, and sample the color on both sides of the guide. If the color number is the same, we move the guide up a bit to find the highest place we can put it and still match on both sides. If the color number is different, we move it down a bit until it matches. The color we sampled, about 465 pixels down in our comp, was

#403E8A. We'll slice down to that guide, and since it is a gradient, we'll export it as a jpg with the name main_back.jpg.

Modifying the Columns

1. In Code view of our XHTML document, highlight both columns as well as the mainContent div and the clearing element.

2. On the Common pane of the Insert bar, choose Insert Div Tag.

3. In the dialog, choose "Wrap around selection" and give the ID the name of mainWrap.

4. Click New CSS Style and choose to add the style to the three-ColLiqHdr.css style sheet. Click OK.

5. Go to the Background pane and navigate to the image we just created setting it to repeat on the x axis (horizontally).

6. Set the background color to the color the gradient ended on—#403E8A.

This lets us have any amount of content in the portion of our page containing the mainContent div and side columns. If the page is extremely short, it will end, still showing the image, before the background color starts. If the page is very long, it will continue on seamlessly with the solid background color. Users can't tell where the image ends and the color, created with CSS, begins.

T   *Due to an odd little bug in Dreamweaver, you'll need to have your page in Code view to select the three divs. If you are in Split view, Dreamweaver will change your selection to contain* only *the first column. Why? We don't know. Just take heed.*

T   *To keep your CSS sheet in a logical order, use Dreamweaver's new CSS management features to move the #mainWrap rule up above the #sidebar1 and #sidebar2 rules. In the CSS Styles panel, click the All button, click the #mainWrap rule at the bottom of the list and drag it up above the #sidebar1 rule. Drop it. It's now moved within your actual CSS page.*

FIGURE 4.12 You can see how well our CSS background blends—it looks like one graphic!

Dealing with Margins

In a Mozilla-based browser (this includes Firefox) or as shown in Figure 4.12, there's an odd space where the overall body background color shows through above the area where the `mainWrap` background graphic starts. This is a perfect example of one version of **margin collapse**.

When two vertical margins meet, and the margined elements have no padding or borders specified, the largest margin takes precedence over the smaller. When both margins are the same size, the space rendered is the size of one of the margins—not the two added together. This is why you can zero the top margin of an element, yet still have space between elements

Margin collapse occurs when two margins touch. One margin, the smaller of the two, will disappear (or collapse), allowing the larger margin to take precedence. For example, when you have a heading followed by a paragraph element, the margin that is larger will be rendered—the margins are not added together. Sometimes this appears as a space between divs, caused by the margin of the first or last element escaping outside the div itself and pushing the div away from the div next to it. Believe it or not, this is correct behavior—it's not a bug. But in this case, it's unsightly.

There are three basic ways to prevent margin collapse, and the page design determines the best method to use. In our case, we're dealing with the top margin of the h1 that is protruding outside the `mainContent` div. We can either get rid of the top margin on the h1, leaving only the bottom margin; add the **padding-top** property to the `mainContent` div; or add a border to the div. Both the border and the padding will keep the margins from interacting.

The first option won't work for us. Again due to margin collapse, even if we remove the top margin from all paragraph and headings, the bottom margin would continue to hold the elements away from the element above them.

Sometimes padding or borders aren't an option due to the design. In that case, we'd have to use the zeroing method. But for this design, our two side columns already have padding at the top and there's a nice amount of space before our headings start, so we'll use the padding method with the **#mainContent** rule. It now looks like this:

```
#mainContent {
    margin: 0 24% 0 23.5%;
    padding-top: 10px;
}
```

The Illusion of Columns

In Chapter 2 (our fixed-width layout), we looked at a simple way to use one graphic and create the effect of two or three, full-length columns called faux columns. This time, we'll use a different method since this layout doesn't have full-length columns and we're dealing with percentage widths.

T   *If you'd like to create two or three equal length columns within a liquid, percentage-based layout, it's quite doable! Please refer to Zoe Gillenwater's free article at Community MX—Creating Liquid Faux Columns. http://www.communitymx.com/abstract.cfm?cid=AFC58*

Let's analyze the comp. We've got three background images to place: the triangles and the two drop-shadowed column tops. We can't slice the two drop-shadowed areas as one image since the width of the middle area is flexible. (And remember, only one background per customer please—errr—per element, that is.) We've already placed a background on the `mainWrap` div. That leaves the `sidebar1`, `sidebar2` and `mainContent` divs with no backgrounds yet declared. It's quite obvious that the triangles in the right corner can only go on the `sidebar2` div since the `mainContent` div is margined away from that area.

That makes it pretty simple to see what to do from here: the left column, `sidebar1`, will need the drop-shadowed column separator as shown on our comp on the left side of the `mainContent` area. That means the `mainContent` div gets the drop-shadowed column separator from the right.

Positioning the Backgrounds

Moving back into your image editor, slice each of these three areas as tightly as you can. For the drop shadows, slice from the lighter column area to the other side of the shadowed area, staying as close as you can. Vertically, slice until the area where the color becomes solid and the shadow ends. Export the triangles as side2_back.jpg, the left column area as side1_back.jpg and the right column as content_back.jpg. These are now named for the column they'll be attached to which makes it easier if you have to come back to the site later.

N   *Remember to turn off any layers with text sitting on top of a graphic you're slicing. You'll add the text within Dreamweaver.*

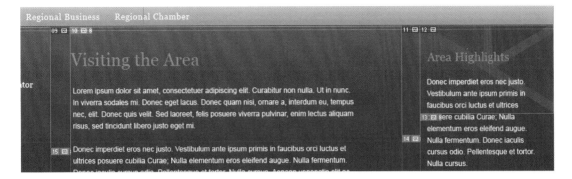

FIGURE 4.13 Notice slice 9, 11 and 12 in our Photoshop comp

Back in Dreamweaver we'll add each of these to our page on the div for which they were just named. Each should be set to **repeat-none** and they should be positioned to the top and right. We're also going to set a **min-height** slightly taller than the graphic within so the graphic doesn't end abruptly if there is too little content in the side columns.

The code should look like this:

```
#sidebar1 {
  float: left;
  width: 22%;
  padding: 15px 0;
  background: url(images/side1_back.jpg) no-repeat top right;
  min-height: 200px;
}
#sidebar2 {
  float: right;
  width: 23%;
  padding: 15px 0;
  background: url(images/side2_back.jpg) no-repeat right top;
  min-height: 145px;
}
#mainContent {
  margin: 0 24% 0 23.5%;
  padding-top: 10px;
  background: url(images/content_back.jpg) no-repeat right
top;
}
```

Min-height works in all current browsers, including Internet Explorer 7. But it isn't supported in IE 6 or below. In those browsers, we can imitate the same behavior using the height property. IE will expand a box to contain its content, so if the column has more content, it will simply grow longer. If it has less, it will remain at the height given. We only want to do this for IE 6 and lower, though, so we'll need to use an Internet Explorer Conditional Comment within the head of our document:

```
<!--[if lte IE 6]>
<style type="text/css">
  #sidebar1 { height: 200px; }
  #sidebar2 { height: 145px; }
</style>
<![endif]-->
```

Refer to Chapter 2 for more information about Internet Explorer Conditional Comments.

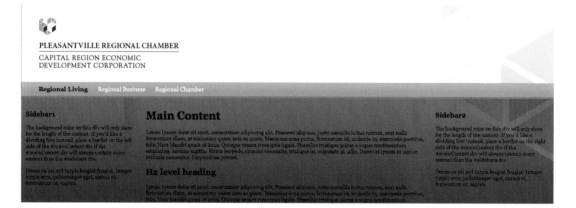

FIGURE 4.14 Previewed in a browser, it's looking like columns—but their content spills out!

Tweaking the Columns

Now is the time for all good designers to come to the aid of their columns. Though we graphically have our nice drop-shadowed, columned look, the measurements aren't exactly right. Viewing the designer's vision in Photoshop, we see that the alignment of the left column (sidebar1) is the same as the navigation and header above it—40 pixels from the left. The right column appears to have about 30 pixels on the right side.

With percentage-based layouts, we never want to add padding to the actual column itself. Instead, we want to use margin or padding

N *If you choose to set actual pixel values for the side columns, instead of allowing them to be fluid like the center, you could place the padding on the columns themselves. It would be quite easy then to calculate the amount of margin needed on the* mainContent *div. Our designer has asked that the columns remain fluid like the rest of the design.*

on the elements within the columns. Remember, the actual width of an element is the width value *plus* the padding and border. If we add 40px of padding to the left column, currently set at 22%, our actual width would be 22% + 40px—a number we can't be sure of at all! Thus, margining the middle mainContent div away from the column is risky at best.

Let's start on the right column, since it's simpler, then we'll move over to left column, changing the paragraphs to a list and positioning them properly. We've already measured in Photoshop and seen that, in the right column, the approximate space we want from the right side is 30px.

In your style sheet, you'll find a compound list of selectors:

```
#sidebar1 p, #sidebar1 h3, #sidebar2 p, #sidebar2 h3 {
    margin-left: 10px;
    margin-right: 10px;
}
```

Since we want differing margin values, we'll separate the right and left sidebar selectors and only make the change in the sidebar2 values.

1. Turn on the CSS Layout Outlines from the Visual Aids toolbar.

   Note that the shadow separating the mainContent from sidebar2 is actually contained in the mainContent div.

2. Leave the left margin as it is, and give the right margin the 30px value.

   ```
   #sidebar1 p, #sidebar1 h3 {
       margin-left: 10px;
       margin-right: 10px;
   }
   #sidebar2 p, #sidebar2 h3 {
       margin-left: 10px;
       margin-right: 30px;
   }
   ```

   When previewed, you'll see that we haven't changed the actual width of **sidebar2**. We've simply decreased the line length. The mainContent div's content is still too far to the right, but we'll adjust that in a moment.

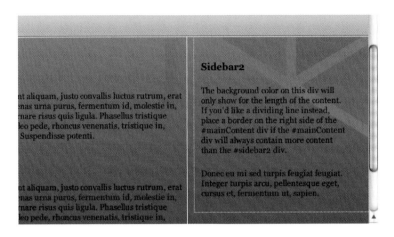

FIGURE 4.15 The right column is in the right place—the **main-Content** spacing is still off

While this is starting to come together, it would be nice to see the fonts in their proper colors and styles, wouldn't it? At times, that makes it easier to visualize the design more accurately. Since all the paragraph text is white except the footer, an efficient way to get a better view is to create a type selector for all paragraphs. When we move to the footer later, we'll simply assign a different color value there.

3. Change the **p** elements to use the Arial font set within Dreamweaver and also give it a line height of 1.5 to match the comp.

    ```
    p {
        color: #FFF;
        font-family: Arial, Helvetica, sans-serif;
        line-height: 1.5;
    }
    ```

    If the line-height *value is given no unit of measurement, it is calculated as a multiple of the font size. The value 1.5 is comparable to 150%.*

4. In the same way, since all headings are the same #FF9F00 color, create a comma-separated list of heading type selectors:

    ```
    h1, h2, h3, h4 {
        color: #FF9F00;
    }
    ```

Adding the Badge Image

The last element to place in the right column is the Walking Tour badge. Obviously, we could do as we have been doing and simply slice this image in an image editor and export it. But we're going to do something slightly different this time. (If you don't have access to Photoshop, please export the badge from the graphics editor of your choice.)

1. Open the design in Photoshop, locate the Walking Tour layer group and open it in the Layers panel. Cmd-click on the icon for Layer 1 in the layer group to select the area of the badge image. Select the Walking Tour layer group in the Layers panel and choose Edit > Copy Merged.

   Photoshop creates a merged (flattened) image containing all of the elements within the layer group's active selection area and places it on the clipboard.

2. In Dreamweaver, place the cursor at the end of the text in the third paragraph and tap the Return key to create a new paragraph. Choose Edit > Paste.

   Dreamweaver recognizes that the content on the Clipboard is not text, but rather an image and opens the built-in Fireworks optimization dialog. We can now set the optimization level for the image.

3. Click the small window pane icon divided into four sections in the lower right of the dialog.

   The 4-up view lets us compare different compression settings side-by-side. You'll notice that the GIF 256 has a smaller compression size, but the gradient background doesn't look as nice. Comparatively, the default JPG compression of 80% looks good.

4. Click on the page that has the 80% optimization to make it active, and click OK. Name the image walking_badge.jpg and place it in the images folder for the site.

One advantage of optimizing images from Photoshop by pasting within Dreamweaver is that Dreamweaver uses the "headless Fireworks" optimization engine. Since Fireworks creates smaller file sizes, this makes our page weight even lighter.

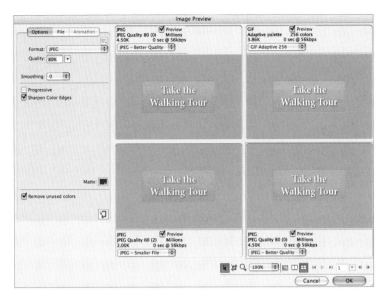

FIGURE 4.16 A The headless Fireworks optimization within Dreamweaver

Dreamweaver prompts you for alternative text for the image just as it did when we placed the logo earlier.

5. Enter text that is descriptive of the image such as, "Take the walking tour" and click OK.

Of course anytime that we are dealing with a website, there is always the chance that the client will change their mind about an image or piece of text. Changing text is easy since it is part of the HTML, but with images, we're forced to go back to the original image file—whose name and location we hope we remember—and then make the requested change, re-exporting and potentially placing the file in the layout again.

With the new Photoshop integration, Dreamweaver takes the guesswork out of the process. Compare the badge image on the page to the Photoshop comp. Do you notice any difference? In the Photoshop comp the badge image has a drop shadow that is missing in the image on the page. Unfortunately when we used the automatic pixel selection for the layer in Photoshop, it did not select the pixels that make up the drop shadow effect.

Let's correct that now. Notice in the Properties inspector that there are two Photoshop (or, if the image came from Fireworks, Fireworks) icons. The one in the bottom row of the inspector

T *If you have closed the original Photoshop or Fireworks image, Dreamweaver launches the application and opens the file. However, Dreamweaver has no way of indicating to the other application what the selection area or slice was that was used to create the image, so you'll need to manually reselect it. We're crossing our fingers that future versions of the applications might bring us this functionality.*

T *If you want to re-optimize the image, you can select the image and click the Optimize icon in the Edit section of the inspector. This reopens the optimization window, but the source image for the new optimization is the original Photoshop or Fireworks image in its entirety. You'll have to use the slice tool in the optimization dialog to re-slice the desired section of the graphic and this can be difficult. A better bet is to delete the image from the page and start over.*

N *If you're thinking to yourself that we could have used the copy/paste technique during the creation of the page logo or background images, you're right! But since this is a book about CSS and Dreamweaver, we didn't want too many of our exercises to require you to use Photoshop.*

identifies the path to the original Photoshop file which was used to create the image.

6. Click the icon in the Edit section of the inspector.

   Dreamweaver opens the original file in either Photoshop or Fireworks, depending upon the original file type.

7. Back in Photoshop, click Layer 1 in the Layers panel in the walking tour layer group. Be sure nothing is selected in your Photoshop comp by choosing Select > Deselect. Choose Layer > New Layer Based Slice. Choose Edit > Copy.

8. Back in Dreamweaver, choose Edit > Paste again.

   This time Dreamweaver simply updates the graphic without taking us through the optimization dialog. In other words, Dreamweaver assumes that we would like to use the same optimization on the image that we applied before.

It's also possible to drag an entire PSD out of Bridge (choose File > Browse in Bridge) and drop it into a Dreamweaver layout. Just remember that you'll be placing a flattened version of the entire file into Dreamweaver. But this can be quite handy if the image is a photograph or simple image that you need in its entirety on your page.

Creating the Left-hand Navigation

With more accurate visuals all set, it's time to work on the left column. This column is slightly more complicated than the last since the shadow graphic is contained in the right side of the column, and space must be created for the graphic within the column itself. Also, the little marker by the menu item that indicates which page the user is on is all the way against the left side of the column. Because of this, we can't simply margin the overall list: instead, we'll have to use padding on the list items themselves. Let's see how that works.

1. Remove all content in the `sidebar1` div and replace it with an unordered list of links using the link names given in the Photoshop comp.

Remember that since we want to use the same current page indicator trick we used on the horizontal menu, each list item needs a unique ID:

```
<ul>
  <li id="visiting"><a href="#">Visiting the Area</a></li>
  <li id="moving"><a href="#">Moving to the Area</a></li>
  <li id="maplocator"><a href="#">Interactive Maplocator</a>
</li>
  <li id="directory"><a href="#">Business Directory</a></li>
</ul>
```

Since we removed the heading and paragraph elements from `sidebar1`, we don't need the selectors for them.

2. Remove the `#sidebar1 p` and `#sidebar1 h3` selectors.

3. Create a descendant selector and zero the browser defaults. Also increase the text size slightly since the menu text in the comp is larger:

```
#sidebar1 ul {
  margin: 0;
  padding: 0;
  list-style: none;
  font-size: 105%;
}
```

Many times, we'd create the space on the left of the menu with a left margin on the `ul` itself. However, with this design, we want to be able to add the visual indicator all the way on the left side of the page, so we can't move the entire list over. We have two other elements to choose from though. We can either move the list item itself, or the link within it. Before we give you the answer, think about which one you would put it on—and why...

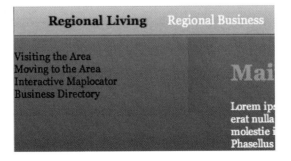

FIGURE 4.17 We've got the list sitting right up against the left side of our page.

Okay, time's up! If you chose to put the padding on the link within the list item, you made the same choice we did. If you chose the list item itself, you're not wrong: remember, there are many ways to do the same thing with CSS. But we chose the link because, when we add the CSS to create the page indicator, it will not only add the graphic on the left, it will also change the color of the link. Since we'd have to create a selector to change the link color, using it to add the graphic as well is efficient, more so than creating another set of rules just for the graphic. For this reason, we'll put the padding on the link element.

Styling the Menu Links

Ready to style the links?

T *We could have written the above selector as* #sidebar1 a *(leaving out the* li *portion of the cascade). It would have selected the links within the list items. It would have also selected any other link that might be put in that column later, or in other pages in the site which use the same layout. So being specific here can be helpful down the road.*

1. Set the display to block, the color to white, remove the underlines, and set the padding to 5px for the top and bottom and 40px on the left to match the alignment of the elements above.

```
#sidebar1 li a {
    display: block;
    padding: 5px 0 5px 40px;
    color: #FFF;
    text-decoration: none;
}
```

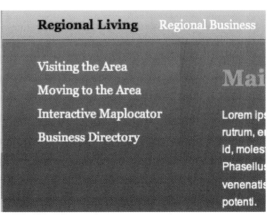

FIGURE 4.18 We've got the correct color and spacing for our vertical navigation now

We set the display to block just like we did in the horizontal navigation, since we want the entire link to be clickable.

If you look in a browser, you'll see that the alignment of the top of the `ul` is a bit high. We also know we need to account for the 33px wide graphic that creates the shadow on the right of this sidebar.

2. Give the `ul` a top margin to move it down and a right margin to keep the text out of the graphic area:

```
#sidebar1 ul {
    margin: 15px 35px 0 0;
    padding: 0;
    list-style: none;
    font-size: 105%;
}
```

Since our comp width is 1066px, let's make the columns match up as closely as possible within a 1024px browser width. Obviously, this is based on percentages, so those column widths will ultimately ebb and flow, but we'd like our initial settings to be close to what the artist envisioned.

3. Increase the left column's width by 1%, giving it a total of 23%.

```
#sidebar1 {
    float: left;
    width: 23%;
    padding: 15px 0;
    background: url(images/side1_back.jpg) no-repeat top right;
    min-height: 200px;
}
```

Placing the Page Indicator on the Vertical Menu

We'll indicate what page the user is on the same way we did before: by placing a class on the link.

First we need to get the arrow graphic. You can use the arrow.gif file that you downloaded from the Web site, or you can slice the arrow from the Photoshop document. But instead of zooming in very close on the little arrow to slice it out, select the "arrow path" slice in the body layer group, and use the layer-based slice technique discussed in *Adding the Badge Slice*. Copy and paste the arrow anywhere in the Dreamweaver document, optimizing the image as arrow.gif. Set the darkest purple background area as the transparent color. Since the graphic is so small, we won't need to worry about a matte color. Delete the image from your Dreamweaver document.

1. Put arrow.gif and the #FF9F00 color on a descendant selector. Align the gif to sit in the vertical center of the text.

   ```
   .visiting #visiting a {
      background: url(images/arrow.gif) no-repeat left center;
      color: #FF9F00;
   }
   ```

N *If you place the graphical indicator on the vertical center of the list item's link, if the user's text is large and it wraps to the next line, the graphic will be centered on both lines. You can also align it to the top for your own designs.*

2. Place the .visiting class for the vertical menu on the body element along with the .living class that's already there for the horizontal menu.

   ```
   <body class="living visiting">
   ```

   You can put more than one class on an element if you separate them with a space. This can be quite useful at times.

3. Create all the other descendant selectors for the vertical menu. Follow the same pattern we just used:

   ```
   .visiting #visiting a, .moving #moving a, .maplocator
   #maplocator a, .directory #directory a {
      background: url(images/arrow.gif) no-repeat left center;
      color: #FF9F00;
   }
   ```

4. Finally, use the same orange color for the vertical menu hover state as used on the headings and page indicator.

   Remember again, whenever we define a hover state, we also want to define the active and focus so that users with alternative methods of navigating your site can also see where their focus is.

   ```
   #sidebar1 li a:hover, #sidebar1 li a:active, #sidebar1 li
   a:focus {
      color: #FF9F00;
   }
   ```

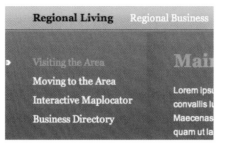

FIGURE 4.19 The final vertical menu with page indicator

Styling the mainContent Area

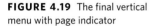 *Remember that padding is inside the div and margin is outside.*

We'll have our columns looking perfect when we make a simple adjustment to the `mainContent` div. The shadow creating the right column is contained within the `mainContent` div so, unfortunately, using a margin would actually make the column itself appear wider. (Feel free to experiment with that to see how it looks).

Using padding will leave our graphic where it is, but will move the content within the div away from the right edge. Since the designer has given a rather wide margin to the text in `mainContent`, we'll use about 100px of right padding and see if that achieves the desired result.

```
#mainContent {
    margin: 0 24% 0 23.5%;
    background: url(images/content_back.jpg) no-repeat right
top;
    padding-top: 10px;
    padding-right: 100px;
}
```

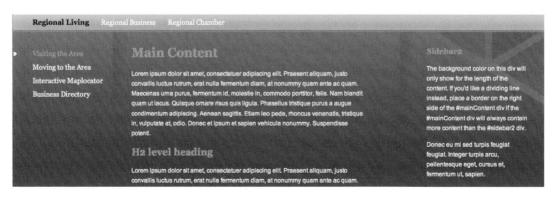

FIGURE 4.20 Our columns and menu should now match our comp nicely

Getting to the Bottom of it— Styling the Footer

We're very close to being done. But we need to get rid of the gray background in the footer so that the footer will use the background color from the page.

And we still have the issue of the two 10px stripes of color between the main area and the footer to contend with. But that's fairly easy—and image-free! All we need is a couple of borders.

1. Delete the gray background from the `#footer` selector using your method of choice.

2. Place a `#2D2D70` 10px line above the footer using a 10px top border.

3. Set the left padding to 40px (like the left column) and the right padding to 30px (like the right column).

    This will ensure that our alignment matches the upper areas. Since the margin of the `#footer p` element already has a 10px top and bottom margin, we'll leave the top and bottom **padding** zeroed here.

    Using shorthand, the code looks like this:

    ```
    #footer {
      padding: 0 30px 0 40px;
      border-top: 10px solid #2D2D70;
    }
    ```

    Now, remember our three columns are placed in a single div called `mainWrap`. We'll use that div to place what appears to be the topmost border of the footer. However, it will actually be the bottom border of the `mainWrap` div.

4. In the `mainWrap` div, place a `#36357D` 10px line at the bottom of the div, with 20px of padding at the bottom.

    This gives us the following code:

    ```
    #mainWrap {
      background: #403E8A url(images/main_back.jpg) repeat-x;
      border-bottom: 10px solid #36357D;
      padding-bottom: 20px;
    }
    ```

Floating Left and Right

With the stripes created, let's turn our attention to the content within the footer itself. We have a copyright and an unordered list of links. One is on the right side and the other is on the left. It's not uncommon to want to align elements both left and right. There are several ways to accomplish this—from absolute positioning to floating one or more elements.

For our footer, it seems simplest to float the unordered list and leave the **p** element on the left. Let's put the XHTML code into our page first. Because a floated element must precede the element you want it to sit next to, place the **ul** before the **p** element in the source order:

```
<ul>
  <li><a href="#">Home</a></li>
  <li><a href="#">Site Map</a></li>
  <li><a href="#">Contact Us</a></li>
</ul>
<p>Copyright 2007 Pleasantville Regional Chamber. All rights
reserved</p>
```

Let's quickly look at the CSS code beginning with the footer's **p** element. We previously created a **p** type selector that is controlling the color and **font-family** for all **p** elements on the page. The footer is the one area where the **p** elements differ. They're not white, nor are they Arial, so we must override those properties with this new, more specific selector—**#footer p**. We'll also give the **p** element a width of 59% so that it only covers a little more than half the page—even if the text size on the page is a good deal larger than we designed for.

```
#footer p {
  margin: 0;
  padding: 10px 0;
  width: 59%;
  color: #5C5A99;
  font-family: Georgia, "Times New Roman", Times, serif;
}
```

Since we've built two menus already, it should be pretty simple for you to create this one. Structure it like the top horizontal navigation, but style the links as in the vertical menu.

1. Start as we do all lists, by zeroing the defaults. Float the list right, and give it a width of 39%.

   Notice that the 59% width added with the 39% gives us 98%. Staying below a full 100% width assures us that we won't run into something like float drop later.

```
#footer ul {
  margin: 0;
  padding: 0;
  list-style: none;
  float: right;
  width: 39%;
}
```

2. Float the list items themselves to the right just as you did the `ul`.

```
#footer li {
  float: right;
}
```

   Floating them to the left would cause them to begin 61% from the left of the page since the `ul` is set to a 39% width.

3. Set the links to `display: block` (to keep them clickable for the full width), style them with the proper color and 10px padding and remove the underlines. Finally, create a compound selector to set the hover/active/focus color.

```
#footer li a {
  display: block;
  padding: 10px;
  color: #5C5A99;
  text-decoration: none;
}
#footer li a:hover, #footer li a:active, #footer li
a:focus {
  color: #FF9F00;
}
```

venenatis, tristique in, vulputate at, odio.
Copyright 2007 Pleasantville Regional Chamber. All rights reserved
Contact Us
Site Map
Home

FIGURE 4.21 With the footer complete, we're down to some simple styling

Putting on the Final Touches

Our page is looking great and with just a few more styling touches, we're done! First, we want to make sure the links on the page aren't the default blue. We'll make them white with underlines. For our hover style, we'll remove the underline.

```
a {
   color: #FFF;
   text-decoration: underline;
}
a:hover, a:active, a:focus {
   text-decoration: none;
}
```

In the comp at the middle bottom of the mainContent area, there's a link styled with the same little triangle indicator we placed on the vertical navigation. In times like these, we need to find out what our graphic designer had in mind. Does she want a specific link style? Or is she indicating that all the unordered lists should have this indicator instead of a regular bullet? In this case, all unordered lists should be styled with the graphic instead of the bullet.

To do this, we'll use code similar to the code for the page indicator on the vertical navigation. Since we've already defined the color and font-family in the p element, we'll add the ol and ul for the mainContent div to that same p selector.

```
p, #mainContent, #mainContent ol {
   color: #FFF;
   font-family: Arial, Helvetica, sans-serif;
   line-height: 1.5;
}
#mainContent ul {
   margin: 0;
   padding: 0;
   list-style: none;
}
#mainContent li {
   background: url(images/arrow.gif) no-repeat left center;
   padding-left: 15px;
}
```

The only thing left to do is style and size our headings. We've changed the text for our headings in the XHTML page to the same words as the comp, to help us visualize. Since our designer gave all the headings a normal weight, we can add the `font-weight` property to the heading selector we already created, to control the weight of all our headings at once. The sizing will have to be changed separately.

```
h1, h2, h3, h4 {
   color: #FF9F00;
   font-weight: normal;
}
```

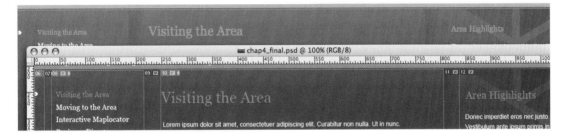

FIGURE 4.22 Comparing our headings to the comp

The h1 and h3 in the sidebar are smaller than the designer envisioned. We'll adjust those now:

```
h1 {
   font-size: 225%;
}
h2 {
   font-size: 175%;
}
h3 {
   font-size: 150%;
}
h4 {
   font-size: 135%;
}
```

If the sizes of your headings are consistent within the various divs, writing a simple type selector works nicely. If you want the size of the side column's h3 *to be different than an* h3 *within your* main-Content *area, using a descendant selector works better.*

Your page is complete! Take a look at it in your browser and admire your work.

So what have you've accomplished in this chapter? You've learned how to deal with percentage-based layouts and to overcome the challenges that margin and padding give in these layouts. Additionally, you've learned how to effectively use background images within percentage-based columns; style both horizontal and vertical menus without the use of inline images; and create a current page indicator. Finally, we've explored the use of Photoshop CS3, together with Dreamweaver CS3 to optimize or streamline the production process.

Creating a More Complex Design with Elastic Layouts

AS WEB DESIGNERS and developers, we generally have a lot of smart and professional reasons for building a site the way we do. We position and size page elements to direct the focus of users, making it easy for them to find what we want them to see and to do what we want them to do. We carefully design and develop what we plan to be an enjoyable, engaging experience for our audience—and a profitable one for our client.

But let's pause for a moment and consider the situation for some of our site visitors: in particular, those with low vision. We're not talking about blind people, but rather those with trouble viewing text comfortably at default font sizes. This includes a large percentage of people in their late thirties or older (your authors included!), as well as people with eyesight issues that aren't age-related.

Although not all of these users are savvy enough to know how to manipulate font sizes in their browser, many are—and those with exceptionally poor vision almost definitely are. But when increasing the font size in a browser, the width of the layout usually constrains the text. Text becomes big in comparison to everything else on the page, and line lengths can become ridiculously short, making online reading a difficult and frustrating exercise.

Checkpoint 3.4 of the W3C's Web Accessibility Initiative (WAI) Web Content Accessibility Guidelines (WCAG) 1.0 recommends the use of relative units. See http://www.w3.org/TR/WAI-WEBCONTENT/wai-pageauth.html#tech-relative-units

Yes, it's pretty inconvenient, not to mention inconsiderate, of users to be less than perfect, grow older than their thirties, or for whatever reason have low vision. The spoilsports! But the good news is that we can design accessible web sites that will allow more design precision and scale—with text, layout and even images—while retaining the proportions of our intended design. These layouts are referred to as being "elastic" due to their overall stretchiness.

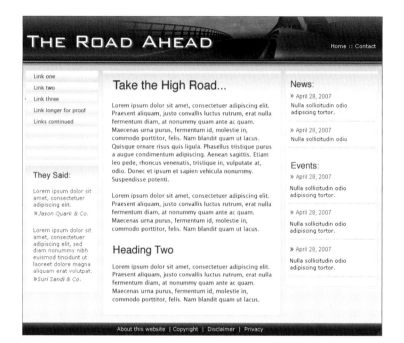

FIGURE 5.1 The comp for our fictional travel site.

In this project, we are building a web site for a fictional client, a travel agency specializing in land-based travel.

Create a folder called **TheRoadAhead**, and define the site, making the folder you just created the site root. Be sure to place the sliced images in the images folder.

Let's roll!

What is Accessibility and Why Should I Care?

An accessible web site is a site that doesn't exclude user groups from accessing the site's content. It is not merely about catering to blind people; an accessible web site embraces all aspects of making content available in as many formats, to as many people, in as many user agents and devices, as possible. Truly accessible content can be accessed and processed independently from its visual appearance in a browser.

Writing well-structured, semantic code is the first and most important step in providing accessible web sites. Fortunately it's not hard to do and nor is it expensive to implement! It enables alternative devices, including mobile devices as well as screen readers, to render content appropriately and according to their own standards and specifications. It also assists people with all kinds of disabilities—the blind and deaf, quadriplegics, people with motor difficulties or arthritis or carpal tunnel or any other condition that makes using a mouse or keyboard challenging, and yes, even those who simply need glasses to see clearly. And the list goes on: web accessibility also includes internationalization and the arrangement and writing of content in such a way as to assist those with poor language skills or cognitive difficulties.

What web accessibility is:

Web accessibility is about making sure the content of a web site is accessible to as many people on as many devices and as many user agents as possible.

What web accessibility is not:

Web accessibility is not about duplicating experience.

Why should I care?

- **Humanistic principles:** caring that people with disabilities or using alternative devices have as much right and need to access the content of a web site as those who are totally fit and sitting at desktop computers with the most modern equipment.

- **Business principles:** people using alternative user agents are your customers, too! Why exclude them? In fact, when a web site is built accessibly, buying online can be much easier for a person with a disability than leaving the house.

- **Anti-discrimination laws:** these are becoming more widespread and more strictly enforced and litigation can be costly to a business in terms of time, money, reputation and goodwill.

The New Document

Let's begin with one of Dreamweaver's built-in elastic layouts and modify it for our client.

Open the New dialog and in the Blank Page section, select 3 column elastic, header and footer layout. Set the DocType to (X)HTML 1.0 Transitional and in the CSS Layout drop-down list, select Create

T *If this were a real client, we would be sure to use good keywords in the title of our page so that the search engine spiders would find them relevant and even delicious, and would come back often! It's always a good idea to feed the spiders well.*

New File and save the file in your site under the default name of `thrColElsHdr.css` (or change it to whatever you desire). Save the (X)HTML page as `index.html`.

Title the open (X)HTML document "The Road Ahead :: Travel the Roads", either using the Title input in the Document toolbar or directly in the head section of the (X)HTML code.

Resetting the CSS defaults

In this project we are only going to be working with a three-column layout, so we don't need the `thrColElsHdr` prefix on all our rules. If you've forgotten how to remove it, head back to Chapter 4 and apply the instructions in *Simplifying the CSS Selectors* to the `thrColElsHdr` prefix. Delete this class from the body tag in the (X)HTML document too.

In this chapter, we're going to use a new method of zeroing out the default settings in the different browsers to give us a solid starting point.

1. Open the `thrColElsHdr.css` file.

2. Add the following code to the top of the document:

```
html, body, div, span, applet, object, iframe, h1, h2, h3,
h4, h5, h6, p, blockquote, pre, a, abbr, acronym, address,
big, cite, code, del, dfn, em, font, img, ins, kbd, q,
s, samp, small, strike, strong, sub, sup, tt, var, dl,
dt, dd, ol, ul, li, fieldset, form, label, legend, table,
caption, tbody, tfoot, thead, tr, th, td {
  margin: 0;
  padding: 0;
  border: 0;
  outline: 0;
  font-weight: inherit;
  font-style: inherit;
  font-size: 100%;
  font-family: inherit;
  vertical-align: baseline;
}
```

Remember to define focus styles! ─────

```
:focus {
    outline: 0;
}
body {
    line-height: 1;
    color: black;
    background: white;
}
ol, ul {
    list-style: none;
}
table {
    border-collapse: separate;
    border-spacing: 0;
}
caption, th, td {
    text-align: left;
    font-weight: normal;
}
blockquote:before, blockquote:after,
q:before, q:after {
    content: "";
}
blockquote, q {
    quotes: "" "";
}
```

Tables still need 'cellspacing="0"' in the markup ─────

N *We know you can't copy/ paste from the book and that's a heckuva lot of code to type. If you prefer, you can copy the code from Eric Meyer's site (as well as read more details about why it's written in the way it is) at http://meyerweb.com/eric/ thoughts/2007/05/01/reset-reloaded/ (or use the resource page for this book to access the link.)*

The code above is a nifty way to combat some potential cross-browser issues, as well as to simplify the CSS, in one hit. Our thanks to the inimitable Eric Meyer for this technique. If, as the design progresses, we want to change any of these values, we will simply add the new value to the relevant rule further down in our style sheet.

N *In your own sites, you may not use all the selectors included in this block of code. But using this CSS reset technique means that if you add selectors at any point in the future, the groundwork is done to avoid unexpected surprises.*

As you remember (you do remember, right?) from our review in Chapter 1, specificity being equal, the last declaration on the page for any given selector overrides any previous declarations and will be applied by the browser. However, in the majority of cases, setting these values in a block of code at the top of the style sheet means we don't have to set the same values individually, later.

Creating a Reset Snippet

This reset is so handy, let's add it to our Dreamweaver Snippets for future re-use. To do so:

1. Highlight the reset code in the CSS document.

2. Select the Snippets tab in the Files panel.

3. In the interests of snippet organization, we'll create a new folder for CSS snippets (that is, if you're not so organized that you already have one!). Make sure none of the existing folders are selected. (If one is, click in the area at the bottom of the list of folders and the selection will clear.) Click on the New Snippet Folder icon at the bottom of the Snippets pane. Name the new folder CSS.

4. Click on the Add Snippet icon at the bottom of the Snippets pane or right-click the selected code and choose Create New Snippet from the contextual menu.

    In the dialog that appears, you will see that the CSS code you previously highlighted is already inserted in the text area.

5. Name the snippet CSS Reset, give it a description if you wish, and choose the Insert block radio button. Click OK.

T *To reuse this snippet, simply place the cursor wherever you wish the snippet to be added, open the Snippets pane and double click on the snippet. It will be inserted at the cursor. And if you're really into time-saving aids in Dreamweaver, you can even add a keyboard shortcut to the snippet. To do this, choose Keyboard Shortcuts from the Dreamweaver menu (Mac) or the Edit menu (PC). You'll need to duplicate the default shortcut group by clicking the Duplicate set button. Give your new set a name, then choose Snippets from the Commands drop-down list. Locate your new snippet and assign a keyboard shortcut by pressing the plus "+" button. Press your desired shortcut keys and then click the Assign button. Viola! Now you've always got the snippet at your finger tips!*

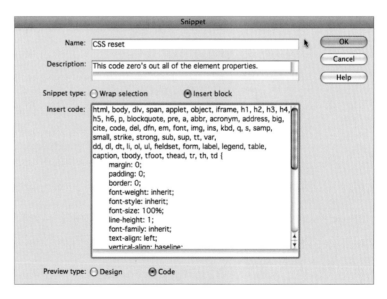

FIGURE 5.2 Our handy CSS reset code will always be available to us as a code snippet.

While we will further define many styles in our style sheet, some of the declarations that zeroed margin and padding now become duplicated CSS. These can be cleaned up as we come across them, to avoid making the style sheet unnecessarily large. When deleting anything, be sure to test each change, ready to Undo if required. Sometimes styles influence, or are influenced by, other styles in a way that is not obvious at first glance.

It's Just a Jump to the Left

Centered pages can actually appear to jump depending on whether or not a scrollbar is present. It's not an actual movement, but it looks as if it is, because the layout is in a slightly different position in the browser window. This can be very disconcerting when it's not obvious to the user (and especially the designer) what is happening, and it may be perceived as a design flaw. But not to worry, there's a quick fix!

Since we don't want to remove the scrollbar from all pages (that would be silly), we're simply going to give every page a scrollbar. The code below will apply a height of 100% to the body and html elements—and then add a margin of 1 pixel. Add it to your page right below the reset:

```
html, body {
   height: 100%;
   margin-bottom: 1px;
}
```

The margin adds 1 pixel to the full height of the viewport, and thus, creates a scrollbar. Even small pages, with very little content are convinced they have just a pixel more than will fit. It's not ideal, but neither is the layout jump. We've decided to go with the lesser of two evils. Save and view the page.

Tweaking the Reset

Don't worry about the loss of the font-family in Dreamweaver's Design view. It's still there in browsers and you can be sure we'll be resetting it to match our comp in a later rule anyway.

We want to be judicious about customizing the CSS reset: often, it doesn't make sense to do so. But in this case, since our designer chose a blue for the headings and text, we'll set the color universally in the body element. For many designs, though, there are enough differences in color between elements that leaving the body at the default black makes more sense.

1. Click inside the (X)HTML document and choose **<body>** on the tag selector. In the CSS Styles panel (Current view) select the first single body rule in the Rules pane.

    Do not select the first rule of the CSS reset, which also includes the body element, since it also embraces many other elements.

2. In the Properties pane, change the color property to a value of #336.

    Click into the page to view the changes. Why is the text still black? Our page came with a default body rule. In it, the text is declared to be black. That rule comes after the reset rule we just edited. Since they have the same specificity, our default rule is overriding our changes.

    As described in Chapter 2, this is shorthand for the longer #333366. The color displayed will be exactly the same for both, however it is easier and more efficient to use the shorter version.

3. Select the second single body rule in the Rules pane. In the Properties pane, select the color property and click the trashcan icon to delete (or right-click and choose delete).

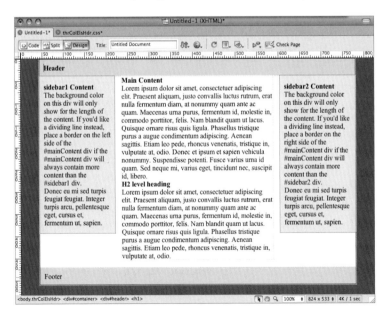

FIGURE 5.3 After applying the CSS reset, some of our styling has been lost.

Now the text on our page is colored blue to match our comp. But due to the reset rule, it has no default margin or padding. Don't worry about that for the moment, we'll have everything peachy in a bit.

Before we go on, let's review the basic structure of the page. A container with a specified width is centered in the browser window. Within it is a header and footer, each with a fixed height and a three-column content area. The center column has no width specified and uses side margins to clear the two, narrower side columns. The side columns are floated and have set widths. This is exactly like the basic structure of the other CSS layouts we've used thus far: nothing new, here. Or is there?

The Significance of the Em Unit

This particular layout is special because the widths on the divs are set in em units, rather than in the more common pixels or percentages. In print, an em is a unit of measurement based on the width of the uppercase letter M, which varies for different fonts. Em unit measurements have been in use for typesetting since movable type was invented—and no, we're not talking about the blogging software! A browser interprets 1em to equal the default font size of the browser, which (unless it has been changed by the user) is 16px (regardless of the font-family specified).

The em is Relative

Unlike pixels, an em is a relative unit. Since an em unit is based on font size, the actual width of a div (or size of an em) changes if a font declaration is set directly on the div or if the overall font size is increased by the user. In contrast, divs sized using percentages, also a relative unit, calculate their size based on their parent element.

In other words, when using ems for layout, the dimensions of the layout expand or contract depending on the user's font size: the overall proportions of the page and its contents remain the same. A person viewing your page with a default font size of 32px sees the same number of words per line as the person with a 12px, 16px or 25px default.

Let's take a quick peek before this gets too confusing.

1. Head back to our `index.html` page and preview it in a standards-compliant browser (meaning—not Internet Explorer—we never go there till the end of a project).

2. Using your browser of choice's method, increase the text size (Ctrl+/Cmd+ on Firefox and Safari).

   Notice how the entire layout resizes—not just the text? That's the beauty of the em. Unless you set a maximum width, your user has full control—and perfect line lengths!

TEXT SIZING

All the CSS layouts in Dreamweaver have a body rule with a font-size value of 100%, meaning 100% of the browser's default font size. Since 1em is also equivalent to the browser's default font size, for all practical purposes, a font-size value of 100% equals 1em. When we set font sizes elsewhere in our (X)HTML document in em units, the sizes are relative to this value.

DIV SIZING

Some developers set font-sizes directly on divs to size everything within them down by the same, relative amount. We won't enter the debate of whether that's best practice, but we will discuss when it's safe—or not—in elastic layouts. Since the container holds all other divs in the layout, setting a font-size on the container resizes everything within it the same relative amount. This gives us consistency.

However, if the side columns are given differing font sizes, their widths relative to each other will vary. In fact, doing this can completely break your layout. Let's look at this in Dreamweaver to make it crystal clear.

1. Select the `<div#sidebar1>` in the tag selector.

2. From the left edge of your document window, click, hold and drag a guide out to the left edge of `sidebar1`. Do the same thing for the right side of the `sidebar1`.

3. Place your mouse between the two guides (you don't have to click). Press your control key (PC) or command key (Mac).

   Dreamweaver tells you the actual pixel width between the two guides. Ours measured 177px.

4. In the CSS Styles panel, add the `font-size` property to the `#sidebar1` selector and give it a value of `.8em`.

   You'll notice an instant shrinkage of not just the fonts, but the overall div width. But the `mainContent`, whose width was not affected, retains a margin using the em unit sizing that descends to it from the container. So we have more white space between the `sidebar1` div and the `mainContent` div than we anticipated.

FIGURE 5.4 The overall width of `sidebar1` has decreased, yet the rest of the page remains the same

5. Move the guide, which should be sitting out in the margin of the `mainContent`, back to the `sidebar1`'s right side where it belongs.

6. Measure the actual pixel space using Ctrl/Cmd again.

   Although both sidebars have an overall width of 11em units, the size of `sidebar1` has shrunk to 142px, while `sidebar2` remains at the original size. Imagine the problems you'd have if all the divs had their own font-sizing—especially if they were all floated. Buyer beware!

7. Remove the `font-size` you just placed on `sidebar1` since, as you can see, this is definitely not a safe way to size our layout.

To avoid this scenario, the best practice is to put the `font-size` on the containing div only. The `font-size` is then applied uniformly to all contents of the page. From there, you can change the `font-size` on block elements within the individual containers of the page, such as the `p` and `heading` elements themselves. This won't change the overall div size.

Limitations of em-based layouts

Here are a couple more things to consider when designing with em-based layouts:

Images are generally assigned a fixed pixel width (even if no `width` property is set, the browser calculates the image's width in pixels). Though we can set the width of an image using em units, and thereby allow them to scale with the font size as well, most images will only scale nicely to a point. After that, they can start to look somewhat ugly and pixelated. We'll look at scaling images in more detail later in this chapter.

Due to the expansive nature of em widths, your design must allow for horizontal growth. As the layout resizes beyond the width of the viewport, a horizontal scrollbar appears. Workarounds have their own limitations and we'll consider these later in this chapter as well.

Even with a few things to keep in mind, the accessibility and flexibility of em-based layouts make them very attractive indeed.

Some Overall Type Adjustments

Now that you understand how fonts are sized, and how em units are applied, let's style the container of our page.

Typically, the browser default font size, which we've left at 100%, is too large for most developers, clients and users. We're going to scale the font-size down on the container.

1. Click to place the cursor anywhere in the (X)HTML document and select `<div#container>` from the tag selector.

2. In the `#container` rule, click the Add Property link in the Properties section and set the font-size to 0.8em.

It is often quicker to simply type the unit of measure in the value field after typing the value rather than clicking and selecting the unit of measure from the adjacent drop-down list. Dreamweaver honors the value typed into the field even if another unit, for example pixels, is pre-selected in the drop-down list.

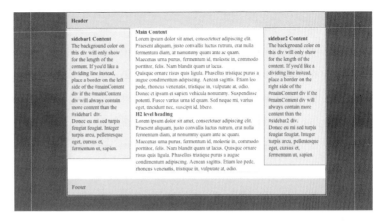

FIGURE 5.5 You can see by Dreamweaver's guides that the overall width of the container has decreased due to the change in font size.

Currently our style sheet has **#container** set to **46em**, which under normal circumstances would be the approximate equivalent of 736 pixels, where **1em** is the default browser font size of **16px**. As soon as we reduced the font size on the **container** element, the page shrank in width. But according to our designer's comp, we want it to take up to 760 pixels (or its em equivalent) when the page loads, so that users with default font sizing set will see a page that fits nicely in a 800px wide screen resolution.

1. Select the **#container** rule in the CSS Styles panel's Rules section again.

2. Set the width property to **59.375em**. (A very odd number indeed!)

   You can see the changes reflected in the CSS file (with the comments removed here to avoid clutter):

   ```
   #container {
       width: 59.375em;
       background: #FFFFFF;
       margin: 0 auto;
       border: 1px solid #000000;
       text-align: left;
       font-size: 0.8em;
   }
   ```

Wondering how we calculated that? Here's the math. By default, 1em = 16px. The font size on #container is 0.8em To get the pixel equivalent for the actual font size used in the page, we multiply the default pixel size by the em unit we've given the div—16 x 0.8 = 12.8px. So 1em in the container is about 12.8px. We want the overall width to be around 760px, so we simply divide that by the pixel number we arrived at (per em). 760 ÷ 12.8 = 59.375em. Easy, right?

DEFINING OUR MAJOR TYPE ELEMENTS

Now that we've got our overall font size and container scaled down, we'll turn our attention back to the compressed page we were left with after our CSS reset. Let's redefine our **p** element as a start.

1. In the CSS Styles panel, click on the New CSS Rule icon. Choose Tag and type **p** into the Selector box (or choose **p** from the drop-down list). Click OK.

2. In the Type section, add the fonts `"Lucida Grande"`, `Verdana`, `Arial`, `Helvetica`, `serif`.

3. Next to Size, type in **1em**. Alternatively you can type 1 and select ems from the drop-down list. Either method works. For the line height, type **1.5**. Line height defaults to pixels so select `multiple` from the drop-down list.

4. In the Box category, for Margin, uncheck the check box next to "Same for all" and add a `margin-top` of **0.4em** and a `margin-bottom` of **0.7em**. Click OK.

5. Switch to the open style sheet document and scroll to the bottom of the file. If your Dreamweaver preferences are set to display CSS shorthand, you'll see this rule added at the bottom:

```
p {
    font: 1em/1.5 "Lucida Grande", Verdana, Arial,
Helvetica, serif;
    margin-top: 0.4em;
    margin-bottom: 0.7em;
}
```

We are going to reuse this font selection, so it makes sense to add it to the drop-down list. In the drop-down list, select Edit Font List to open a dialog box where individual fonts can be selected, grouped together and placed in the list. (Specific instructions for this are included in Chapter 2 if needed.)

The 1em before the forward slash refers to the font size, and the 1.5 after the forward slash refers to the line height.

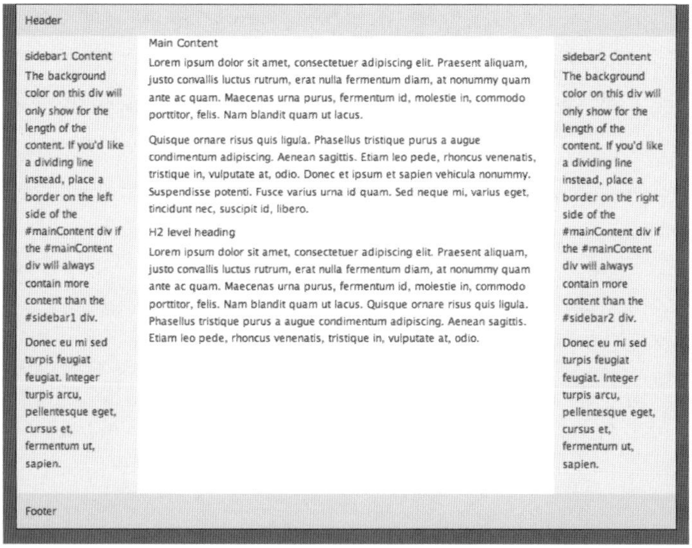

FIGURE 5.6 We can see the increase in line height as well as the color applied to text on the page.

STYLING THE HEADINGS

Switch back to the (X)HTML document and highlight the heading, Main Content. In the tag selector, we can see this is an <h1> heading. But the rule shown for the h1 in the CSS Properties pane is the compound first reset rule and h1 is listed as only one of many other selectors. We'll create a separate, specific h1 selector.

1. With `<h1>` selected, click on the New CSS Rule icon at the bottom right of the CSS Panel.

    Dreamweaver suggests a descendant selector of `#container #mainContent h1`. All of our content is in `#container` so it's overly specific to include that as part of the selector.

2. Delete `#container`, leaving `#mainContent h1` and click OK.

3. In the Type category, set the font to `Helvetica, Arial, Verdana, sans-serif`. (Add these fonts to the font list via the Edit Font List dialog for later re-use.) For size, type in `1.8em`. For weight, choose `normal`. Click OK.

    Our main heading is now much larger but not as bold as a typical `h1` because we overrode that behavior with the `weight:normal` declaration.

    The style for `h2` should be identical to that of `#mainContent h1`, except that the size should be set to 1.6em. We could go through the process of creating the rule using the methods we used so far, or, we can do it even faster. Hmm… we vote fast!

4. Switch to All mode in the CSS Styles Panel, and select the `#mainContent h1` rule that we just created.

5. Right-click and choose Duplicate. Name the selector `#mainContent h2` and click OK.

    The rule is added at the bottom of the style sheet below the `h1` rule.

6. With the new rule selected, change the value of the font-size property to `1.6em`. (Remember it's in shorthand.)

7. Let's also add a bit of padding to the top of the `h2` elements by clicking the Add Property link and typing `padding-top` and assigning the value `0.7em`.

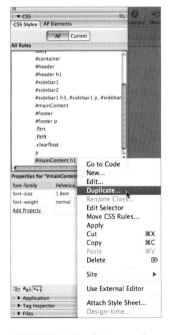

FIGURE 5.7 Duplicating a rule saves a lot of time.

N *The distance created by this top padding, along with a zero bottom padding, creates a visual association between the heading and the content directly below it.*

The CSS layouts in Dreamweaver all have a **h1** and **h2** element in the **mainContent** area, while the sidebar areas use an **h3** for their headings. Of course, we might want to add a **h3** to the **mainContent** area as well. Therefore, we'll create a rule for all **h3** elements regardless of their source location.

8. Duplicate the **#mainContent h1** rule again. Rename it to make it a simple element selector—**h3**.

9. Set the **font-size** of the new rule to **1.5em** in the Properties section of the CSS panel.

Now, we've created three simple rules to handle the **h1**, **h2** and **h3** elements on the page.

```
#mainContent h1 {
    font: normal 1.8em Helvetica, Arial, Verdana, sans-serif;
}
#mainContent h2 {
    font: normal 1.6em Helvetica, Arial, Verdana, sans-serif;
    padding-top: 0.7em;
}
h3 {
    font: normal 1.5em Helvetica, Arial, Verdana, sans-serif;
}
```

Though the headings are nicer, our page looks a bit gray and boring right now. Don't panic. Some small image files, and some smart CSS, and we'll have it looking as nice as our comp in no time.

The Visual Transformation

This is where the fun begins. Our framework for the page is established. All the basic CSS properties have been zeroed out and set to our liking. Now all that remains is to begin to add and style the actual page content. First up, let's get rid of all that ugly gray!

Styling the Header

We'll feel much better about our page when we have a nice logo in place. We're going to add the logo to the header, but as a background image so we can keep the nice gradient that extends down the page, behind any text we later add to the page's content.

1. Click to place the cursor inside the header of the (X)HTML document, select `<div#header>` from the tag selector, and head back to the CSS Styles Panel. Click the Edit Style button to bring up the Edit dialog box.

2. In the Background section, remove the background color of `#DDDDDD`. We want the background to be transparent.

3. Click the browse button and navigate to the `logo.jpg` in the image directory of your site.

4. Set repeat to `no-repeat`, set the horizontal position to `left` and the vertical position to `top`.

5. Remove the values from the Padding section. Click OK.

   Naturally we don't want the existing heading text shouting Header at us, so we'll first change that to our company name, The Road Ahead—be sure not to delete the `<h1>` element while editing the text.

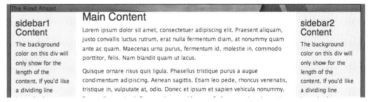

FIGURE 5.8 Well, at least we have a little slice of the header showing!

Since we're using a background image that incorporates the logo, we want the company name accessible to those who won't see the logo. Let's use a trick to move the name off the screen but still keep it accessible to devices that read the text.

6. Make sure the cursor is placed inside the `<h1>` element in `<div#header>` and then click the Edit Style (pencil) icon in the CSS Styles Panel.

7. In the Box category, remove the padding and margin values.

N   *Setting the width makes sure the name doesn't appear on the left side of the screen when a very large font size is used.*

8. Go to the Positioning section of the CSS Rule Definition dialog box. From the Type drop-down list, set the position to **absolute** with a width of **80em** and set the left property in the Placement section to **-100em**.

We now have the following rule in our style sheet:

```
#header h1 {
    width: 80em;
    left: -100em;
    position: absolute;
}
```

FIGURE 5.9 Egad! Now the whole thing has completely disappeared!

But what just happened to our page?! Suddenly the sidebars have decided they want to be completely on top of the header!

As has happened in previous chapters, we've been slapped by the principles of positioning. We know that when an element is absolutely positioned, it moves out of the document flow and other elements around it no longer react to its presence, and so attempt to move into its space. Before we positioned the **h1** element in the header, the header's space was reserved on the page (although, with the text so small, it wasn't much space). But the moment that the header's content, in this case the **h1** element, received positioning information, the header collapsed because the elements that came next in the flow, namely the sidebars, no longer perceived it as needing or using any space.

W   *Warning! From here, we'll assume that you have gotten familiar with the way in which elements are selected in Dreamweaver, i.e., "click to place your cursor in an area of the page, then select X in the tag selector". You've only done it a thousand times at this point, so for brevity's sake, we'll begin to simply say "select X with the tag selector"— unless there is a real need for more explicit instructions.*

The same effect would have occurred if we had floated the **h1** element because, while a floated element is not completely taken out of the flow of the document, other floated elements attempt to move in around it.

In order to reserve the header's space on the page, and make it the height of the background image within it, we'll give it a height.

1. Select **<div#header>** on the tag selector. (Since the header is completely collapsed, you may have to select the header from code or split view.)

2. Click Add Property in the CSS Styles panel. Type, or choose from the drop-down list, the property height. Give it a value of **110px** (the height of the background image).

Don't worry about the fact that Dreamweaver is not respecting the height of the header yet, it will! All browsers show the project looking like Figure 5.10.

FIGURE 5.10 The height has forced the sidebars to begin 110px from the top of the container.

When the page is viewed in a browser, our sidebars are beneath the header, just where we want them. The logo is in the background of the header, the header text is gone, and our page is looking more like our comp all the time.

The Header Illusion

Our comp has the header color spanning the full screen, yet the header on our page is constrained by the #container and #header elements. This is easily remedied by applying a horizontally-repeating background image (of the same gradient as our logo image) to the body element. The visual effect makes the header area appear seamless—as if it extends from the left to the right of the browser.

1. Select <body> in the tag inspector. In the CSS Styles Panel, click the Edit Style button to edit the body selector.

2. In the Background category, set the background color to #FFF.

3. Navigate to the tile.jpg background image in the images directory of the site.

4. Set repeat to repeat-x, the horizontal position to left and the vertical position to top.

The background color on the side columns prevents the background on the body "behind" it (above it in the cascade) from showing through. We don't need to specifically set a background color on container, sidebar1 and sidebar2 because, as per the rules of CSS, they have a default transparent value, which is exactly what we want!

We have one more tweak to make before our header looks the way we want it to look.

5. In the CSS Styles Panel, open All mode and select `#container`.

6. In the properties for `#container`, select the background property. Right-click and choose delete. Do the same for the border.

7. Repeat for `#sidebar1` and `#sidebar2`. We don't need that ugly gray color anymore!

Preview your page in a browser.

FIGURE 5.11 Now we're getting somewhere...!

Adding Inline navigation

Before we complete the header division of the page, we need to add two links: Home and Contact. Most navigation is actually a list of choices (thus often called a menu) and this is no exception. Let's start with the markup, and then style it.

1. In order to place our code exactly where we want it, in the Code section of Split view, place the cursor between the closing `</h1>` tag and the closing `</header>` tag.

   Make sure not to separate the comment noting the end of the header from its closing tag. `<!-- end #header --></div>`

2. In the Property inspector, click the unordered list icon.

   Viewing the code, you can see that an unordered list, including one set of list item tags, has been added on a new line under our `<h1>` element.

Notice that Design view now matches what we've been seeing in the browsers. Dreamweaver sometimes likes to have content in a div to give it a height.

3. Place the cursor between the newly created `<li></li>` tags and type the name of our first list item, **Home**. Click in the Design view section, and the word Home appears in the header.

   It's not where we want it, but we'll sort that out shortly, using CSS.

4. In Design view, place the cursor at the end of the word Home and press Enter or Return. We are now on not just a new line, but also in a new list item element. Type the second list item, **Contact**.

   In the Code view section, our header now contains the complete list.

   ```
   <div id="header">
   <h1>The Road Ahead</h1>
   <ul>
   <li>Home</li>
   <li>Contact</li>
   </ul>
   <!-- end #header --></div>
   ```

   Now let's add the links.

Since we don't have a contact page yet, a placeholder hash mark (#) will give us the look of a link until we create the real one.

5. In Design view, select Home. In the Property inspector, in the Link input field, type a placeholder hash mark (#).

6. Select Contact, and in the Link field, type **#**.

   Our code is looking great, but the visual appearance of the list is far from ideal. It's time for some more CSS goodness!

FIGURE 5.12 We've got a list, but not a very pretty one...in fact, we can barely see it in Design view!

STYLING THE INLINE NAVIGATION

The CSS reset removed margins, padding, bullets and all other styling that might apply to lists. We'll create a separate unordered list selector in our style sheet and build the style up from this starting point.

1. In the CSS Styles panel, click the New CSS Rule icon. In the dialog box, select the Advanced radio button, and in the Selector name field, type #header ul.

   Once again, we'll add this to our external style sheet.

N *We are using pixels here because the height of the header is defined in pixels to allow for a background image defined in pixels. A pixel margin on the list provides consistency of positioning against the image background.*

2. In the Box category, select right from the Float drop-down list. Uncheck the Margin "Same for all" box, and apply a top margin of 55px. Click OK.

If you glance at the document in Design view, you'll see that the list is now aligned to the right. That's a step in the right direction.

Making Dreamweaver Play Nice

Dreamweaver is a great tool with good visual rendering—most of the time. Every now and again however, it encounters a property or rule that causes some indigestion. The ingenious Dreamweaver engineers anticipated this and created a handy tool to use in those situations called **Design-Time Style Sheets** (DTSS), as described in Chapter 4.

We used a process of elimination and some detective skills to decide *which* property needed to be added to fix the rendering. By removing chunks of code, both (X)HTML and CSS, we discovered that the technique used to pull the **h1** in the **header** off the screen was causing problems in Design view. When we placed content inside the header (the unordered list), Dreamweaver rendered the height of the header. But when we floated that list, we lost that goodness since unless a float is cleared, the container doesn't know where it ends.

A simple fix would be to add a clearing element in the (X)HTML, but we don't want to add unnecessary code that the browsers don't need. But, remember, a float can contain or enclose another float. Adding the float property to the heading is another fix: we tried it, and voila! Dreamweaver rendered it perfectly. But in browsers, it's broken. This is the perfect case for a DTSS!

1. Create a new CSS document (File > New > Blank Page > CSS)

2. Create a single rule (be brave, type it in by hand!).

```
#header {
   float: left;
}
```

3. Save and name your file.

   We use `dtss.css` just so we can quickly remember what that style sheet contains.

4. With your html page in front, click on the context menu on the right corner of the CSS Styles panel and choose `Design-Time`.

   You can see in the dialog you can both add, and remove CSS pages.

5. Click the add button over the "Show only at design time" text area. Navigate to the page we just created. Click OK

   Dreamweaver is now giving us a view very similar to the browsers!

FIGURE 5.13 Dreamweaver tamed!

Though floating our list took us in the right direction, we still need our list to be on a nice, even horizontal plane. We'll style the list item elements to take care of that.

1. Create another new CSS rule, this time naming the selector `#header li`.

2. In the CSS Rule Definition dialog, go to the Block category. For display, choose `inline` from the drop-down list.

   This setting causes the list items to display side-by-side.

3. Go to the Box category and uncheck the "Same for all" box for padding. Allocate a right padding of `0.3em` and a left padding of `1.5em`. This nicely spaces our inline list items, with a comfortable distance from the right side of the header. Click OK.

We've made progress on the positioning, but the font and colors leave something to be desired—in fact, they're downright unreadable! Thus far, we haven't needed to choose how to display the font in the header, because the **h1** element is positioned off the screen. But let's set a font family and a font size, and apply a color specifically for links in the **#header** div. Let's use the same font as in the paragraph text.

1. Duplicate the rule for the **p** selector. (You remember that trick, right? If not, go back and re-read *Styling the Header*.) Choose All mode in the CSS Styles panel, right-click **p** in the list, and choose Duplicate. Name the new selector **#header a:link**. Be sure to switch the radio button to Advanced. Click OK.

2. Select our new **#header a:link** rule. Delete the margin declarations that were applied to the paragraph by selecting each of them in the CSS Styles panel, Property pane. Then right-click and choose Delete (or simply press the trashcan icon while the declaration is selected).

   We've gotten rid of what we don't want, now we'll add what we need.

3. Click the Add Property link. Set the color property to #FFF. Set text-decoration to **none**.

   These styles will also apply to visited links for this navigation list. Instead of duplicating the rule, let's simply add **#header a:visited** to the **#header a:link** rule, creating a compound selector.

4. Select **#header a:link** in the All view of the CSS panel, then right-click and choose Go To Code. This will place the cursor in the rule in our external style sheet. Place a comma directly after the selector name, then type in **#header a:visited**, leaving a space before the declaration block. We now have the following rule added to our style sheet:

```
#header a:link, #header a:visited {
    font: 1em/1.5 "Lucida Grande", Verdana, Arial,
Helvetica, serif;
    color: #FFF;
    text-decoration: none;
}
```

T *With a compound selector, make sure you never leave a comma at the end of the comma delimited list. If you do, some browsers will ignore the entire rule.*

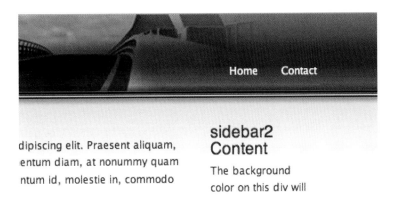

FIGURE 5.14 Now the list is looking more like a navigation bar.

We'll do something similar for the hover, active and focus states of the links. We know in advance we're going to use a compound selector, so we'll plan for that from the start.

1. Create a new rule by clicking on the New CSS Rule icon, select the radio button labeled Advanced, and name the selector: #header a:hover, #header a:active, #header a:focus

2. In the Type category, set the decoration to underline and the color to #95B2E3. Click OK.

   There is just one more thing to attend to before our inline navigation is complete. Our designer placed a visual separator between the two links. We created an image from it, but we won't (of course!) place it directly into the (X)HTML. To reproduce this, we'll create a special style for the second (Contact) list item.

3. Create a new CSS rule, .deco.

4. In the Background category, browse to the background image dots.gif. Set repeat to no-repeat, horizontal positioning to left, and vertical positioning to center.

5. Return to your (X)HTML document and place the cursor in the word Contact in the header navigation. Click its parent <li> element in the tag selector. From the Style drop-down list in the Property inspector, choose deco.

   The visual separator has now been inserted between our two links—although because the elements are inline, Dreamweaver doesn't show this to us.

T *We've found that leaving the Selector Type set to Advanced at all times allows us to create any kind of selector we need. Dreamweaver won't gripe about you creating a class in an element (tag) selector or tell you your class formatting isn't correct when you place it into the Tag category. Choosing Advanced lets you create everything from simple selectors to the most complex sibling or descendant selectors. You're only limited by your knowledge!*

6. Save the (X)HTML page and the CSS file and preview the page in a browser.

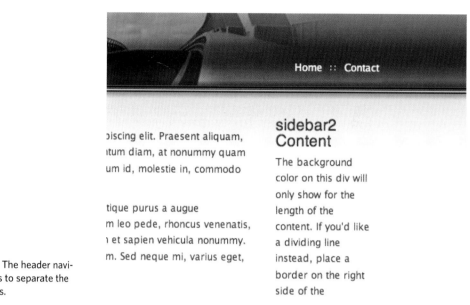

sidebar2
Content

The background
color on this div will
only show for the
length of the
content. If you'd like
a dividing line
instead, place a
border on the right
side of the

FIGURE 5.15 The header navigation with dots to separate the navigation items.

Great! Our simple navigation list is now in place and styled correctly using CSS.

The Main Content

T *Be sure you choose em units when you change margin and padding values that were previously set to zero. When a zero value has no unit set, opening it in the Edit CSS Style dialog will not automatically add a unit of measurement. Though zero can be written with no unit of measurement, any other value requires a unit to be specified. When initially adding a value, Dreamweaver will default to pixels. It's only in the case of a pre-existing number, with no unit of measurement (like zero) that Dreamweaver does not automatically add a unit of measure.*

The main content area of this web site is largely already in place, but we do want to adjust the margins and padding to retain our clean layout and avoid overlaps with the sidebars when we begin to edit them.

1. Select `<div#mainContent>` with the tag selector. Click the Edit Style icon and select the Box category. Under Padding, set the Top and Bottom fields to **1em**, and the Right and Left fields to **2em**. Under Margin, leave the top at **0**, and set the right to **16.5em**, the bottom to **1.5em**, and the left to **14em**.

2. In the Border category, apply a `1px solid #E6E6FF` border.

3. Move to the Background tab and browse for **box_top.jpg**. Select it and set repeat to `repeat-x`.

In our code, the rule for `#mainContent` will now look like this:

```
#mainContent {
    margin: 0 16.5em 1.5em 14em;
    padding: 1em 2em;
    border: 1px solid #E6E6FF;
    background: url(../images/box_top.jpg) repeat-x;
}
```

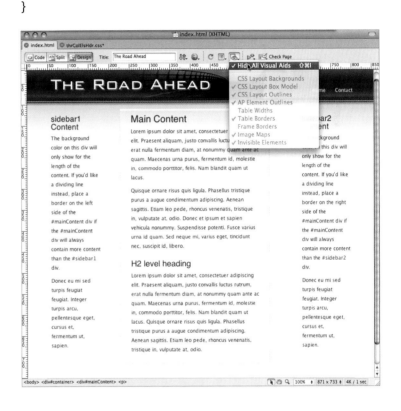

FIGURE 5.16 With Dreamweaver's Visual Aids turned off, we can see the effects of our changes.

FORMATTING IMAGES

Almost no page today is devoid of images. Within our comp, our designer hasn't inserted any images, but we can assume by the layout that they are likely to occur in the `mainContent` area. We'll add one to give our client an idea of what it might look like.

Inserting an image is easy, but images in em-based layouts are special, and we must pander to them a little. Ideally, we want any images in the content to scale along with the text when the text is resized. But images on the web are made up of pixels and are fixed in size. Applying stretchiness to them via ems really only works to a point—after which, they can look too large and pixilated, or else too small and indistinct, depending on how they're scaled. In other words, we are not actually making the image larger and therefore clearer, as may be the case with scaling font size. We are scaling each pixel, which can degrade the overall quality of the displayed image.

Still, we can scale with relative success to a degree, so let's experiment with an image now.

1. Place the cursor to the left of the first word in the second paragraph in mainContent. Click on the Insert Image button in the Insert panel and locate globe.jpg. When presented with a text insertion field for Alt text, type Globe of the world.

Note that Dreamweaver automatically inserts the image dimensions. But we're going to set the image size with CSS.

The globe, a small image, is now at the beginning of our second paragraph. It doesn't look really good there, so it's time to set up a new style for our image.

2. In the Property inspector, notice the size of the image. The image is 80px by 80px (a 1 to 1 aspect ratio). We're going to strip these values out and apply the size via CSS. Remove the two instances of 80.

3. In the CSS Styles Panel, create a new selector called #mainContent img.

4. In the CSS Rule Definition dialog box, from the Box category, set the height and width to 6.25em each. Set float to right.

The new style is now at the bottom of our style sheet:

```
#mainContent img {
   float: right;
   height: 6.25em;
   width: 6.25em;
}
```

That's it! Our image will now float right and have dimensions in scalable ems.

5. Save the page and the CSS file and test it in your browser. Increase and decrease the text size, and get a feel for the way the flow of the text around the image remains consistent—and also the level of image degradation that occurs.

> **N** *If an image is placed into the document that is purely decorative and has no real meaning for a non-sighted user, it's best to leave the alt attribute empty. But empty doesn't mean we don't add it at all! It means we put the alt attribute into the image, but leave it with empty quotation marks (i. e.,: alt=""). This keeps assistive technology from annoying a blind reader by reading the name of your image—especially if you're dealing with a dynamic site with long, meaningless names.*

> **N** *This rule will style all images placed in the mainContent area, which means the initial size and proportions of each image to be displayed in this area must be the same. If we want to size each image placed in the mainContent area individually, we would need to use individual classes.*

> **N** *We chose the value of 6.25em, not through any kind of rocket science, but through a simple mathematical calculation. 1 divided by the text size times the number of pixels for the width (or height) of the image equals the number of ems for the dimension. In our case, that gave us 6.25.*

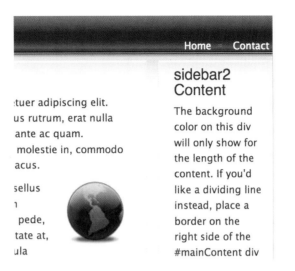

FIGURE 5.17 The image has scaled with the text (as seen in Firefox). We've increased the font size three times.

Belly up to the Sidebars

We'll now tweak the sidebars to the width we want and set them up for the neat (we didn't just say "neat", did we?!) display of the content they will contain.

1. Select the `<div#sidebar1>` in the tag selector. In the CSS Styles panel, in Current mode, look at the properties for this sidebar in the CSS panel. The width is set to **11em**. There is no need to open the CSS Rule Definition dialog box here, although you can certainly do so if you wish. It is easier, however, to just click on the number 11 that represents the **11em**, and type in our desired width of **13em** instead.

2. Still in the Properties section, click on the values for padding and replace them with **0 0 1.5em**.

    Remember, this uses CSS shorthand: the first zero sets the top padding, the middle zero sets the left and right paddings, and the **1.5em** sets the bottom padding.

3. Select the `<div#sidebar2>` on the tag selector. Click on the Edit Style button and open the CSS Rule Definition dialog box. (We have more work to do on this div so this time it's easier to use the dialog.)

4. In the Box category, change the width to 13em and set the padding to Top: **0.7em**, Right: **0.8em**, Bottom: **1em**, Left: **1.5em**.

Be careful to change the units here, as by default they are set in pixels, which won't give quite the effect we're after with the values we've chosen!

5. Switch to the Background category and browse for the background image, **box_top.jpg**. Set repeat to **repeat-x**.

6. Switch to the Border category. For style, select **solid** from the drop-down list. For width, type in **1**, which will default to units of pixels, which are our desired units in this case. Set the color to **#E6E6FF**.

FIGURE 5.18 With the sidebars properly sized, we're ready for the content.

And with that, we've got the basic work done on our sidebars. Time to add our content to them.

The Main Site Navigation

The main navigation of our web site also utilizes an unordered list. This list is located in **sidebar1,** the left column. Each list item looks like a button, and the color of the link text changes on hover.

As with the header navigation, we'll begin by coding the list markup, and apply all of the visual effects using CSS after the list code is complete.

1. In the Code view pane of Split view, place the cursor to the right of the line that reads `<div id="sidebar1">`. Click on the Unordered List icon in the Property inspector.

   An unordered list with a single list item is inserted below that line.

2. The cursor is now between the `<li></li>` tags, so type in the text for our first link, Home. Click inside Design view to see the text.

3. Placing the cursor to the right of the word Home in Design view, press Enter or Return, and type the next menu item, About. Continue in this manner to create new list items for Services, Archives, Resources and FAQ. The code should look like this:

```
<div id="sidebar1">
  <ul>
  <li>Home</li>
  <li>About</li>
  <li>Services</li>
  <li>Archives</li>
  <li>Resources</li>
  <li>FAQ</li>
  </ul>
```

4. Create links by highlighting each list item in Design view, one by one. Use the Property inspector to add hash marks (#) as placeholders so the list items look like links.

Adding a Background to the List Items

So far, the list looks plain—quite far from wonderful—so let's work some CSS magic.

1. Create a new rule and name the selector `#sidebar1 li`.

2. Switch to the Background category. Set the background color to #FFF then browse for the **nav_back.jpg** image and select it. Apply a value of **repeat-x** to repeat, and set the horizontal position to **left** and the vertical position to **bottom**.

   This background image is going to create a shadow effect. When the layout is resized and the text increases, causing the li element to grow accordingly, we need the shadow to remained anchored at the base. The top of the image color is white. So making white the background color of the li will give us a seamless transition.

3. Switch to the Box category and insert a width of **100%**. This ensures the list item takes up the entire width of its containing block, sidebar1. In the same section, uncheck Margin's "Same for all" box and set the Bottom field to **0.2em**.

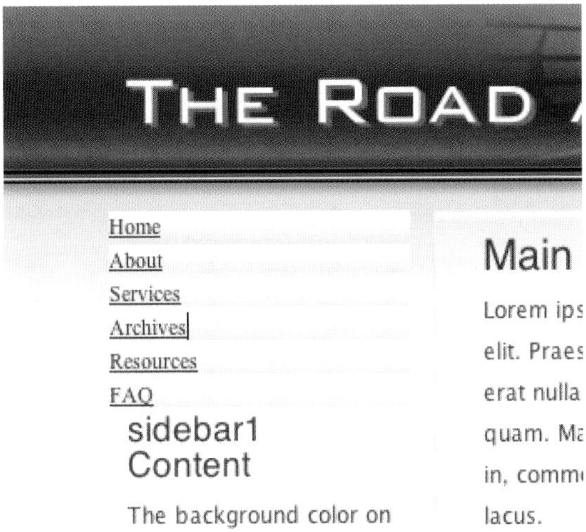

FIGURE 5.19 The list elements have a background, but are still way too small.

Styling the Links Themselves

Our links still don't look right. They're too small and the text needs some styling.

1. Create a new rule with a compound selector of #sidebar1 a, #sidebar1 a:link, #sidebar1 a:visited.

2. Set the font to the font set we created for the paragraphs: "Lucida Grande", Verdana, Arial, Helvetica, sans-serif and the size to **0.95em**. Set the color to **#336** and decoration to **none**.

3. For the display property, select **block**.

   The a element is an inline element by default. When it's converted into a block element, it fills the width of its parent element (in this case, the li element) making the whole list item appear to be a clickable link.

4. Adjust the padding, by setting the top to **0.5em**, the right to **1em**, the bottom to **0.3em**, and the left to **1.5em**.

5. Set a 1px wide, solid border with the color #E6E6FF. Click OK.

6. Add another new CSS rule and name the selector **#sidebar1 a:visited**. For this rule, set the color to #55628B.

7. Add a final new CSS rule for our main navigation links, and name the compound selector **#sidebar1 a:hover, #sidebar1 a:active, #sidebar1 a:focus**.

8. Set the color to #A23378. Add a background image of **arrow.gif**. Set repeat to **no-repeat**, the horizontal position to **4px**, and the vertical position to **50%**.

T *When your code appears to be correct and you just cannot figure out why the CSS does not render correctly, it is usually a specificity issue! Check to see what other rules are influencing the rule with the problem. The Rules pane in Dreamweaver can help: with the problem tag selected and displayed in Current mode, the CSS rules affecting that tag will be listed in Rules view under the Rules pane. Click on them to see what properties and values are taking effect. For more detailed information about the rules of specificity, Andrew Tetlaw has an excellent article on Sitepoint: The Great Specificity Swindle*

FIGURE 5.20 Wow! Look at those sexy rollovers!

Using the <cite> Element

Let's move further down the column and allow our client's satisfied customers to speak out. We are going to create a Testimonials section.

1. Directly after the closing `</ul>` tag of the main navigation, insert a new div tag by choosing the Insert Div Tag tool from the Common section of the Insert panel. In the dialog, type `quotes` in the ID field.

   We now have the following lines in our code:

   ```
   </ul>
   <div id="quotes">Content for id "quotes" Goes Here</div>
   ```

   Dreamweaver so nicely reminds us where the content should go.

2. Remove the words "Content for id "quotes" Goes Here" and select and drag, or copy and paste, the closing div tag so it closes the new div immediately before the end of the column enclosing all the content within:

   ```
   </div>
   <!-- end #sidebar1 --></div>
   ```

3. We already have a placeholder level 3 heading. Change the heading text from `sidebar1 content` to `They Said:.`

N *The cite element should not be confused with the cite attribute. The cite attribute is applied inside the blockquote or other block level tag such as p to provide a URI reference to the source of the quote.*

Our testimonials will take the format of a quotation, followed by a new line containing the author's name. The name will be indented and italicized to make it obvious to visual users that it is not a part of the quote. For non-visual users or non-graphical user agents, we will use the (X)HTML `<blockquote>` tag to indicate quoted text and the `<cite>` tag to indicate a reference to another source. In this case the `<cite>` tags will enclose the author's name, but be aware that `<cite>` should also be applied to names of publications, including legal documents and legislation.

As always, let's start by writing the code, and style it later.

1. Highlight the first paragraph of sample text in the sidebar. Right-click and choose Remove tag `<p>` from the menu.

2. With the text still highlighted, right-click again and choose Quick Tag Editor.

   The cursor is placed inside a `<` and `>` pair, ready for you to type in the name of the tag you wish to use. But as you begin to type, Dreamweaver tries to suggest the tag it thinks you are trying to find.

3. Start to type `blockquote` into this field, and you'll see how quickly this very tag is suggested. Scroll through the list if necessary to select the correct tag or, if Dreamweaver's guess is correct, press Enter to select the highlighted tag and then press Enter again to close the dialog box.

    Once you get the hang of this it becomes a very fast method of wrapping tags around page content.

4. De-select the text then click inside it. From the Property inspector, select paragraph.

    This will place the paragraph tags back inside the `blockquote`.

Does this step make you think we're mad? (You'd be right, but not for the reasons you may think!) The reason we removed the `<p>` tags before wrapping the `blockquote` around the text is because the tags must be properly ordered. In order to meet the W3C's specifications for `blockquote,` the `<p>` tags must be inside the `<blockquote>` tags. The specifications say that in a strict (X)HTML doctype, `blockquote` must contain another block element and the `p` element fits the bill perfectly. If we left the `<p>` tags in and simply added `<blockquote>` tags, the `<blockquote>` would be placed inside the `<p>` tags instead of the other, correct way around.

1. In the Design view pane, type some dummy text over the existing text in the first paragraph—we'll use:

    `Lorem ipsum dolor sit amet, consectetuer adipiscing elit. Praesent aliquam, justo convallis luctus rutrum, erat nulla fermentum diam, at nonummy quam ante ac quam.`

2. Create a new paragraph beneath our new testimonial and type in a name.

    We've used the name `Thomas Quamley`.

3. Select the name, right-click and choose Quick Tag Editor again, and type `cite,` then hit Enter twice.

    If you created the new paragraph in Design view, be sure to check the source code to confirm that the new paragraph isn't placed inside the `blockquote`. Alternatively, simply choose the `<blockquote>` element and press the right arrow key, then press Enter. This ensures that you are outside the `blockquote` when the next text or tag is entered.

4. Repeat these steps for the second default paragraph in the sidebar, but choose a different name for the second testimonial. We chose `Sim Simley & Co.`

Our lovely, semantic (i.e. meaningful) code is now in place and alternative devices will know that there is a quote with a defined source (in our case, a customer), regardless of how the text is styled in the browser.

Speaking of styling, Dreamweaver has taken it upon itself to style the contents of the `<cite>` tags. Don't be concerned by this. When viewed in the browser, there is no styling. The browser is correct, because we reset the `cite` element in the CSS reset.

We'll style `<cite>` now, along with the `blockquote`.

1. Create a new CSS rule and name the selector `#sidebar1 #quotes`. We are targeting everything in the div we created with the ID of `quotes`.

2. Set the padding as top of `2em`, right of `1em`, bottom of `1.5em` and left of `1.5em`. Set a top margin of `15px`.

The top margin is set in pixels to prevent the gap between the main navigation and the quotes from becoming unpleasantly large if the font is resized.

T *Reusing a graphic as we've done with* box_top.jpg *is a great way to save bandwidth.*

3. Switch to the Background category, and again locate box_top. jpg and select it, and set repeat to repeat-x. In the Border category, set a 1px solid border with the color #E6E6FF. In the Type category, set the font size to 0.9em.

4. Create a new CSS rule for blockquote. Set the top margin to 1.5em.

5. Create another CSS rule, this time for the element cite. In the Background category, browse to arrow.gif, setting repeat to no-repeat, horizontal position to left and vertical position to center. In the Type category, set style to italic. Go to the Box category and add a left padding of 12px.

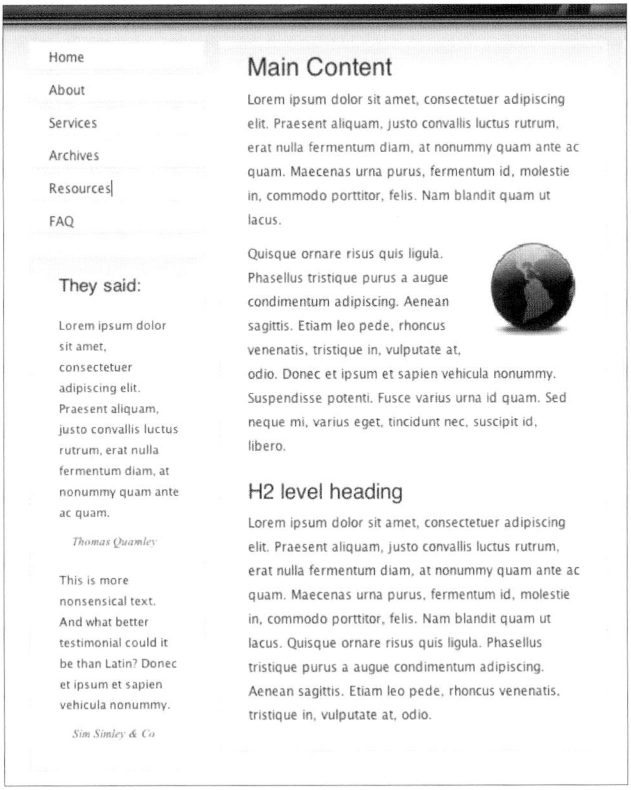

FIGURE 5.22 The styling is coming along.

6. Create a compound selector, naming it #quotes p, #quotes p cite.

   We need to specifically include cite to override its properties in the CSS reset.

7. Set the color to #A23378. In the Box category, set all of the margins to 0.

   Our sidebar alignment is a bit off, so we'll fix that before we leave this area.

8. Switch to the All mode in the CSS Styles panel and click on the compound selector #sidebar1 h3, #sidebar1 p, #sidebar2 p, #sidebar2 h3.

   These items have margin, which is the cause of the weirdness in alignment.

9. With the compound selector highlighted, click the trashcan icon at the bottom right of the CSS Styles panel.

   The entire offending rule is deleted.

And Then a Step to the Right, uh... Sidebar

In the right sidebar, the client has requested that we list the most recent entries on the web site. The column will have two headings, News and Events.

1. Diving straight into the markup, change the default h3 text in sidebar2 to News. Just highlight the existing text and type in the new text over the top.

   Each item will consist of a date and a short extract, with paragraph formatting.

2. Select the first paragraph in the right sidebar and type a date.

   We typed November 22.

3. Select the second paragraph and type in some filler text.

   We typed, "This is the news item that links to more news." You can type gibberish or Latin if you like.

4. Press Return to create a new paragraph and type in a date. Add another new paragraph underneath this date and type in more filler news text.

5. Press Return again, and in the Property inspector change the formatting to h3. Type the name of the second section, Events.

6. In the Events section, create the same two paragraphs. Either create them in the same way or copy and paste them in.

Our second sidebar now has some content in place but needs to be styled.

ADD A LITTLE STYLE

1. Right-click the date in Design view and select CSS Style > New from the contextual menu. Create a class called date.

2. In the CSS Rule Definition dialog box, go to the Type category and enter the color #A23378. Switch to the Background category and browse for and select arrow.gif. Set the repeat to no-repeat, the horizontal position to left, and the vertical position to center. Move to the Box category and set the left padding to 12px.

The padding keeps the text away from our arrow graphic.

3. In Design view, highlight each of the dates in turn and in the Property inspector, use the Style drop-down list to apply the date class to each date.

4. Create another CSS class called info. In the CSS Rule Definition dialog box, go to the Box category and add a top margin of 0.2em and a bottom padding of 1em. Switch to the Border category and create a bottom border only, with a 1px dotted line of the color #D6B0D9.

5. In sidebar2, highlight each of our information paragraphs and use the Property inspector to apply the info class to these paragraphs.

Our design is really taking shape now. The only basic section of the page we have yet to style is the footer.

FIGURE 5.24 The right sidebar is looking great!

Last But Not Least, the Footer

We've reached the final piece of our page puzzle—the footer. At the moment, the width of the footer is constrained by the width of the container. This creates a visual imbalance because the header stretches across the screen. We already have a background image on the body, so we can't use the same element for the footer—one background image per customer, errr, element, please! Instead, let's move the footer outside of the container so that the footer fills the width of the body element.

At the bottom of the (X)HTML document, you'll see this code:

```
<br class="clearfloat" />
<div id="footer">
 <p>Footer</p>
<!-- end #footer --></div>
<!-- end #container --></div>
</body>
</html>
```

1. In Code view, select the footer div tags and their contents and drag them below the closing div for container.

```
<br class="clearfloat" />
<!-- end #container --></div>
<div id="footer">
 <p>Footer</p>
<!-- end #footer --></div>
</body>
</html>
```

   The footer now spans the width of the screen. Now *that* was easy!

   Let's change the footer text to something more appropriate, such as something more common, like a copyright.

2. Highlight the word Footer and type © 2007 The Road Ahead. All rights reserved.

   We can now apply an attractive background that will match that of our header.

3. Select `<div#footer>` in the tag selector. Set the font to `Helvetica, Arial, Verdana, sans-serif`, the Size to `0.7em,` and the color to `#CCC.`

4. Move to the Background category and browse for and select `foot.jpg.` Set repeat to `repeat-x`, horizontal position to `left`, and vertical position to `top`. Set the background color to #272E42.

5. In the Block category, set the Text-Align field to `center`.

6. Move to the Box category and under Padding, set top to `0.75em` and right, bottom and left all to `0.5em`.

The CSS should look something like this:

```
#footer {
    padding: 0.75em 0.5em 0.5em;
    background:#272E42 url(../images/foot.jpg) repeat-x left top;
    text-align: center;
    color: #CCC;
    font: 0.7em Helvetica, Arial, Verdana, sans-serif;
}
```

This padding matches the left alignment of the elements in the divs that appear above it.

7. Save the page and the CSS file and preview it in a browser. Experiment with increasing and decreasing the size of the browser font and notice that everything scales beautifully.

FIGURE 5.25 And with that, it's done!

Quick IECC Tweaks

Remember at the end of Chapter One, we discussed the Internet Explorer Conditional Comments (IECC) that add a fix to our page to correct the inconsistent rendering of margins between browsers? Since we used Eric Meyer's CSS reset in this layout, all our browsers are rendering the same zero values. Thus, we don't need the padding-top on any of the rules in the IECC. We'll remove them now, leaving only the `#mainContent { zoom: 1; }`.

Our basic page construction is done! The hard part is over. Now it's just a matter of adding the additional site content. Let's move on and build a simple contact form, linking to it from the header navigation.

Creating and Styling an Em-Based Form

We're going to use our basic layout for all of the other pages in the site, but one of those pages needs to contain a contact form. Customers and potential customers can use the form to contact our client (using a form helps avoid some spam), but the form needs to scale with the rest of the page layout.

Even within our em-based page layout, using the em unit to layout forms allows an extra degree of flexibility and accessibility. The form field expands and contracts when the font size is adjusted, so the user can still fit the same number of characters into the field and it will look the way it's meant to look, whatever the size of the font.

A Brief Form Refresher

A **fieldset** groups related form fields together. The fieldset defines a form control group, grouping associated form controls together in a logical way. Fieldsets may be nested.

A **legend** supplies a heading for the form as a whole. The legend should be short, concise, and totally relevant to the fieldset. The legend will be read by a screen reader (in verbosity mode) before *each* label, (for example, "Your Details: Name. Your Details: Address") so it should be brief and make sense when read in the context of the label.

The expression **"label for="** associates a form field's label with the field itself.

Used properly, these elements increase a form's usefulness and accessibility.

Coding the form

Submitting a form generally requires back-end programming, which is beyond the scope of this book. Imagine, if you will, that we're just building and styling a basic form, using XHTML and CSS, and then handing it off to a back-end developer to implement the form submission process.

1. Using `index.html` as our basic structure, choose File > Save As and save the file as `contact.html`.

2. Change the heading `Main Content` to `Contact Us`. In the paragraph below Main Content, type: `We will never share your details with anyone else (except where required by law).`

   Where a full privacy policy is unavailable, it helps to add a line or two in summary on the Contact page.

3. Delete the subsequent paragraphs and headings in the `main-Content` area.

   Each form field must have a correctly marked up label so that user agents can make the connection between the form control and its label, even when the connection is not visually obvious. This makes the difference between a form making sense—or not—to users relying on screen readers or other alternative devices.

   We'll establish this connection between our labels and form controls by assigning both the label and the form control an ID of the same name.

4. Place the cursor into your privacy statement, select the `<p>` on the tag selector and hit the right arrow key.

   This takes you out of the current p element so you can place the form below it.

5. Using the Forms section of the Insert panel, click the leftmost button, the Form button, which inserts the basic tags for the `form` element.

   A red-dotted rectangular outline appears around the cursor and in the code.

N *if you don't see the red outline, go to View > Visual Aids > Invisible Elements and make sure it's turned on (or use the Visual Aids drop-down on the Document toolbar.*

6. Leave the cursor in place and locate and click the fieldset button in the toolbar.

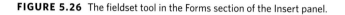

FIGURE 5.26 The fieldset tool in the Forms section of the Insert panel.

A dialog box appears asking for the form's legend.

7. Type Your Details.

A form may contain many fieldsets that group specific types of form information to make them more logical. Access keys can be used to target specific fieldsets in a long and complicated form, although these are probably best avoided until cross-browser support improves.

We also want to let the user know which form fields are mandatory. Making the minimum information needed mandatory assures our client of at least getting basic contact information.

8. With the form legend text still selected, press the right arrow key. This moves the insertion point after the `</legend>` tag. Create a new paragraph by pressing the Return key and type the following: Fields marked with * are mandatory.

Now we'll turn our attention to inserting the input fields and their labels.

9. In Design view, create a new line. If paragraph formatting has been applied, remove it either manually or right-click and choose Remove Tag `<p>` from the contextual menu.

We are using Design view because the dialog box to add elements is slightly different in Design view from the dialog box to add elements in Code view.

10. Click the Text Field button in the Insert toolbar. Or choose Insert > Form > Text Field. In the Tag Editor dialog box, assign an ID of name, a label of Name *, and make sure the radio button "Attach label tag using 'for' attribute" is selected. Leave the other settings at their defaults. Click OK.

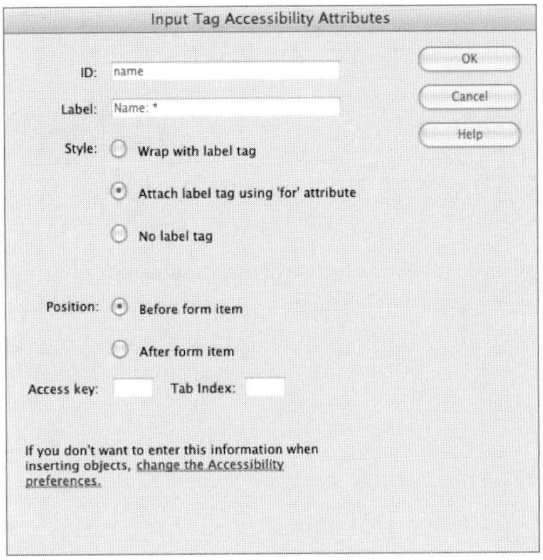

FIGURE 5.27 Input tag dialog when inserted from Design view.

11. Continue to build and modify the form in this way, adding text fields and associated labels for address, phone number, and email. Add a text area with the associated label Your Message:.

```
<form action="" method="post" enctype="multipart/form-data"
name="form1" id="form1">

    <fieldset>

    <legend>Your Details</legend>
    <p>Fields marked with an * are mandatory.</p>
    <label for="name">Name: *</label>
    <input name="name" type="text" id="name" />
    <label for="address">Address:</label>
    <input name="address" type="text" id="address" />
    <label for="phone">Phone:</label>
    <input name="phone" type="text" id="phone" />
    <label for="email">Email: *</label>
    <input name="email" type="text" id="email" />
    <label for="message">Your Message: *</label>
    <textarea name="message" id="message" cols="45"
rows="5"></textarea>
    </fieldset>
</form>
```

Adding a submit button will complete our form.

12. In Design view, place the cursor to the right of the Your Message text area. Select `<fieldset>` on the tag selector. Click your right arrow to exit the fieldset.

If you look at Code view, your cursor will be between the closing fieldset tag and the closing form tag.

N *If using a Strict doctype, the Submit button must be placed within a fieldset in order for the page to validate.*

13. In the Edit Tag dialog box that appears, apply an ID of `submit` and leave the Label field blank. Select the radio button that is labeled No Label Tag. Click OK.

The button is added to the end of the form as a `submit` type of input.

T *It makes no functional difference whether or not the name and ID are given identical values, but making them identical can help to avoid confusion.*

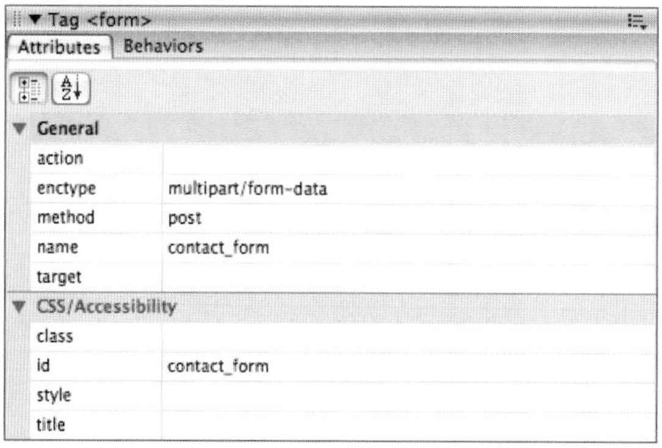

You can use the Tag Inspector (Window > Tag Inspector) to add to and edit all of the form tags. Look at our actual `<form>` tag. By default, it has a name and an ID of `form1`.

FIGURE 5.28 Dreamweaver's Tag inspector gives us yet another way to edit the attributes of our form elements.

N *When an element, including a form element, is selected, its attributes are visible in the Tag inspector and also in the Property inspector. Use whichever is easiest for you, but be aware that the Tag inspector offers a greater range of options which may be required in more complex forms or web pages.*

Our code is just right at this stage, but the visual result when viewed in Design view (or a browser) is less than perfect. Let's fix it with some more CSS goodness.

FIGURE 5.29 Our form in its default condition.

Styling the Form

We need to create five new form-related rules to cater to the elements we have just added to our (X)HTML.

1. Create a new CSS rule for the `fieldset` element. Apply a `1px solid` border with the color `#336`. Apply a padding of `0.8em` to all sides except the right, which should have a value of zero.

    The padding is simply to keep the contents of the fieldset away from the edges and border.

    There's nothing wrong with having some right side padding—in fact, it's desirable. But because IE7 renders the border on the fieldset outside the padding (making it so the top and right borders don't meet up properly), we're leaving it at zero. Another option would be to include the padding for other browsers in the regular CSS document and then override the right padding using an IECC for IE7.

2. Create a CSS rule for the `legend` element. Set the font size to `1.5em`.

3. Create a selector for the `label` element. Set the display property to `block`. Set the top margin to `0.5em`.

4. Create a compound selector `input, textarea`. Set the top and left borders to `1px solid #336`, and the right and bottom borders to `#978EBA`. Set the background color to `#D9DEE8`, the width to `21em`, and give it `.2em` of padding.

    The background color makes it visually intuitive to put the cursor in an input field. The padding simply gives the form a bit of breathing room.

5. Create another CSS rule for `textarea`, and set a height of `8em`.

    The Submit button has taken on the same width as the rest of the inputs. It looks really weird! Plus, since the button is outside the fieldset, it needs some margin to move it down a bit. We'll need to create a CSS rule for this single input element, and since the Submit button already has an `id` assigned, we'll use this id in our selector.

We are applying all font sizes, margins and paddings in ems so they will expand and contract relative to the font size, maintaining the proportions of the page and of the form. The form itself is a block element and as such will fill the width of its parent unless otherwise specified.

The label element is usually an inline element, but changing it to a block display forces the text field to a separate line below the label.

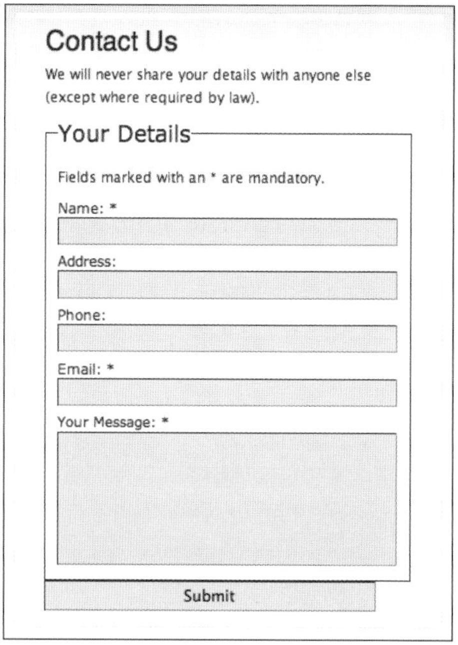

FIGURE 5.30 The wildly wide Submit button.

T *If your submit button has more words than ours, simply adjust your width. Since the button is created with em units, it'll get larger as the text size is larger. With em units, you need have no worries about cutting off some text!*

T *Since a radio button and check box are also form inputs, our general styling for an input will be adopted by those elements as well. It's likely that style won't translate well (especially background colors and borders), so we find it useful to create a class to counteract those properties and values that are unsightly. We apply the class to our radio buttons or check boxes and they change back to a more attractive rendering.*

6. Create a new CSS rule for the selector. Give it a width of **8em**, and a top and left margin of **.8em**.

This will give the Submit button the same alignment from the left side of the fieldset and also a little breathing room at the top. The submit button now has its own unique size, differentiating it from the rest of the inputs.

Be aware that the default styling for form elements varies wildly from browser to browser. Even though we've zeroed some of our defaults, giving us a more level playing field, what can be done with various elements still varies. Safari is the most different; locking us down to its inherent OS look. (Yes, we'd *love* to see this change!). Other browsers vary in the way they apply certain properties and values, so unless you stick with the basics, you'll rarely achieve the same look from browser to browser.

7. Create a new compound rule for `input:focus, textarea:focus` and give it a background of `#E5EBF4`.

```
input:focus, textarea:focus {
  background: #E5EBF4;
}
```

This lighter background color shows when the text area has focus making the field appear to the visual user to "light up" a little. Unfortunately, Internet Explorer does not show `:focus` pseudo classes on anything except links so the IE user won't see the change. But it doesn't hurt anything and the other browsers will have a nice enhancement.

FIGURE 5.31 The address field lights up when the cursor is placed inside.

N   *Remember, the <em> tag is for emphasis. It gives emphasis visually by creating italics. The em unit is the unit of measure we've been working with—so you know all about that!*

N   *Don't forget to add the appropriate em tag in the sentence about required fields at the beginning of the form controls.*

INDICATING REQUIRED FIELDS

One last touch: those asterisks representing required fields are actually quite important, so let's wrap them in <em> tags for emphasis, and color them red as an added extra for sighted users.

1. Wrap the asterisks in <em> tags by highlighting the asterisk and then using the key command Ctrl+I/Cmd+I.

2. To style the asterisks, create a new descendant selector, and name it `form em`. This rule will apply to all em elements that occur within a `form` element.

T *There's no need to use classes when you can easily target an element with a descendant selector.*

3. Set the color to #C00 and set the font-weight to **bold**.

With that, our form styling is complete! You'll see differences between Dreamweaver and the various browsers, so be sure to test in each browser.

```css
fieldset {
  border: 1px solid #336;
  padding: .8em 0 .8em .8em;
}
legend {
  font-size: 1.5em;
}
label {
  display: block;
  margin-top: .5em;
}
input, textarea {
  width: 21em;
  background: #D9DEE8;
  border-top: 1px solid #336;
  border-right: 1px solid #978EBA;
  border-bottom: 1px solid #978EBA;
  border-left: 1px solid #336;
  padding: .2em;
}
textarea {
  height: 8em;
}
input#submit {
  width: 8em;
  margin-top: .8em;
  margin-left: .8em;
}
input:focus, textarea:focus {
  background: #E5EBF4;
}
form em {
  color: #C00;
  font-weight: bold;
}
```

Adding Form Validation

At this point, we have a nice working form—well, it will be working after our co-worker puts the dynamic code in! However, we have one last enhancement to add to the form using Dreamweaver's new built-in Spry form validation—a time saver to be sure.

You'll remember that we set several fields as required fields but we need to enforce that. And we asked visitors to provide their phone number, but we need to make sure that they provide it in a properly formatted, 10 digit North American format of (XXX) XXX-XXXX. While we could rely on our back-end programmer to provide this functionality, we can also build it directly into the form using a new feature of Dreamweaver CS3, the Spry framework for Ajax.

We'll talk more about the Spry framework for Ajax in Chapter 6, but for now, let's use a bit of its functionality to enhance our form.

The Name field has been designated as a required field. In other words, we don't want to allow someone to submit the form if they have not provided this information.

1. Select the textfield `name`.

2. Switch the Insert panel to the Spry category and click the Spry Validation Text Field icon.

FIGURE 5.32 The Spry Validation Text Field icon.

The Spry Validation Text Field tool creates a `<span>` around the input field. This `<span>` provides the functionality, via JavaScript, to validate that the user enters text into the field. The Required checkbox is checked by default, so we don't have to do anything further.

FIGURE 5.33 The Spry Validation Text Field tool provides advanced functionality for ensuring that a visitor enters the proper information.

Let's next ensure that the visitor provides the properly formatted telephone number.

3. Select the **phone** textfield.

4. Once again, click to select the Spry Validation Text Field from the Insert panel.

   The phone number is not required, but we want to make sure that if the visitor enters their phone number, it is properly formatted.

5. In the Type drop-down list, select Phone Number.

6. From the Format drop-down list, select US/Canada.

   We also want to let the visitor know exactly what we are expecting from them.

7. In the Hint field, enter (123) 456-7890.

   This value gives the visitor a visual indication of what is expected, but disappears as soon as they tab or click into the field.

8. Check the Enforce pattern checkbox.

   Using this checkbox causes the browser to automatically enter the parentheses and dashes without the visitor needing to do so by hand.

9. Uncheck the Required checkbox.

   Finally, we need to establish when the validation will occur.

10. In the Validate on section, place a check mark in the Blur checkbox.

    The Blur option tells the browser to validate the field if the visitor either clicks or tabs out of the field.

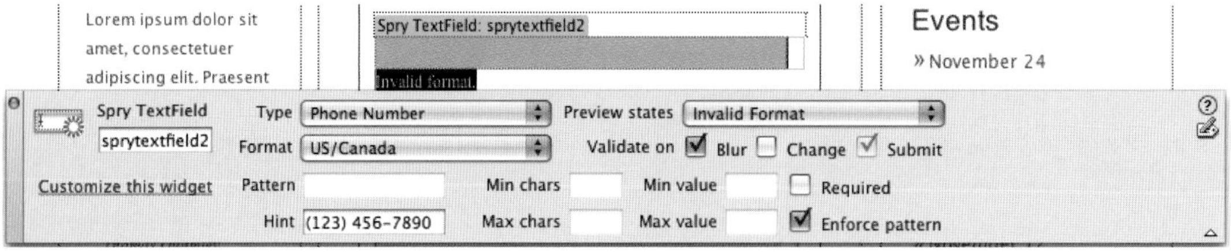

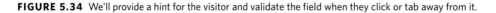

FIGURE 5.34 We'll provide a hint for the visitor and validate the field when they click or tab away from it.

11. Create the Spry region for the email field, select Type email address, validate on Blur and leave the Required box checked.

12. Create a Spry Validation Text Field for the Comment field, just as we did for the Name field and simply leave the Required check box checked.

13. Save the file and click OK to copy the required JavaScript files into your site.

    By default, Dreamweaver places the Spry CSS and JavaScript files into the root of your site.

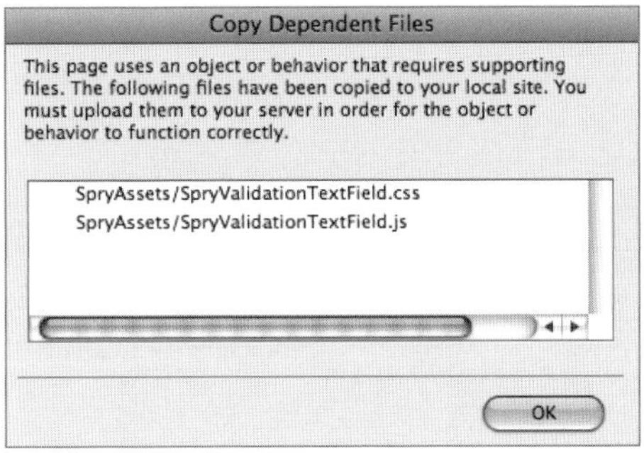

FIGURE 5.35 The Spry frame-work for Ajax provides a number of pre-built JavaScripts that need to be copied to your server.

14. Preview in a browser and experiment with an empty name field, a mis-formatted email or incorrectly entering a phone number.

FIGURE 5.36 That was the easi-est form validation ever!!

Creating and Styling Accessible Data Tables

Pure CSS layouts have become so commonplace in the last two or three years that it can be difficult to remember how to design tables at all, let alone how to style them to display data in a meaningful way. Fortunately, Dreamweaver CS3 makes creating standards-compliant and accessible data tables really easy.

This table can easily be adapted for other uses: for example, timetables, catalogs, employee directories, and so on.

For businesses servicing customers from physical premises, it's always a good idea to have the business's opening or office hours clearly visible on the web site. These details are frequently placed on contact pages. We're going to go a step further than simply listing the office hours. We're going to provide a nicely formatted table so customers can see opening times at a glance.

For our fictional client, the office opening times are varied. The office is open on Monday and Friday mornings and afternoons, Tuesday and Thursday afternoons and evenings, and Wednesday and Saturday mornings only. The office is closed on Sundays.

We need a grid displaying the days of the week as headings on one axis, and morning, afternoon and evening headings on the other axis. The time of day will be in the horizontal headers, so we'll need 3 columns for those. The days of the week will be in the vertical headers, so we'll need 7 of those.

We'll also shade the opening times for fast and easy visual identification.

Let Dreamweaver Do the Heavy Lifting

Make sure that both the Layout tab of the Insert toolbar and the Tag inspector are open. We're going to rely on these to make our table building fuss-free.

With `contact.html` open in Split view, place the cursor in the Code view pane just after the form we created, but before the closing `</div>` tag of `mainContent`. This is where we'll place our Opening Hours table.

1. Click the Insert Table button in the Insert toolbar.

A dialog box pops up immediately offering us all kinds of options for our new table. We choose the options, and Dreamweaver CS3 builds the table. That seems like a good deal to us!

We need to define the numbers of rows and columns our table will contain. We've already established that we need three columns for the time of day, and seven rows for the days of the week. These numbers don't take into account the header row and the header column, so we need to add one to each number.

Accessibility and the Anatomy of a Data Table

A correctly marked up data table has basic components that should *always* be present for the benefit of screen readers and other devices. These components are the `caption` and `th` elements, and the `summary` attribute.

From an accessibility viewpoint, the most important thing to remember when building data tables is to ensure that data is associated with the appropriate header in the table. This is easy to achieve visually for sighted users. But for users of screen readers, except in the most simple of data tables, the association must be explicitly indicated in the code in order for a screen reader to speak the header/data relationship to the user.

This is done using a combination of the table header element, `th`, by setting `id`s on the header, and by adding these `id`s to the `headers` attribute in the related data cells. Sometimes using `scope` together with `col` and/or `row` works, but using a combination if `id` and `headers` is a more reliable method.

All tables have an opening `<table>` tag and an associated closing tag. This in itself isn't enough to determine whether the table is being used for data or for layout. The most useful ways to let screen reader users know that the content of the table is data is through the use of the `caption` element and the `summary` attribute.

The `caption` element is placed directly after the `table` element and encloses the table's title. The `summary` attribute is applied to the `<table>` tag and provides helpful information for the screen reader user about how to understand the table. For example, as well as a brief description of what correlating data the table contains, the `summary` tag might also be used to warn the screen reader user when there are two or more rows or columns of header data. Tips like this can make the user's path to acquiring the required information much smoother.

Even so, tables with single rows or columns of headers are far easier for screen readers and their users to decipher than those with multiple levels, so it's a good idea to avoid complexity in data tables wherever possible. We'll keep our table very simple for that reason.

With a more complex table, however, it is necessary to explicitly make a connection between data cells and the relevant header. To do this, give each `th` element an `id`, and for each `td` (table data) element that relates to that header, apply a `headers` attribute containing the value of that `id`.

Be aware that the headers attribute can contain multiple values. It should contain a value for each `th` associated with it.

T *If you forget to allow for the headers, you can always use Dreamweaver to add an extra row or column. Place the cursor in a cell that will be adjacent to the new row or column. Right-click and select Table > Insert Rows or Columns from the contextual menu. Alternatively, simply change the number of rows/columns using the Property Inspector.*

2. In the first section of the Table dialog box, Table size, insert the values of **4** and **8**.

3. Remove the border of 1 pixel that Dreamweaver inserted by default, and leave the other options in the Table size section blank.

4. In the Header section, select the fourth option of Both, since we need headers on both axes of the table.

5. In the Accessibility section, give the caption a value of `Office Hours` and type in the summary:

   `Office opening hours categorized as morning, afternoon and evening for each day of the week. There is a single header row and a single header column.`

Giving the Table Dimensions

We'll start on the CSS now, because the table is too narrow for comfort. Let's set a width on the table.

N *On some web sites, two or more tables of different styles and purposes could be located in different sections of the page. If that were the case here, we would use appropriate Advanced selectors and/or CSS classes. In our case, all we need is a simple* `table` *selector because we know we won't be using tables on our site except for data and that they will always be in the* `mainContent` *area.*

1. Create a new CSS rule for the `table`.

2. Set a width of **100%** for the table. Apply a **1px** solid border with the color **#336** and set the border-collapse to `collapse`.

   Our table has expanded to fill the width of its parent, `mainContent`. We've applied the collapse value to the borders so that they render as a single border—not a double.

   Click inside the top left table cell in the Design view pane. Look at the Code view pane and locate the cursor. It is inside the first `<th></th>` tag pair. We know this is the horizontal row of headers across the top of the table, because the attribute `scope` has been applied, with a value of `col`. This tells us that the table header cell heads a column.

T *Take a moment to hover your mouse over different areas of the table, including the edges. You'll quickly discover that hovering over the leftmost edge of a row highlights all the cells in the row, and that hovering over the topmost edge of a column highlights all the cells in the column. If you take it a step further and click, the entire row or column is selected.*

3. Leave the top left cell blank, and type the following into the top row of cells: `Morning`, `Afternoon`, and `Evening`.

4. Again skipping the top left cell, fill in the days of the week down the left column of the table.

   There are some spacing issues, but ignore them for now. We'll fix them shortly when we style the table using CSS.

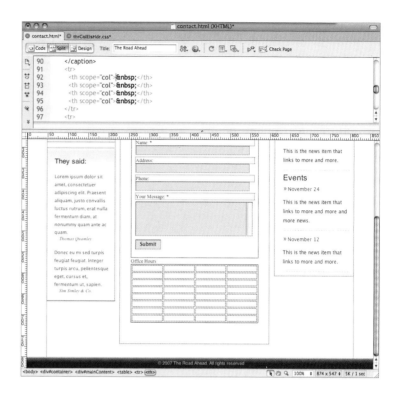

T *Use the Tab key to move the selection to the cell on the right of the current cell, instead of continually reaching for the mouse to re-position the cursor.*

FIGURE 5.37 The scope attribute is identifying the table cell as a header for a column of data.

N *When space is tight, abbreviate the table headers and mark them up accordingly with the* ‹abbr› *tag. Screen readers will read out the title attribute of* ‹abbr› *tags. There is also an* abbr *attribute specifically for use in* th *tags that has its own special use. When the header text is long and repetition would be tedious, an abbreviation of the long header text can be defined in the* abbr *attribute. On the first occasion the* th *is encountered, some screen readers will read it out in full but subsequently will read out only the abbreviated text in the* abbr *attribute.*

Dreamweaver has again decided to display parts of the page with its own styles, ignoring those in our style sheet. By default, table headers are displayed by browsers in a font weight of bold. However, we removed this default in our CSS reset rules. Dreamweaver is also ignoring the fonts we have set. Previewing the page in a browser will display the table using the CSS from our style sheet. The table header will have a font weight of normal and our selected font will display correctly. When using the CSS reset method, be aware of this issue so you are not deceived into thinking you've set a style, when in fact it's only Dreamweaver CS3's rendering engine that did so.

We need a way to indicate when the office is open. As blocks of time are going to be selected, an indicator that visually fills each cell would be ideal. To achieve this, we can highlight the cell with a background color, using CSS.

But wait a second—what about the users of screen readers? After all, they won't benefit from the display of a background color.

For non-sighted users we'll put the words Open or Closed in the appropriate cells so a screen reader user will know the office is open at the day and time corresponding with that particular cell. This also means that a key to explain the highlighting is unnecessary for sighted users.

5. In Design view, type into each cell of the table its status of either Open or Closed. For Sunday, insert a single Closed for the morning period. We'll work more with Sunday shortly.

Office Hours

	Morning	Afternoon	Evening
Monday	Open	Open	Closed
Tuesday	Closed	Open	Open
Wednesday	Open	Closed	Closed
Thursday	Closed	Open	Open
Friday	Open	Open	Closed
Saturday	Open	Closed	Closed
Sunday	Closed		

FIGURE 5.38 Our table with the opening times for each day.

Providing Additional Feedback For Accessibility

The table structure is deliberately simple, but let's still apply the markup that allows screen reader users to discover the relationship between table cells and their headers.

We'll give each th an id, and each table cell a headers attribute containing a value identical to that of the id of the associated th. We will do this using the Tag Inspector, so make sure it is open and in Attributes mode.

1. In the (X)HTML document, click in the th cell containing the word Monday. Select th in the tag selector. In the Tag Inspector, expand the CSS/Accessibility section. Set the id attribute by clicking in the field to the right of id and typing the word mon. Press Enter to apply the new id.

2. Do the same for the other days in the header column, obviously using the appropriate day name as the value for each id.

3. Assign an **id** to each of Morning, Afternoon and Evening in the header row across the top of the table. For example, Morning would have an **id** of morning. Continue until each header cell in the table has an **id**.

   In the same way, we will now assign the values we just set for each **id** as the values of the **headers** attribute in each table cell. Each table cell has two corresponding headers and will therefore have two values for the **headers attribute**. When a screen reader selects the table cell, it will use the values for the **ids** and **headers** attributes to establish the relationship between that cell and its two headers.

4. Click inside the first **td** cell, which is the one to the right of the **Monday th** and beneath the **Morning th**. Select the **<td>** in the tag selector if it is not already selected, and look over at the Tag Inspector.

   You will see that **headers** is listed under the Attribute tab.

5. Type in two values for **headers** – **mon morning** – and **make sure the values are separated by a space**. These values are identical to the values of the **ids** on the corresponding **th** elements.

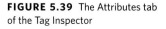

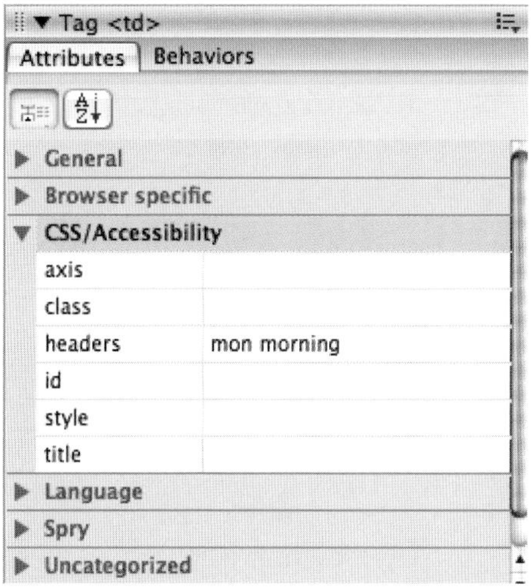

FIGURE 5.39 The Attributes tab of the Tag Inspector

6. Follow this procedure to give all cells containing data a **headers** attribute.

Before we move on to styling the table with CSS, we'll perform one little act of housekeeping to make our table easier to understand. On Sunday, the office is closed all day. We currently have the word **Closed** once, which keeps things nice and clean, but it is only in the Morning cell and the Afternoon and Evening cells are empty. Those cells actually do represent either an Open or Closed status so it's not an ideal situation.

```
<tr>
    <th id="sun" scope="row">Sunday</th>
    <td>Closed</td>
    <td> </td>
    <td> </td>
</tr>
```

Instead of repeating the word Closed three times for that day, we will combine the Morning, Afternoon and Evening cells to indicate that the Closed status spans all three.

7. In Design view, place the cursor in the cell that represents Sunday Morning and which contains the word Closed. Drag the mouse from this cell over to the right side of the table.

You will see that the cells it passes through are selected.

8. With these cells selected, right-click and choose Table > Merge Cells or simply press the M key.

Now, there is a single cell for Sunday.

9. Change the text to read **Closed All Day**.

A look at our code shows the changes.

```
<tr>
    <th id="sun" scope="row">Sunday</th>
    <td colspan="3">Closed All Day</td>
</tr>
```

Dreamweaver has applied a **colspan** of **3** to a **td**, creating a single cell combining the original 3 tds instead of using 3 separate **tds**.

Styling the Data Table

Let's start right at the top of the table and style the `caption` element. Captions can be problematic to style consistently across browsers so we'll keep our styling very basic. We already reset its properties in our CSS but a space above the caption would visually separate it from the form, and we also want the text to be larger.

1. Add a new CSS rule for the element `caption`.

2. Set the font-face to `"Lucida Grande", Verdana, Arial, Helvetica, sans-serif,` and set the size to `1.5em`. For padding, set top to `1em` and bottom to `0.2em`.

   The caption now displays in Dreamweaver in our chosen font, and has a spatial association with the table below it.

   We need to move the `th` and `td` cell contents away from the edges of their cells and spread them out a little more. We'll also apply borders, thus creating a visual grid and making it easier for sighted users to identify the required information.

3. Add a new CSS rule with an Advanced selector of `th, td`.

4. For padding, set top and bottom to `0.1em` and left and right to `0.4em`.

   Add a border in order to display the rows and columns as a grid.

5. Switch to the Border category and add a `1px` solid border with a color of `#336`.

   We also need to create a style for `th` alone, to clearly and visually differentiate between the header cells and the table data cells.

6. Add a new CSS rule for the `th` element.

7. Set the font-size to `.85em`. Set the font-weight to `bold`, and the color to `#D9DEE8`.

   In Design view, we can see that Dreamweaver has applied some cell spacing of its own, but when viewed in the browser, the table displays as intended. Dreamweaver maintains this additional space in order to help us more easily select elements of the table—while disconcerting perhaps, it does serve a purpose.

Fields marked with an * are mandatory.

Name: *

Address:

Phone:

Invalid format.

Email: *

Invalid format.

Your Message: *

Submit

(except where required by law).

┌─Your Details─────────────────

Fields marked with an * are mandatory.

Name: *

Address:

Phone:
(123) 456-7890

Email: *

Your Message: *

Submit

Office Hours

	Morning	Afternoon	Evening
Monday	Open	Open	Closed
Tuesday	Closed	Open	Open
Wednesday	Open	Closed	Closed
Thursday	Closed	Open	Open
Friday	Open	Open	Closed
Saturday	Open	Closed	Closed
Sunday	Closed All Day		

Office Hours

	Morning	Afternoon	Evening
Monday	Open	Open	Closed
Tuesday	Closed	Open	Open
Wednesday	Open	Closed	Closed
Thursday	Closed	Open	Open
Friday	Open	Open	Closed
Saturday	Open	Closed	Closed
Sunday	Closed All Day		

FIGURE 5.40 The table appears to have more space in Dreamweaver (on the left) than in a browser.

Finally, in order to highlight the table cells that signify that the office is open, we can create a class that we'll apply just to the relevant **td** cells.

8. Add a new CSS class called **open**. Set the background color to #EFE5EB.

9. In Design view, place the cursor inside the first **td** that contains the word Open. This is the cell to the right of the header Monday and below the header Morning. Drag the mouse to select that cell and the one immediat ely on its right, which also contains the word Open. Holding down the Ctrl key, continue to select all the cells containing the word Open.

10. In the Property inspector, click on the Styles drop-down list and choose the class **open**. Alternatively, right-click on the group of cells that are selected and choose CSS Styles>open from the contextual menu.

A pale pink background has now been applied to all of the office opening times, drawing the eye to the most important data for sighted users, and our table is complete.

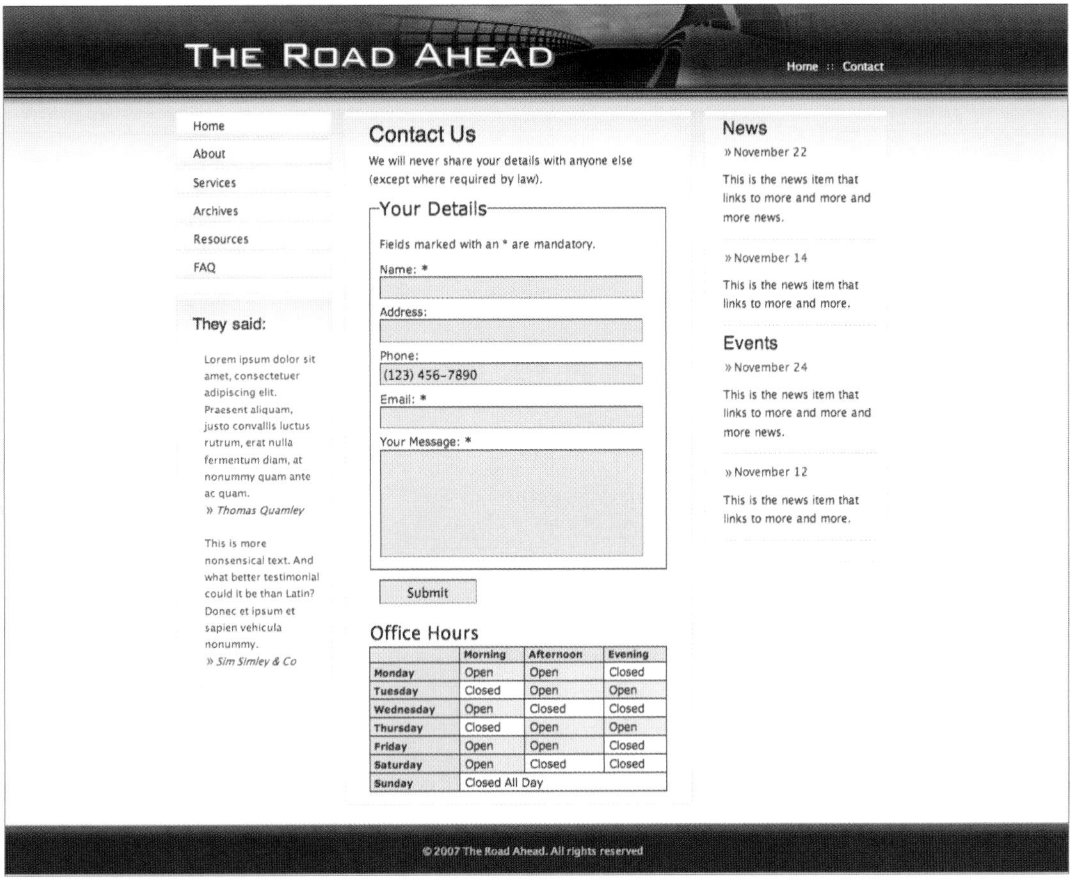

FIGURE 5.41 Our completed page as viewed in Firefox.

Do You Feel Accomplished?

In this chapter, you've used one of Dreamweaver's default elastic layouts to create and style a generic page and a contact page with data table and form. You've learned that containers with em widths will expand and contract according to font size, maintaining the intended page layout and proportions. You've also learned how to save and use Snippets. You have created an accessible form and an accessible data table, both of which will expand or contract with the layout.

Give yourself a gold star for a job well done!

Building a Gallery Site with CSS and Spry

IN THIS CHAPTER, we'll create a site for a fictitious client, Rive Gauche Galleries. Along the way, we'll use and combine different CSS layouts in a single site, as well as explore the world of progressive enhancements using the Spry framework for Ajax.

As an art gallery, one requirement for Rive Gauche is that the site display a large number of graphics without a lot of scrolling, and at the same time offer a larger detail image without opening additional browser windows or linking to other HTML pages. Because of the amount of information to display, the client would like the content area of the pages to expand as the browser's viewport is widened. While we're at it, the owner would like us to ensure that the site's layout integrity is maintained when the browser agent's text size is increased or decreased—like many of us, he finds the small text on many web pages uncomfortably hard to read. Finally, the client also wants a form that potential customers can use to contact them.

Our client's site was originally built in the late '90's, and looks its age. Yep, we've got our work cut out for us.

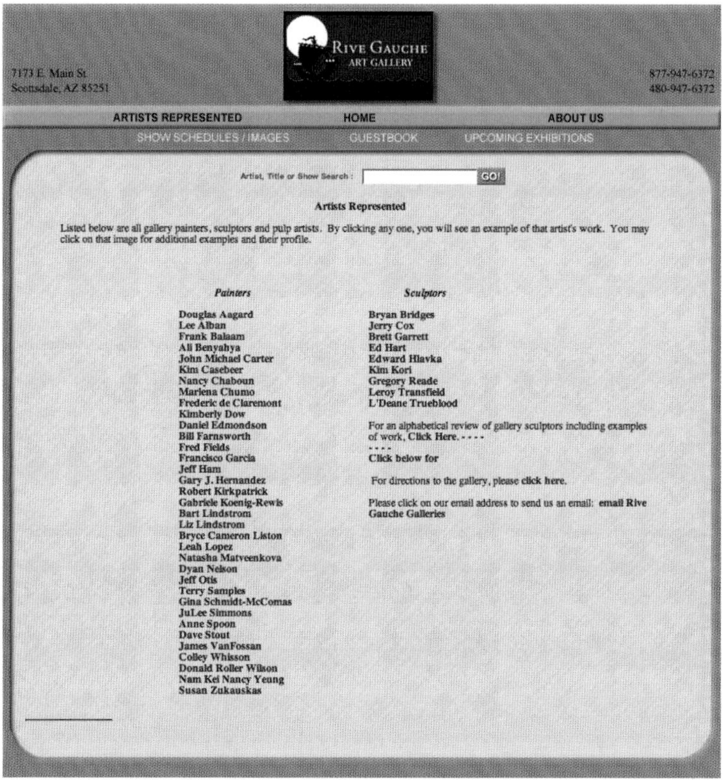

FIGURE 6.1 The client's old site—did the web really look this bad in the 90's?!

Selecting the Proper Starter Layout

Since the page needs to both expand with the browser agent's viewport width and expand or contract with the change of text size in the browser agent, there's only one type of starter layout to use—the hybrid layout. We simply need to decide upon the number of columns and we'll be ready to go.

FIGURE 6.2 The comps of the gallery pages pose a challenge.

But should we use a two-column or three-column layout? For the home page, it's fairly easy to see two columns. The navigation could be in the left column and we could then divide the main content section to accommodate the thumbnail images and text. But the artists' page has a column of text on the right. No need, though, to reinvent the code equivalent of the wheel: we can simply use two separate CSS layouts and combine their rules.

1. Create a Dreamweaver site called Chapter_6 and copy the tutorial files into it, or use your own images.

2. Create a new document using the New Document dialog. Select the 2 column hybrid, left sidebar, header and footer layout. Ensure that XHTML 1.0 Transitional is selected as the DocType.

3. Choose to create a new style sheet file for the layout. Change the name of the style sheet from the default of twoColHybLtHdr.css to mainStyles.css and save it in your new site.

4. Save the HTML page as index.html.

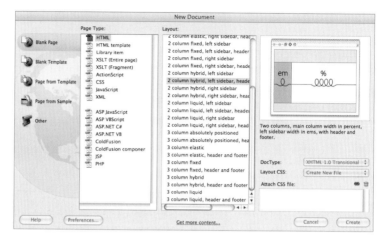

FIGURE 6.3 The hybrid layout allows the page design to adapt both to a browser agent's window width and to changes in the browser agent's text size.

Building the Initial Framework

Since we're giving the body a black background, even though the #container will have a white background, we want to change the text to a contrasting color on the body element. If any user agent has trouble displaying any of our values, we want to be sure we have contrasting colors on the divs that are displayed. Thus, the text on the body is changed to white (since it's on a black background) and the text on the #container is defined as black (since it's on a white background).

The initial framework of all the pages within the site is relatively simple and by this point, you should feel comfortable creating it. Therefore, we'll simply do a quick review.

1. Remove the background color from the sidebar. Apply black (#000) as the background color to the body of the page, and change the padding on sidebar1 to 0px.

2. Change the background color of the header and footer to black (#000) and the text to white (#FFF).

3. Remove the border from the container. Change the width of the container to 100% and the text color to black (#000).

4. Create a new rule for all h1, h2 and h3 elements as follows:

```
h1, h2, h3 {
  font-weight: normal;
  letter-spacing: -.05em;
  line-height: 1.1;
}
```

5. Remove Verdana from the font-family of the body rule. Add the line-height property set to 1.5 to give the text on the page an airier feel.

```
body {
    font: 100%/1.5 Arial, Helvetica, sans-serif;
    background: #000;
    margin: 0;
    padding: 0;
    text-align: center;
    color: #FFF;
    }
```

6. Place the cursor in the header and use the tag selector to remove the **h1**. Go ahead and delete the word "header" from here as well.

7. Because we've deleted the **h1** and will not be using it in this site, it's probably a good idea to switch to the All view of the CSS panel now and delete the `.twoColHybLtHdr #header h1` rule. You can do this by selecting the name from the list, right-clicking and choosing Delete.

8. Place the logo.gif in `<div#header>`. Apply 30 pixels of left and right padding and 10 pixels of top and bottom padding to the header rule.

9. Assign `"/index.html"` as the image's link in the Property Inspector.

   Remember that visitors to a site generally expect the logo to be a link taking them back to the home page of the site. This link takes the user back to the index page at the root level of the site.

   You'll notice that (although it's really hard to see on the black background) the image now has a blue line all the way around it, indicating that it is a link. So we'll need to remove this— unless you just really like your images outlined in blue!

10. Create a new rule for images within a link element, `a img`, and set the border to **none**. Your code should look like this: `a img {border:none;}`

11. Add `logo_traditional.gif` as a background image to the header rule. Set it to **no-repeat**, with a right horizontal position and center vertical position.

    Another look at the comps (it's always a good idea to refer back to your comp now and then) reveals that we need to create a bit of separation between the header/footer and the content area by adding a red line and a bit of air.

12. Add a bottom border to the header rule. Make it **solid, 6px** and **#AD2027**. To hold the content away from the bottom of the header, add **margin-bottom:50px**.

13. For the footer, we'll want the same padding as in the header, so set padding to **10px 30px** and then add a **border-top** using the same properties as we used for the header.

14. Last but not least, we'll add the gallery address and phone numbers to the footer. The default text color of the page is black, and on a black background that could cause some serious readability issues! Change the color for the **footer p** rule to white (**#FFF**) and add the following text to the footer:

    +1-800-123-4567 +1-800-987-6543 12345 Main St. Scottsdale, AZ 85251

    From the comp, we can see that the text appears to be two text blocks, one on the left and one on the right. It's very easy to achieve this effect using a float. Since we want the telephone numbers to appear on the right, they are ahead of the address in the source code order.

15. Wrap the telephone numbers in a `<span>` element. Assign a class of **fltrt** to the span using the Property Inspector or in code. Add the font-size property to the **footer p** rule and set it to **0.7em**.

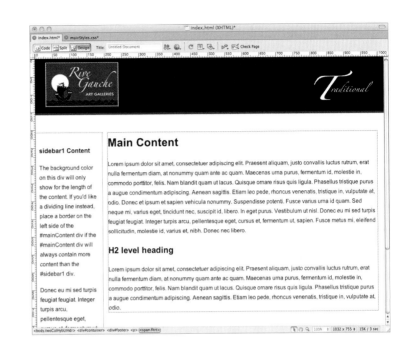

FIGURE 6.4 With the initial framework for the index page in place, we're ready to rock!

Lights, Camera, Content...

If you simply drag the cursor in Design view from the h2 to the end of the text to select it and then press delete, the h2 element may be left on the page. We don't want that, so make sure it's completely removed.

Before we begin to tackle the navigation, let's get the simple main content area out of the way. Based on our comp, the content area is nothing more than some text and three images.

1. Delete the placeholder text from the beginning of the h2 heading to the end of the final p element in the mainContent area.

   As we look at the page, something is not quite right. With the exception of the text in the footer, the text on our page is much larger than it is in our comp. But, as always when working with the CSS layouts, the best practice is to change the font-size on individual elements, rather than changing it globally using the body element.

2. Using the CSS Panel or your preferred method, create a new rule for the paragraph elements of the mainContent area:
   `#mainContent p`

3. Set the font-size to **0.8em**. So that the layout more closely resembles the comp, either break the remaining dummy text into several paragraphs, or copy/paste the text from the finished index page.

4. Save the page (and remember, if the CSS file is open, you'll need to save it as well) and preview it in the browser.

Because this is a hybrid layout, it should fill the viewport, as well as adjust to the browser's default text size. Experiment with this by changing the width of the browser window. Notice that the mainContent text adjusts accordingly. Try increasing and decreasing the size of the browser's font. Notice that the width of the sidebar adjusts as well.

Hmmm...did you see that? Do it again—open the browser to the full width of the screen. Whoa! That's not good! Look how long those lines of text are in the mainContent area. Text is less readable when the line exceeds 80 characters. Combine that with our smaller text size and you have to admit that this is not good.

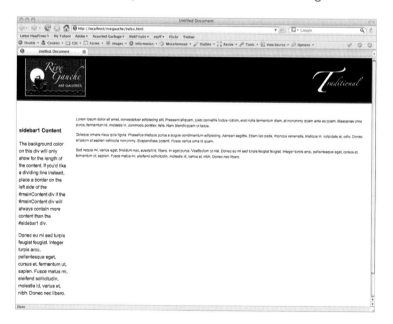

FIGURE 6.5 Even without going fullscreen, the line length of the content area is waaaay too long!

To limit this behavior, we'll use the **max-width** property. The problem with this approach is that a certain browser (that'd be Internet Explorer for those of you who've been sleeping through the book) only began to support this property in version 7. So, we're going to need a dual approach—one for standards-compliant browsers and one for the other guy.

Using max-width and min-width

Let's get our standards-compliant browsers happy first. In addition to keeping the length of the line from becoming too short, we'll also use `min-width` to make sure that the window can't be collapsed so far that we get a really short line.

1. Place the cursor in the mainContent element and click to select the `.twoColHybLtHdr #mainContent` rule in the Rules section of the CSS Panel's Current view.

2. Click the Add Property link in the Properties section of the CSS Panel. Type `max-width` and give it a value of 62em.

3. Select the container rule in the CSS Panel, click Add Property again and enter `min-width` as the property with a value of 60em.

4. Save your pages and preview in Firefox or Safari (or your standards-compliant browser of choice). Expand and contract the browser window and you'll notice our maximum and minimum widths kicking into play.

So now that we've solved the line width issue for our favorite browsers, we need to solve the problem presented by Internet Explorer 5.5 and 6.

Getting IE's Attention—min/ max width Enforcement

Unfortunately, Internet Explorer has no simple way to solve our issue—or, perhaps more accurately stated, no standards-compliant way. But there is a workaround, known as an **expression**. An expression is an IE-only property that uses Javascript within your CSS file. It needs to be placed in an IECC and actually allows us to get close to the max-width and min-width standard.

Since it gets us where we need to go for IE 6... what the heck. Let's do it.

We picked this value by experimenting with how wide we personally felt the lines could still be easily read. We also didn't want too much whitespace to the right of the text, so a narrower (but probably more readable) width wouldn't work. We chose to constrain the width using em's instead of pixels to allow for changes in the font size by the viewer.

1. Switch to Code view and scroll towards the top of the document until you locate the IECC (Internet Explorer Conditional Comment). The code block begins with: `<!--[if IE]>`.

2. Add the following code above the closing `</style>` tag with the IECC:

```
.twoColHybLtHdr #container { width: expression(Math.
max((document.documentElement ? document.documentElement.
clientWidth : document.body.clientWidth)/16,
960/16)+'em'); }
```

What in the world is all that?! Well, it's actually not as scary as it looks. Let's walk through it, piece by piece, remembering that because we've placed the code in the IECC, only Internet Explorer will read it.

First, we're telling IE to locate the element defined by the descendent selector `.twoColHybLtHdr #container` and then get ready to set its width property. Next, we use IE's proprietary `expression();` statement, which basically says "we're about to give you some JavaScript to execute."

The core of the expression uses the JavaScript Math class. `Math. max()` takes two comma-delimited arguments and determines which argument is bigger. As arguments we're giving it `(document. documentElement ? document.documentElement.clientWidth : document.body.clientWidth)/16` and `960/16`.

The first argument is a basic true/false statement that asks whether the viewer's browser is running in Standards mode or Quirks mode. The statement `document.documentElement` is asking, "is this true?"; in other words, does this browser know what we're talking about when asking about the document's DOM? The question mark ends the question or condition. This is then followed by the true and false options, separated by a colon (:).

In our case, the true statement `document.documentElement .clientWidth` states that we are interested in the width of the document, or in this case, the browser viewport in a browser running in Standards mode. The false statement is exactly the same, just running in Quirks mode. Finally, note that the true/false statement is enclosed in parenthesis, indicating that we want to determine this outcome before we continue.

N   *Remember, 1em is equal to 16px based on the default base font size used by modern browsers.*

After we've determined the width of the viewport through either the Standards mode or Quirks mode, we then divide the resulting pixel value by 16. Now, did you hear that? The width value is delivered in pixels—this is our only choice—but we're dealing with a hybrid/liquid layout and want to measure our value in ems. That's why we're dividing the result by 16. Dividing the pixel value by 16 gives us the equivalent value in em spaces.

Our second argument is **960/16.** You'll recall that for standards-compliant browsers we limited the min-width to 60em. Grab your calculator and do the math... 960 divided by 16 is 60.

So basically, we've told the Math.max function to determine which is larger, the current width of the viewport (in pixels, but divided by 16 to give us the em equivalent) or 60.

Once we've determined which value is greater, we're adding "em" to the total to let the browser know that the value is using this unit of measure.

N   *Are you wondering if there is a* Math.min *function? Yes, there is. It would limit the maximum value (in our case the width) that could be applied to an element. So...* Math.max *gives us a minimum whereas* Math.min *would give us a maximum. Now, that makes perfect sense!*

With that, we've now assigned the width value to the container element, telling Internet Explorer to respect the same min-width value of 60em that we assigned to our standards-compliant browsers. If the viewport is larger than 60em, the page content will continue to fill the viewport. Once the viewport shrinks to less than 60em, the content will not shrink beyond its defined 60em width.

Not Too Far... Constraining the Content Area for IE

With the overall width of the page container constrained, we need to ensure that the line length of our mainContent area doesn't become too long if the window is opened wide.

Create a new line in the IECC after the rule that we just created and add the following code:

```
.twoColHybLtHdr #mainContent {width: expression(container.
clientWidth > 1220 ? "62em" : "auto"); }
```

We're asking Internet Explorer to find the `.twoColHybLtHdr` `#mainContent` element and assign a width to it based upon the result of an expression. Our expression uses syntax that's similar to the previous expression: if this is true, do this, otherwise do something else.

Stepping through the code, `container.clientWidth > 1220 ?` asks IE if the width of the element identified as container is greater than 1220 pixels. If this is true, it sets the width of mainContent to 62em. Otherwise—when the container's width is less than 1220—it sets the width of mainContent to auto. This means that as the viewport decreases below 1220, the content of mainContent will continue to reflow to fill that remaining space.

Of course, since we set a min-width (or its IE equivalent) on the overall container, it only reflows until the overall width of the container element reaches its minimum value.

We've now conquered Internet Explorer 6. So what about version 5.5 or earlier? Well, that's where it gets a little... um... less successful. For Internet Explorer 5.5 and below, our solution has a serious side effect: the page is no longer a hybrid/liquid layout. IE 5.5 and below can't understand the first argument value in the rule for the container element. Therefore, those browsers select the second argument as the value. In this example, our page width would be 960px regardless of the viewport width. If the viewport is wider than 960px, black margins will appear on the left and right of our layout.

Remember that `.clientWidth` *delivers its results in pixels.*

In researching this particular step in our workflow, we initially wanted to use the second syntax (without all that `Math.max` stuff) for the overall width of our container. That would have looked like this:

```
.twoColHybLtHdr #container
{width: expression(document
.documentElement.clientWidth
< 960 ? "60em" : "auto"); }
```

Unfortunately, however, this won't work for our example. It would have worked if we'd only wanted to constrain the value of the container element, but we also needed to determine how to size the mainContent element. Using the value "auto" would have resulted in the browser reporting a value of 0 and that wouldn't have worked.

FIGURE 6.6 Internet Explorer 5.5 turns a semi-deaf ear on our solution.

Spread Out the Pictures

With the overall framework of the content area set, our comp indicates that we have three images that need to be added to the index page above the main text. You'll also notice that the images seem to be evenly spaced across the defined area. But wait... that same relationship needs to be maintained even as the mainContent area is resized according to our min-width and max-width values. No worries—a little bit of floating magic will do the trick.

1. Place your cursor at the beginning of the text in mainContent inside the p element.

2. Either click the Insert Image icon from the Insert panel or drag front_1.jpg, front_3.jpg and front_2.jpg in order onto the page. (Don't forget to add the title of the picture as the image's alt attribute.)

   Notice that the images are not in numerical order. We'll explain this later.

3. Click, drag and highlight all three images. On the Property inspector, select Paragraph from the format drop-down.

4. Create a new class, `.centered,` in mainStyles.css to use for the `<p>` element wrapping the images. Assign it the **text-align: center** attribute, and add a bit of padding to the left and right: **padding: 0 5%**. Add a bottom margin: **margin: 0 0 30px 0**.

5. Place the cursor within the `<p>` element wrapping the images (on the tag selector, be sure you've selected the p element and not one of the images). Use the Property Inspector to assign the newly created .centered rule to the `<p>` element.

   According to our comp, we'll need to make our images stand out a bit with a red border.

6. Create a descendent selector for images within the `<p.centered>` element.: `p.centered img`. Give the rule a 1 pixel solid border: **1px solid #AD2027**, and in order to move the border off of the image, add 4 pixels of padding: **padding: 4px**.

FIGURE 6.7 Our images need some space.

Our images are looking good, but they're still sitting right next to each other; a little floating and we'll be in business.

7. Click to select the image on the left, and with the image selected, use the Property Inspector to assign the `.fltlft` rule to the image.

8. Click to select the middle image, front_3.jpg and using the Property Inspector, assign the `.fltrt` rule to the image.

Okay! Things are looking good. We have one last page element to create—the navigation.

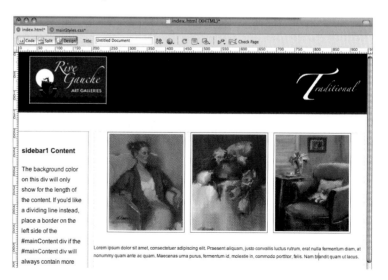

FIGURE 6.8 Nicely spaced images and we're ready for some navigation.

You'll remember that we mentioned earlier that we were not placing the images on the page in numerical order—at least not by their names. Front_2.jpg is a non-floated element (and is aligned to the center of the page using the `text-align: center` *value we gave the p.centered class that contains it. We want the front_3.jpg to move to the right and the front_1.jpg to move to the left of the front_2.jpg image. Both of these images must come before front_2.jpg in the source order since it's a non-floated element.*

Directions, Please…

For the navigation on the site, our designer has specified a vertical navigation bar. No problem… except that at least one section of the site, the gallery section, needs sub-navigation to distinguish between the different types of art available. The client has asked for 2 sub-sections initially. In order to keep things as clean as possible, we decided upon a fly-out sub-menu.

Fly-out menus pose some inherent challenges. The biggest is making the information in them reachable for all users, even when JavaScript has been turned off or is simply not supported.

Enter the Spry framework for Ajax.

What is the Spry framework?

Ajax (short for Asynchronous JavaScript and XML) is really just a fancy way to describe the action when a page requests information (mostly from an external source, but also from within the page) and updates a specific area of the page without causing the traditional page refresh. If you'd like to learn more about it, there's tons of information in books and on the web, but the inner workings of Ajax are beyond the scope of this book. We're just going to use the tools provided within Dreamweaver CS3, specifically the Spry framework.

So what is the Spry framework? In order to implement Ajax within a page, designers have had two choices—write the JavaScript by hand or use a framework. A framework is basically a collection of scripts, but most frameworks are written by and for programmers, and unless you're a JavaScript guru and dream at night of manipulating the DOM, it can be excruciatingly painful to implement them. In contrast, the Spry framework was developed with designers in mind and with the CS3 release, is built into Dreamweaver. A new section of the Insert panel entitled Spry gives us direct access to a number of Spry objects that we can add to the page without coding.

Adobe is continuing to develop the Spry framework, independently of Dreamweaver. The web doesn't hold still and the traditional 18-24 month cycle of Dreamweaver updates isn't fast enough for the enhancements that are possible with Spry. So before doing anything else, let's make sure that you have the latest version of the software.

Go to labs.adobe.com and find the Spry area. As of this writing, the current release of the Spry framework is version 1.6. There are (again, as of this writing) two download links to choose from. One link downloads the entire framework , complete with documentation, an updater for Dreamweaver CS3 and sample files. This will provide you with the JavaScript files that we'll use later in the chapter. The other download link is for an extension to Dreamweaver CS3 that will only update Dreamweaver CS3 to understand the additions to the framework and provide code hinting and syntax coloring for the new items, but does not include the framework files themselves.

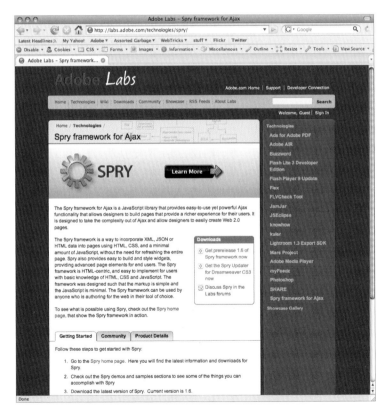

FIGURE 6.9 The Spry page on labs.adobe.com provides two download links—one for the framework itself and a second for an updater for Dreamweaver CS3.

Download the complete framework, unzip it and double-click on the extension in the Dreamweaver folder to update your copy of Dreamweaver CS3.

If you've already used some of the Spry widgets in your site, Dreamweaver will not overwrite the older files without permission when you add the widget again. You must go to Site > Spry Updater... and choose which widgets to update. Dreamweaver will make a copy of the old files and add the new ones.

We'll be using two features from Spry 1.6 in this chapter. Although the extension updates Dreamweaver's understanding of the new features, it doesn't provide new icons or tools in the Insert panel, so we'll be doing a bit of hand-coding—but don't worry, we'll take it nice and slow and explain the steps as we go.

Creating a Spry-based Navigation

A quick look back at our comp tells us that we're going to need the navigation in the sidebar1 area.

1. Click to place the cursor in the sidebar1 element. Select All and delete the contents of the element. Switch to the Spry section of the Insert panel.

   The Spry section has three parts. The first contains tools for adding data to a page. This data is provided by XML. The second section contains some tools for working with forms, such as form field validators. The third section contains the Spry widgets, or interface elements, that shipped with Spry 1.4, which is the version built into Dreamweaver CS3.

   One of the Spry widgets is called the Spry Menu Bar. That's the one that we want.

2. With the cursor still in the sidebar1 element, click the Spry Menu Bar tool. Dreamweaver asks if you want a horizontal or vertical menu. Choose the vertical option and click OK.

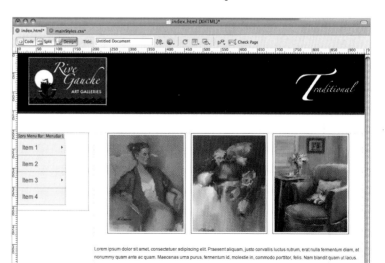

FIGURE 6.10 Our default Spry menu on the page.

We now have a default Spry menu on the page. The four items in the menu are the default menu entries. Two of the items have small triangles to the right of the text, indicating that the entry has a fly-out, or submenu.

Notice also the blue tab above the menu. This doesn't actually appear in the page, but is Dreamweaver's way of indicating that the presence of a Spry widget.

FIGURE 6.11 The Spry Menu Bar can be modified using the Property inspector.

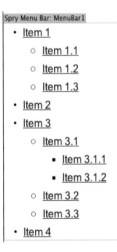

FIGURE 6.12 Without the CSS applied, we can see the menu is a list of links.

FIGURE 6.13 In order for Spry widgets to be used in the site, the corresponding JavaScript and CSS files need to be copied into the site structure.

With the `<ul.MenuBarVertical#MenuBar1>` selected, in the Property inspector, you can see that we can modify the entries. We can add entries, delete entries or reorder the entries, as well as add submenus up to two levels deep. You'll also notice a button entitled Turn Styles Off. Click this button to see its effect. Wow—what just happened?

The menu is now made up of nothing more than an unordered list! This is the real beauty of these Spry widgets—they are nothing more than standard HTML elements, in this case, a list. Each Spry element is styled by CSS to give it its look. (Go ahead and say "cool"—it's okay, we did it too when we saw this the first time!) Turn the styles back on by clicking the button again (now entitled "Turn Styles On").

3. Save your page... just in case. As you do so, you'll notice that Dreamweaver needs to inform you of something—specifically that it's going to need to add some files to your site.

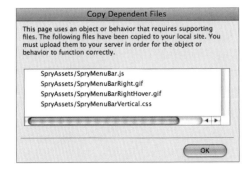

Each Spry widget is made up of HTML elements as we mentioned before. These HTML elements are then styled via CSS. JavaScript provides the interactivity or functionality of the elements. Therefore, Dreamweaver is offering to copy the necessary files into your site structure.

4. Click OK to allow Dreamweaver to copy the files.

   Notice in the root of your site structure a new folder has appeared entitled SpryAssets. This folder now contains the four files that Dreamweaver offered to copy.

   Now all we need to do is modify the menu entries and the associated CSS in order to enhance our page. Let's start with the menu entries.

When you upload your site later, you'll want to be sure you upload the SpryAssets folder to your server.

5. Make sure that the Spry Menu Bar is selected—if it's not, click the blue tab for the Spry Menu Bar and check the Property inspector to see if it reflects that the menu bar is selected.

6. In the first column click Item 1 and change the entry in the Text field to Home. In the Link field, type index.html.

7. In the second column of the Home item, click to select each submenu item and click the minus "-" button to delete them.

8. Change the second menu item to Artists with a link to artists. html.

   The client has requested that this menu entry give the visitor the option of viewing either Painters or Sculptors.

9. With the Artist entry selected in the Property Inspector, click the plus button "+" twice in the second column to add two submenu entries. Change the new submenu entries to Painters and Sculptors with links to painters.html and sculptors. html respectively.

10. Select the third menu item in the first column and change it to Exhibitions with a link to exhibitions.html. Delete the submenu items from this entry as we did for the Home item.

    Dreamweaver informs you that the first submenu item also has a submenu that will be deleted.

11. Click OK. Change the fourth menu item in the first column to Contact with a link to contact.html.

12. Add a final menu item in the first column by clicking on the plus "+" button above that column. Change this entry to About Us with a link to about.html.

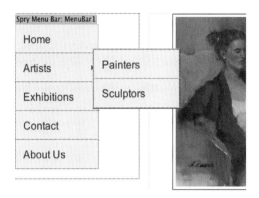

FIGURE 6.14 The modified Spry Menu Bar with the submenu showing.

Styling the Spry Menu Bar with CSS

With the menu entries now set, it's time to style them to match our comp.

In our comp, the menu is aligned with the left side of the logo in the header. The header itself has 30px of padding on the left and right. So it stands to reason that we need to move the menu 30px to the right.

1. Select the entire menu bar by clicking on the blue tab.

In the Current view of the CSS panel, notice in the Rules section that there are two entries for `ul.MenuBarVertical`. The CSS for Spry Menu Bar widget is divided into two sections within the style sheet. One entry describes the layout properties for the widget, while the next entry describes additional attributes. We're going to need to modify a couple of the attributes in the first entry.

2. Select the first `ul.MenuBarVertical` entry in the Rules section of the CSS panel. Change the width in the Properties section to 12em. To push the menu over from the left edge of the window, modify the margin property (currently 0px) to:
`margin: 0 0 0 30px;`

3. Finally, the text size is much too large, so set the font-size property to `0.8em`.

Even though we gave the `<ul>` a width of 12em, our menu items don't seem to have changed. This is because the individual `<li>` elements have also been assigned a default width in the Spry CSS sheet.

4. Click to place the cursor into one of the menu items and then select the `ul.MenuBarVertical li` entry in the Rules section of the CSS panel. Change the width property to 12em.

   We still need to change the background color and text color of the menu items, as well as position the text further to the right and modify the padding within the box. Notice that the next selector in the cascade (in the Rules section of the CSS panel) is the `ul.MenuBarVertical a` rule. This is where we'll find the last bit of basic styling for the menu items.

5. Select the `ul.MenuBarVertical a` rule in the Rules section of the CSS panel. Change the properties of the rule to the following:

```
ul.MenuBarVertical a {
    display: block;
    cursor: pointer;
    padding: 0.5em 0 0.5em 30px;
    color: #000;
    text-decoration: none;
    background-color:#FFF; }
```

The easiest way to save your page and its corresponding CSS files is to right-click on the document tab and choose Save All.

6. If you've not done so recently, go ahead and save the page and preview it in the browser. Remember, if open, you'll also need to save the corresponding CSS files before previewing.

Notice when you mouse over the Artists entry, the submenu appears and it disappears after you mouse off. This is triggered by the SpryMenuBar.js JavaScript file added to the site by Dreamweaver.

But our submenu is not appearing exactly where we want it. It's sitting a bit too high and the left edge of the submenu is overlapping the main menu. To understand how to modify this, you need to understand "where" the menu actually resides when it is not visible.

Remember, when we turned the styles off for the menu, it was nothing more than an unordered list? The submenu items are actually in the source of the page, and in fact, are an unordered list

N   *While it is beyond the scope of this book, you can modify each of the JavaScript files included in the Spry framework. The files are heavily commented so that you know what each section of code does and any precautions you should take when modifying the file. But what kind of things can you do, you ask... Well, one simple modification that we might want to change on our current project is the time it takes for the submenu items to appear/disappear. These values can be found on lines 102 and 103 of the SpryMenuBar.js file:* `this.showDelay = 250; this.hideDelay = 600;`. *The values are in milliseconds, so if we wanted a 1 sec delay, we could change either of the values to 1000. Feel free to open the individual JavaScripts for the Spry framework. Just remember —if you're going to make adjustments or modifications to the files, make a backup first.*

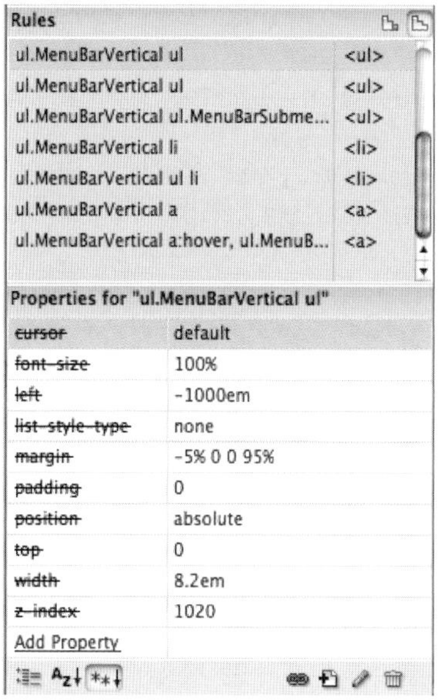

within a parent list item. So, why can't we see the submenu all the time? The answer lies in the CSS—bet you didn't see that coming!

Within the SpryMenuBarVertical.css file, a selector hides the submenus from view until mousing over their parent list item (or menu item) triggers them to show.

Let's take a closer look. With the SpryMenuBar selected, select the Artist entry in the first column of the Property inspector. Next, select one of the entries in column two. Any time we select the submenu entries in the Property inspector, we can also see the element on the page. Place your cursor in one of the submenu items on the page, locate the `ul.MenuBarVertical ul` rule in the cascade of the Rules section in the CSS panel, and select it.

FIGURE 6.15 The magic behind the submenu is actually a left position of -1000em!

Many designers and developers attempt to use the `display:none` attribute to hide elements of the page from the viewer and then use JavaScript to modify the property to show the element. While this is not "wrong"—because there are always multiple ways to solve problems through CSS—it does present a problem for accessibility (and sometimes search engine optimization). An element set not to display is not read by assistive technology. The Spry framework takes another approach, hiding the element by positioning it offscreen. This is done via two properties: `position:absolute;` and `left: -1000em;`.

Okay… then how does the submenu appear and, of equal importance, where does it appear? Once again, this is a function of the CSS, but this time CSS gets some help from JavaScript. When the JavaScript is triggered, it dynamically assigns a class of `MenuBarSubmenuVisible` to the nested `<ul>` that is the submenu.

Take a look at the `ul.MenuBarVertical ul.MenuBarSubmenuVisible` rule in the Rules section. (It should be two entries below the `ul.MenuBarVertical ul` that we just looked at.)

Once the JavaScript has attached the class designator to the element, the browser rechecks the CSS and applies the rule. In this case, it's really simple: `ul.MenuBarVertical ul.MenuBarSubmenuVisible { left: 0; }`. The rule simply changes the left property for the absolutely positioned element from `-1000em` to `0`, thereby moving it back into view.

Since the left property is the only thing that is modified, all of the other properties remain constant from the earlier `ul.MenuBarVertical ul` rule in the cascade. That means `ul.MenuBarVertical ul.MenuBarSubmenuVisible` is responsible for the positioning.

Reselect the `ul.MenuBarVertical ul` rule in the Rules section and take a closer look at the properties and values. Notice the margin property has a value of `-5%` for the top margin. This moves the element up or "above" its normal position which is exactly what we are seeing with the submenu.

The left margin property is set to `95%`, which seems a bit strange. 95% from where? If you remember that this element has been absolutely positioned, then you should also remember that an element that is assigned an absolute position looks for the last positioned parent container to get its point of origin. This element's parent container is the `<li>` defined by the descendent selector `ul.MenuBarVertical li`. Viewing that rule, we see its been given a relative position. Thus, the nested `<ul>` is getting its point of origin from the parent `<li>` and positioning itself 95% from its left edge We'll change the position and move the submenu flush with the item that calls it.

1. Modify the margin of the `ul.MenuBarVertical ul` rule to `margin: 0 0 0 99%`.

Now the submenu appears horizontally aligned with the Artists button. The 99% gives only a slight hint of an overlap to help visually tie the two elements together.

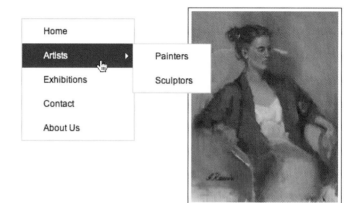

FIGURE 6.16 The menu and submenu are positioned properly—but what's up with the blue mouseover color?!

2. Save the CSS file and preview index.html in the browser to see the change.

Putting the Final Touches on the Menu Bar

Now that you understand that the Spry Menu Bar is being completely styled via descendent selectors of the `<ul.MenuBarVertical>` element, you can quickly finish off the styling to match the comp.

1. Your cursor should be in one of the items in the submenu—if not, place it there and select the last rule in the Rules cascade, `ul.MenuBarVertical a:hover, ul.MenuBarVertical a:focus`.

    You'll notice the lovely blue color that we saw in the browser when we rolled the mouse over the Artists menu item.

2. Change the background-color to `#AD2027`, which is the same red tone that we've used several times.

3. Save the CSS and test the index page in the browser.

    Notice anything? Like, uh, it didn't change anything?! As you know, classes are applied dynamically, and that's causing some issues. The pseudo hover class in our Rules cascade is being overridden by the dynamically assigned class. We'll fix this by hand.

4. Right-click on the `ul.MenuBarVertical a:hover,` `ul.MenuBarVertical a:focus` rule in the Rules section and select Go to Code.

   Immediately below this rule in the style sheet file, you'll see another rule, with the same attributes. These are the selectors that will be used by the dynamically assigned class.

5. In order to consolidate our CSS, copy the selectors `ul.MenuBarVertical a.MenuBarItemHover, ul.MenuBarVertical a.MenuBarItemSubmenuHover, ul.MenuBarVertical a.MenuBarSubmenuVisible` and paste them in the list of selectors for the rule above. Remember to add a comma at the end of the list *before* you paste Delete the duplicate rule you just copied.

   The consolidated rule looks like this:

   ```
   ul.MenuBarVertical a:hover, ul.MenuBarVertical a:focus,
   ul.MenuBarVertical a.MenuBarItemHover, ul.MenuBarVertical
   a.MenuBarItemSubmenuHover, ul.MenuBarVertical
   a.MenuBarSubmenuVisible {
      background-color: #AD2027;
      color: #FFF; }
   ```

6. Save the CSS file and then preview the index page in the browser again. This time, you should see the reddish high-light color when you mouse over the menu entries—including the submenu.

FIGURE 6.17 Now that color looks good on you, Mr. Menu Bar!

Where Am I? Giving Feedback Via the Menu Bar

The visual indicator that lets the visitor know which section of the site they're in is the final bit of polish needed for the menu bar. Our designer has indicated that we need a black background color, white text, and a red bar on the left-hand side of the currently selected menu item.

There are any number of approaches to this type of feedback for the user as we discussed in Chapter 4, but another simple way, if you have access to the menu on all pages, is to define a rule which can be applied to the corresponding menu element. Because much of the styling in this rule will only apply to the menu bar, the selector will be very specific.

1. Create a new rule in the mainStyles.css style sheet and specify its name to be `ul.MenuBarVertical a#selected`.

   You probably know what this means by now. We want the selected ID to affect a link (anchor) that occurs in the unordered list designated as MenuBarVertical.

   To help the item stand out, we'll thicken the text in the link using the font-weight property and make it white on a black background.

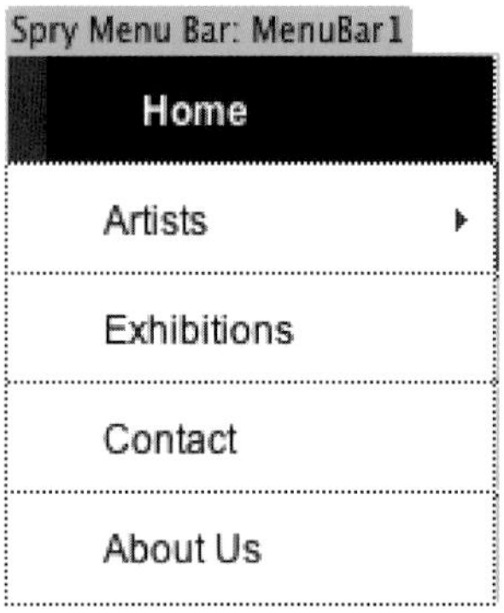

2. Add the following properties and values to the rule:

   ```
   font-weight: bold;
   color: #FFF;
   background-color: #000;
   ```

3. Create the red bar on the left-hand side of the selected item using the border-left property as follows:

   ```
   border-left: 12px solid #AD2027;
   ```

FIGURE 6.18 With the #selected rule applied, due to the box model, the border is pushing the text too far to the right.

4. Place the cursor in the Home link of the menu bar and apply the rule named `selected` from the Style drop-down list in the Property inspector.

You should now see the black background, white text, and red left-hand border. But the text entry is too far to the right. Since the box model includes border and padding, the text is 12px further over due to the left border. The `<a>` element is inheriting padding from a previous rule and adding the border's 12px to it. To figure out where that padding is coming from, use the Summary for selection pane at the top of the CSS panel. Hover over the padding property and Dreamweaver will show you a tool tip that says the 30px of left padding is coming from the `ul.MenuBarVertical a` rule. (`padding: 0.5em 0em 0.5em 30px;`)

We need to create the proper amount of space by subtracting the 12px of left border from the 30px of left padding. That gives us 18px of left padding necessary for this selector.

5. Add `padding-left: 18px` to the rule:

```
ul.MenuBarVertical a#selected {
    font-weight: bold;
    color: #FFF;
    background: #000;
    border-left: 12px solid #AD2027;
    padding-left: 18px; }
```

6. Save the CSS file (and index page, if necessary).

As we add the Spry menu to subsequent pages within the site, we'll change the menu element to which the **selected** class applies to reflect this feedback for the visitor.

And with that, the index page of the site is complete.

FIGURE 6.19 The properly aligned Spry Menu Bar.

A Word about Accessibility, JavaScript and Progressive Enhancement

You probably noticed that the fly-out portion of the menu is relying upon JavaScript to function. That's no surprise—the "J" in Ajax stands for JavaScript! But what about visitors who, for whatever reason, do not have JavaScript capabilities—whether by choice, such as those who turn it off, or by necessity, such as users who rely upon screen readers with limited or no JavaScript support?

In the first versions of the Spry framework, Adobe didn't have an answer: if JavaScript was turned off in the browser, the experience was over—any content that relied upon JavaScript was not delivered to the page. But as we'll see, version 1.6 of the Spry framework addresses these concerns with some, in our opinion, pretty incredible enhancements.

The Spry Menu Bar that we've just implemented continues to function even with no JavaScript present, because only the fly-out portion is controlled via JavaScript. The Artists entry in the menu is linked to artists.html, so visitors without JavaScript can click the link and be directed to the artists page, bypassing the fly-out menu. The artist's page would simply need to make it possible to move on to either the painters or sculptors pages by providing links to them. (Most visitors will choose from the flyout menu and never click on the artist's page link at all, so the fact that it simply contains links to the submenu pages is a good accessibility feature to add.)

This approach is called **progressive enhancement**. We start with a basic, functioning page for all visitors. From there, we build (enhance) the page with additional functionality or interactivity for those users whose browser agent is able to support it.

The bottom line and our mantra must always be "no one gets left behind"!

Combining Two CSS Layouts for Use in a Single Site

The majority of the remaining pages within the site will rely upon the basic two-column layout already established for the index page. However, our designer wants a three-column layout for the artist_detail pages that highlight an individual artist's work.

Of course it's always nice when we don't have to start completely from scratch as we start to work on a new page layout of our site. We've already done a lot of work. Since Dreamweaver CS3's CSS layouts were designed to be easily combined, we'll really only need to worry about elements specific to this single page!

1. Create a new (X)HTML page, selecting the 3 column hybrid, header and footer CSS layout as a XHTML 1.0 Transitional doctype.

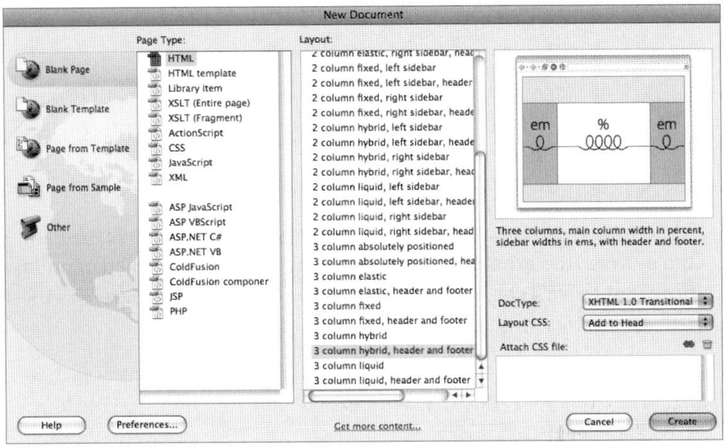

FIGURE 6.20 The basis for this page in the site will be a 3 column hybrid layout with a header and footer.

N *Notice that there's an option in the bottom right corner of the dialog to attach the new document to an existing CSS file. Wouldn't you think that we could attach the mainStyles.css file that we've already created and have a good starting point to continue modifying the page? Unfortunately, this would give us some... uh... unexpected results. (Go ahead—try it. Told you!)*

When you specify "Link to existing file" in the drop-down list, you are telling Dreamweaver that you don't need any of the CSS that would normally be associated with the file. That's a little more than we wanted to do!

In order to combine (our terminology for using the CSS from two distinct CSS layouts) two layouts, we'll need a different strategy.

2. Leave the Layout CSS drop-down list in the New Document dialog set to Add to Head.

3. Click the Attach Style Sheet icon in the lower right corner of the dialog and navigate to your mainStyles.css file.

4. Click OK to create the file and go ahead and save it in your site structure as artist_detail.html.

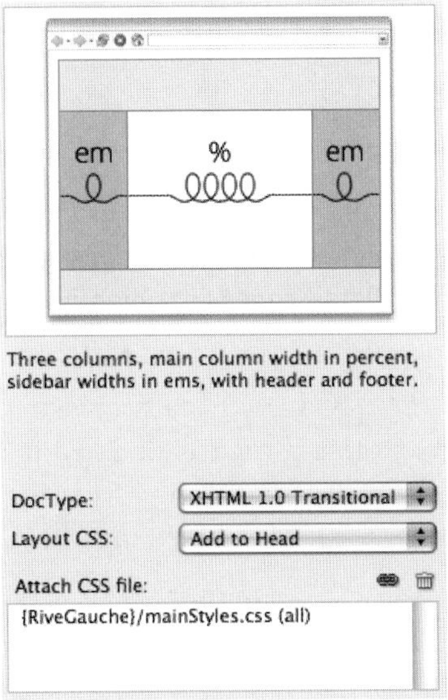

FIGURE 6.21 We can attach an external style sheet to the page while placing the default CSS for the layout in the head of the document.

5. Switch to the All view in the CSS panel. Expand the individual style sheet groupings by clicking the toggle.

Notice that we now have a link to both the mainStyles.css and the `<style>` block in the head of the document containing the default CSS styles that belong to the 3-column layout.

Scroll through the list of CSS rules. Notice anything? Each layout contains basically the same rules. They're simply modified through the specific body class indicating the given layout type. Remember, by default each `<body>` element has a class attached to it that declares what type of page it is.

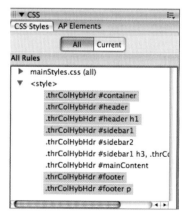

We're going to simplify our styles. It's not as scary as it sounds. You should remember that all the CSS layouts have the same div naming conventions and contain the same basic components. We'll walk you through the process of determining which ones to keep and which can be deleted.

Let's take a closer look. We have a rule for the container element in both the external mainStyles.css file and the internal CSS styles in the header. But the two rules could differ because each is specific to a defined class: `.twoColHybLtHdr #container` and `.thrColHybHdr #container`.

While we could easily append all of our internal styles to the external style sheet (and many people do), it's not a best practice. It results in duplication, more rules to manage than needed, more complicated upkeep and a larger physical file size for user agents.

Let's start by deleting a number of duplicate rules that don't have the extra specificity.

You might have just noticed a change to your page—the body text changed when we deleted the embedded body rule, because it has now taken on the values defined for the body element in the external style sheet. An embedded style always overrides an external rule with equal specificity!

1. In the All mode of the CSS panel, right-click on the following rules in the `<style>` section (the embedded rules) and choose Delete: `body`, `.fltrt`, `.fltlft` and `.clearfloat`.

FIGURE 6.22 There are still a number of redundant embedded rules that we need to remove.

This leaves us with nine embedded rules. But again, we've got some redundancy. We have a specific rule defined for the two column layout's container element giving the values we decided on for the home page. Since the container for both pages should be the same—we want both pages to fill the browser window, have the same background color, etc., we'll remove the page-specific prefix so that it will apply to all our pages.

2. In the All mode, click the name for the `.twoColHybLtHdr #container` rule in mainStyles.css so that it is editable. Rename the rule `#container`, and delete the `.thrColHybHdr #container` rule from the embedded (`<style>`) styles.

   The header, sidebar1 and footer elements will also be the same for all of our pages.

3. Repeat the process above for all rules in mainStyles.css that relate to the header, footer, and sidebar1 since they'll be the same on all our pages. Delete the same rules from the `<style>` block in the three column page.

   If you look at the embedded styles left on the page, you'll notice a compound selector that includes both sidebar1 and sidebar2 rules.

4. Remove the #sidebar1 rules altogether since they're already defined in the linked CSS file. If you like, you can even remove the prefix for the #sidebar2 rules that are left since the two column pages won't include a sidebar2. This simply leaves: `#sidebar2 p, #sidebar2 h3`

   Check the index.html page to make sure that everything still looks the same. If it's still looking good, we know that our modifications to the specificity of our rules haven't had any effect on our original page.

   You should, however, already be noticing several differences to our new artist_detail.html page. There are some spacing differences as well as red borders below the header and above the footer.

5. Finally let's move the remaining three embedded rules into mainStyles.css by shift-selecting the three rules in the All

Notice there are two compound selectors for the side-bars here—one for each layout. You may want to switch to the CSS file to edit this by hand instead of using the CSS panel as Dreamweaver can get a little quirky with the code it can't display in the panel.

mode of the CSS panel and dragging them up to the main-Styles.css area.

6. Click to select the `<style>` element in the All mode of the CSS panel and delete it.

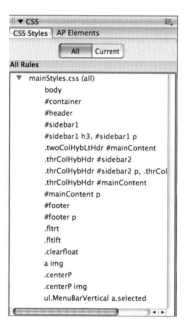

FIGURE 6.23 Our consolidated styles—notice that only a few are specific to a two column or three column layout.

We're now left with an optimized style sheet that works for both a two column and three column hybrid layout.

Common Page Elements in a Flash!

Our next step is perhaps the fastest (and maybe most enjoyable) step in the process—we'll use good old copy/paste to grab the common elements from the index page for the artist_detail page.

1. Switch back to (or open) index.html and select the header element by placing the cursor in the header and clicking `<div#header>` in the tag selector.

2. Choose Edit > Copy and then switch back to artist_detail.html and select its header element using the tag selector.

When copying a Spry menu into a new page, Dreamweaver is smart enough to add links to the JavaScript and CSS files needed. You may, however, find both the vertical and horizontal CSS files included. Dreamweaver includes both since the UI wasn't used to insert the menu. It really doesn't know which menu style is desired.

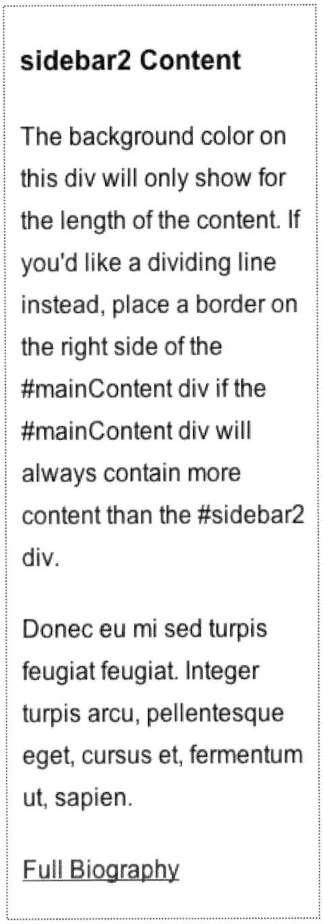

sidebar2 Content

The background color on this div will only show for the length of the content. If you'd like a dividing line instead, place a border on the right side of the #mainContent div if the #mainContent div will always contain more content than the #sidebar2 div.

Donec eu mi sed turpis feugiat feugiat. Integer turpis arcu, pellentesque eget, cursus et, fermentum ut, sapien.

Full Biography

FIGURE 6.24 The sidebar needs some work to match our comp.

T Be very careful when creating a rule when you have more than one style sheet attached to a page. Dreamweaver usually suggests the last style sheet that you've worked with, but not always—especially if you've just linked a new style sheet. Check and double check where the rule is being placed to be sure it's being added to the right style sheet We'll continue to add ours to the mainStyles.css.

3. Choose Edit > Paste to replace its contents with the contents copied from index.html.

4. Repeat the process for the `<div#sidebar1>` and `<div#footer>`.

Now that was easy!

Styling Sidebar2

Before we move into the more complicated (but fun) part of the page, let's get the sidebar2 area properly styled. This area provides details about the particular artist, their bio, and so on.

By default, the sidebar2 div has a width of 11em. Since this is too narrow, we'll widen it, remembering this will require tweaks to the mainContent area as well since it has margins on both the left and right sides.

1. Click to place the cursor into sidebar2 and switch to the Current mode of the CSS panel. Select `#sidebar2` in the Rules section of the CSS panel and change the width property to `13em`.

2. Remove the background property and modify the padding to have a value of 0.

   The `h3` is still not as far up as we'd like, so we'll create a rule to override the default margin of the `h3`.

3. Click the New CSS Rule button in the CSS panel and create a rule for `#sidebar2 h3` with a margin-top of 0.

   We also need to decrease the font-size of the text in sidebar2.

4. Create a rule for `#sidebar2 p` and set the `font-size` to `0.8em` to match the rest of the text on our page.

   Each short description of the artist is designed to end with a link to their full biography.

5. Place the cursor at the end of the text in sidebar2 and then press Return to create a new paragraph. Type the words Full biography, select the text and add a # link in the link field of the Properties Inspector.

N   *Visitors expect links to have underlines, so we'll leave the underline style on the links on our page.*

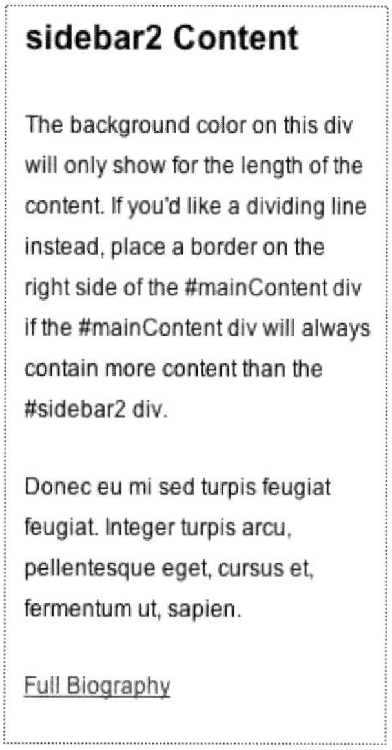

---

sidebar2 Content

The background color on this div will only show for the length of the content. If you'd like a dividing line instead, place a border on the right side of the #mainContent div if the #mainContent div will always contain more content than the #sidebar2 div.

Donec eu mi sed turpis feugiat feugiat. Integer turpis arcu, pellentesque eget, cursus et, fermentum ut, sapien.

Full Biography

FIGURE 6.25 The finished sidebar2 element.

We've used a hash mark to cause the text to render as a link since we won't be creating a page for this. Our new link is the traditional blue, underlined text. But the color doesn't really fit in with our design.

9. Create a new rule **a**.

   We want all text links in the site to take on this style, so the rule has no specificity.

10. Set the color for the rule to **#AD2027** to match the red we've been using throughout the site.

    As you know, any time we modify the width of a sidebar—as we've done here—we need to adjust the margins of the main-Content div.

11. Place the cursor in the mainContent area and use the CSS panel to adjust the margins for the **#mainContent** rule to **0 13em 30px 13em**.

    We've matched the 13em left margin that we also used in the index page's mainContent area.

And with that, we're ready to concentrate upon the picture gallery content for the artist_detail.html page!

Building the Gallery—Part One

The layout of this page needs to be flexible enough to accommodate artists with both large and small portfolios. Our approach will use a welcome new feature within Spry 1.6 that draws upon the page's content and "repurposes" it with additional functionality.

This method takes advantage of our "no one gets left behind" mantra and we'll start by finishing the page design as older browsers and non-JavaScript-enabled browsers will experience it.

1. Delete the content of the mainContent div.

2. Switch to the Common section of the Insert panel and click the Insert Div Tag tool to insert a `<div>`.

3. Type gallery into the ID field and click OK.

This div will hold an individual image and its corresponding title, artist name and price, but we don't need to establish any properties for the div as it will, by default, fill the width of the mainContent element.

Within the image folder in this site, you'll find a number of images entitled IMAGENAME_thumb.jpg. Each of these images has been optimized to a maximum width or height of 138 pixels, making it easier for us to create an appropriately sized container.

4. Delete the placeholder text "Content for id 'gallery' Goes Here" and then click the Insert Div Tag again to add a nested div.

5. Click the New CSS Style button to create the rule for the nested div. Give the rule a name of `.galleryItem`, once again adding it to mainStyles.css.

6. Within the New CSS Rule dialog, specify the following properties and values for the rule:

```
.galleryItem {
    width: 16em;
    float: left;
    padding: 6px;
    border: solid 1px #AD2027; }
```

7. Click OK to create the rule and click OK again to create the div. Select all inside the div and delete the placeholder text.

8. Click the Image tool in the Insert panel or use the menu Insert > Image command. Choose one of the _thumb images— your choice. Add an appropriate alternative text for the image.

9. With the image selected on the page, add a link to the high-resolution version of the image also located in the images folder of the site.

10. Leaving the image still selected, press the right arrow key to position the cursor immediately after the image and then press the Return key to add a `<p>` element.

11. In separate paragraph elements, add a title for the image, the artist's name, the price, and the filename of the high-resolution version of the picture (the name without the _thumb attached).

First Shot

Gabriele Koenig

$1350

7022.jpg

FIGURE 6.26 The ‹div. galleryItem› will be our basic building block for this section of the page.

The completed HTML code for the div looks like this:

```
<div class="galleryItem">
  <p><a href="images/7022.jpg"><img src="images/7022_
thumb.jpg" width="138" height="97" /></a></p>
  <p>First Shot</p>
  <p>Gabriele Koenig</p>
  <p>$1350</p>
  <p>7022.jpg</p> </div>
```

Our basic (X)HTML is here, but obviously we need to add a bit of styling to the contents of the ‹div.galleryItem›.

12. Create a new class .thumbnail and add it to mainStyles.css with the following attributes:

```
.thumbnail {
  width: 144px;
  float: left;
  height: 140px;
  margin: 0;
  text-align: center; }
```

This class will float the `<p>` element containing the image to the left of the text. Notice that we've specified `text-align: center` to cause the images to center themselves within the defined 144px width.

13. Click to select the image in the `<div.galleryItem>` and use the tag selector to select the `<p>` element surrounding it. Apply the `.thumbnail` class to the `<p>` element.

    For the text about each image, we'll use three classes; `.pictureTitle`, `.pictureArtist` and `.picturePrice`.

14. Create three rules with the following properties, adding them to mainStyles.css:

```
.pictureTitle {
  font-size: .9em;
  font-weight: bold;
  padding-bottom: 0.8em;
  margin: 0;
  line-height: 1.2em; }
.pictureArtist {
  font-style: italic;
  padding: 0;
  margin: 0; }
.picturePrice {
  padding: 0;
  margin: 0; }
```

15. Apply the rules to their corresponding `<p>` elements—leaving only the last `<p>` unstyled.

FIGURE 6.27 The `<div. galleryItem>` element— almost finished.

The final `<p>` element contains the filename of the high-resolution version of the image. We'll be using this as we begin to progressively enhance the page, but for now it serves no purpose on the page so we should prevent it from being seen by the browser.

We can either use `display:none` or position the element off screen as we did with the fly-out menu. Since there's no reason for assistive technologies to see the name of the files, we'll prevent it from rendering entirely, using `display:none`.

16. Create a rule `.pictureHirez`:

```
.pictureHirez {
  display: none; }
```

17. Apply the `.pictureHirez` class to the paragraph.

You should see the paragraph and its contents "disappear" from the page.

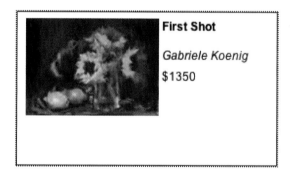

FIGURE 6.28 Let the cloning begin—we'll simply duplicate the `<div.galleryItem>` for each picture in the portfolio.

We've now established the basic building block that we'll duplicate to accommodate as many images as are present in the artist's portfolio. Go ahead and make a few copies, giving them whatever names and prices you like. We chose to use six images.

N *If you're using a dynamic language like ColdFusion or PHP to pull the information into your page, that works perfectly here as well. You'll simply place the code for the repeating regions into the classes we've had you build and the HTML dataset will be created dynamically.*

All set? Notice that the bottoms of the last frames are sitting directly on top of the footer even though we specified that the mainContent element should have a 30px bottom border. Hmm…

Take a look at the code for the `.galleryItem` rule again. One line should jump out at you:

```
.galleryItem {
  width: 16em;
  float: left;
  padding: 6px;
  border: solid 1px #AD2027;
}
```

Pop quiz time—what happens to a container when all of its contents are floated? Since the `<div.galleryItem>` elements are all floated, the mainContent element has no way to know when to grow vertically and in turn, when to apply the 30px of bottom margin to push the footer away from its contents.

We need to clear the element in order to push the footer away.

1. Add a `<br>` immediately preceding the `</div>` tag for the `<div. gallery>` element and assign the `.clearfloat` class to the `<br>`.

The final few lines of the code look like this:

```
<div class="galleryItem">
 <p class="thumbnail"><a href="images/7087.jpg"><img
src="images/7087_thumb.jpg" width="109" height="138" /></
a></p>
  <p class="pictureTitle">Tournesols</p>
  <p class="pictureArtist">Gabriele Koenig</p>
  <p class="picturePrice">$1850</p>
  <p class="pictureHirez">7087.jpg</p>
  </div>
  </div>
  <br class="clearfloat" />
  </div>
  <!-- This clearing element should immediately follow the
#mainContent div in order to force the #container div to
contain all child floats -->
  <br class="clearfloat" />
  <div id="footer">
```

If Dreamweaver prompts you about the JavaScript files that need to be copied into the site structure, click OK.

2. Save the mainStyles.css and the artist_detail.html page.

Preview the artist_detail.html page in a standards-compliant browser. You should be able to re-size the browser viewport and have your galleryItem elements reflow according to the available space on the page.

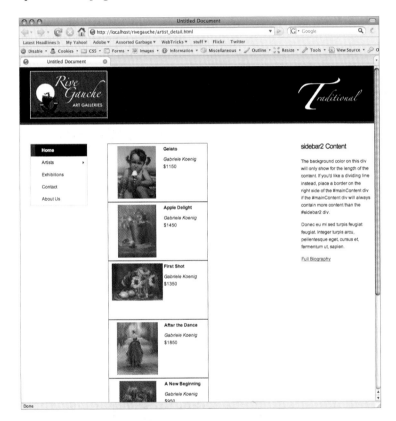

FIGURE 6.29 If we make the browser too narrow, our page doesn't look as good.

But we don't want the page to become too unsightly. Let's limit this functionality to keep the page from being collapsed to a point where we only have one galleryItem on a row.

1. Place the cursor in the mainContent element and select the `#container` rule from the Rules section of the CSS panel.

You'll notice it already contains the min-width rule from our home page.

2. Create a new selector called `.thrColHybHdr #container` and give it a minimum width property: `min-width: 64em`.

   The single `#container` rule will apply to all pages and the descendant selector we just created will override only the min-width property on the three column pages.

3. Save the mainStyles.css file and preview the artist_detail.html again in a standards-compliant browser. Notice that you can no longer make the page too narrow to accommodate the images.

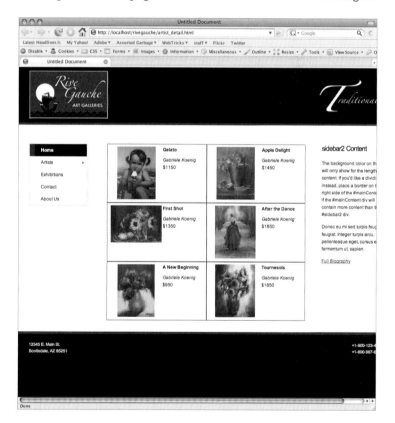

FIGURE 6.30 With a min-width in place, we are assured of having a nice layout even with a narrow browser window.

Progressive Enhancement—
Making the Gallery "Cool"

We now have a nice looking page, regardless of the capabilities of the visitor's browser. Of course, our example only uses six images. Imagine if an artist had a bigger portfolio—say, 12 or 20 pictures or even more. The more images, the more a visitor would need to scroll.

The solution: a progressive enhancement to our page, thanks to the Spry framework. To reiterate, a progressive enhancement builds upon the core functionality of a page, adding features that will be available to advanced browsers, while ensuring that the stage still functions for less capable browsers. Now that we have the core functionality in place, we'll add a different method of displaying the gallery of images.

FIGURE 6.31 Our page (as seen in Firefox) with a Spry Sliding Panels widget to reveal the gallery images.

N *If you've not already done so, please do not pass "go" or read another word without downloading the newest version of the Spry framework for Ajax from labs. adobe.com.*

N *As you explore the Spry capabilities of Dreamweaver CS3, bear in mind that the new features of Spry 1.6 are not visually accessible within Dreamweaver CS3, even after updating Dreamweaver via the downloadable extension. You won't see any icons that represent these tools, and you must use Code view by hand to work with the new features. To explore the use of the visual features of Dreamweaver's support for XML DataSets, we encourage you to check out the excellent articles on Adobe's Developer Connection website at www.adobe.com/devnet.*

The Spry Sliding Panels widget lets us display an unlimited number of images in a limited space. Instead of a link that opens a larger version of an image (as is the case now), even the detail image gets displayed in the page—and without a single page refresh!

In Spry 1.6, we can use an **HTML DataSet** to instruct the browser to read (X)HTML as its data source. This provides us an incredible amount of flexibility because, after all, we're already designing with (X)HTML.

Our particular page is already laid out as standards-compliant (X) HTML and CSS. We'll leverage that page structure, by using it as our data source for our progressive enhancement.

Creating an HTML Data Set

The enhancement that we've already made to the page using the Spry Menu Bar has made some additions to our code. Let's take a quick look at that.

1. Switch to Code view and scroll to the top of the document.

2. Locate the code just above the closing `</head>` tag:

    ```
    <script src="SpryAssets/SpryMenuBar.js" type="text/
    javascript"></script>
    <link href="SpryAssets/SpryMenuBarVertical.css"
    rel="stylesheet" type="text/css" />
    ```

    When we saved our page(s) earlier, Dreamweaver informed us that it would need to copy some files into our site structure. These files were the JavaScript file for our menu, providing its functionality, as well as the CSS that defined the look of the menu.

    Dreamweaver also added a `<script>` tag to link to the JavaScript file and a `<link>` tag attaching the CSS for the menu to our document.

    For our soon-to-be-created Spry Sliding Panels widget, we need to tell the browser what to display in the sliding panel: this information composes our dataset. We'll also tell the browser to load a JavaScript file provided as a part of the Spry framework, in order for it to read and understand the dataset.

N   *As of this writing, the zip file expands as a folder entitled Spry_P1_6_10-01.*

3.   Locate the Spry framework folder that you downloaded from labs.adobe.com. Inside this folder, you will find a folder named "includes."

The includes folder contains many of the JavaScript files for the Spry framework. Keep this folder handy as we'll need several of these files.

4.   Locate the files SpryHTMLDataSet.js, SpryData.js and SpryDOMUtils.js in the includes folder. Copy these files into the SpryAssets folder in your local site.

5.   In the main level of the Spry_P1_6_10-01 folder, open the widgets folder and locate the slidingpanels folder.

6.   In the slidingpanels folder, locate the file SprySlidingPanels.js and copy it to the SpryAssets folder within your local site.

With the JavaScript files now in our local site structure, we need to tell the browser to use these files.

N   *While writing this chapter, we ran into an issue in which nothing seemed to work from here on—in testing the page, the Spry information was not processed. On our system (Mac OS X, 10.5), the problem was a permissions issue on the SpryAssets folder. Changing the permissions to Read & Write for all users using the Get Info command resolved the issue.*

7.   Add the following lines of code to the <head> of the document immediately preceding the </head> tag:

```
<script src="SpryAssets/SpryData.js" type="text/
javascript"></script>
<script src="SpryAssets/SpryHTMLDataSet.js" type="text/
javascript"></script>
<script src="SpryAssets/SpryDOMUtils.js" type="text/
javascript"></script>
<script src="SpryAssets/SprySlidingPanels.js" type="text/
javascript"></script>
```

T   *Be sure if your site definition is set up differently than ours that the path to your SpryAssets folder is properly defined in the links you just pasted in. If you aren't sure, look at the paths used by Dreamweaver when it inserted the link to the JavaScript for the Spry menu.*

In the preceding code, the first JavaScript file, SpryData. js, is responsible for processing the data. The second file, SpryHTMLDataSet.js, creates the dataset and passes it to the SpryData.js file. The third file, SpryDOMUtils.js, will be used a bit later. Finally, the fourth file, SprySlidingPanels.js, provides the sliding panels functionality we're about to implement.

We can now tell the browser to build a dataset using a particular item or items on the page as our source data.

8. Add the following lines of code to the `<head>` of the document immediately following the code from the previous step:

```
<script type="text/javascript"> <!--
var ds1 = new Spry.Data.HTMLDataSet(null, "gallery",
{rowSelector:"div.galleryItem", dataSelector:"p",
columnNames:["Thumbnail", "PictureTitle", "Artist",
"Price", "HiRez"]}); //--> </script>
```

As you can no doubt tell, we're writing JavaScript. The first part of the script `var ds1` is telling the browser to create a variable named `ds1`. We're then telling the browser that this variable will be a HTML dataset that will be processed by the Spry framework.

A Spry HTML dataset is built using several parameters, which are listed in the parentheses. The first parameter, `null`, defines the HTML page to be used as the source of the rest of the parameters. In our case, `null` says "use the page that we are currently on." The second parameter, `gallery`, defines the HTML element that will contain the data. We're telling the browser to find the element with an ID of `gallery`.

The curly brackets provide additional processing options for the selected HTML object. By default, a Spry HTML dataset looks for a `<table>` element, but it isn't limited to using a table. When using a table, the framework processes the rows and columns of the table as the contents of the dataset, using the first row (usually a row of table headers, or `<th>` elements) as the column names of the dataset. But we've just told the browser to look for an element with an ID of `gallery`, and that's a `<div>`. Because we aren't using a table, we need to explain to the browser what elements make up the "rows" and what the "column names" should be.

So, the first parameter in the curly brackets, `rowSelector:"div.galleryItem"`, indicates to the browser that it should look within the `<div#gallery>` element and use each occurrence of a `<div>` with a class of `galleryItem` as a row of data.

The next parameter, `dataSelector:"p"`, defines each `<p>` element within the `<div.galleryItem>` as a piece of data (a column).

Finally, `columnNames:["Thumbnail", "PictureTitle", "Artist", "Price", "HiRez"]` defines the names of the columns that we use to reference the data. It is important to note that the number of column names must be identical to the number of data elements

For more information about using HTML as a source for dynamic data—or even using XML as a data source—spend some time reading the Spry framework documentation and looking at the examples, all included in the zip file you downloaded earlier.

(defined by the **dataSelector**) contained within the row element. In our case, we have five **<p>** elements in each **<div.galleryItem>** element, so we've defined five column names that correspond, namely **thumbnail**, **pictureTitle**, **pictureArtist**, **picturePrice**, and **pictureHirez**.

A Quick Sanity Check

Before moving on, let's make sure that our page works. We won't actually use the following bit of code in our final page, but it's sure nice to know that we've gotten the groundwork done properly.

1. In Code view, locate the start of the mainContent div.

2. Add a **<p>** element immediately before the opening **<div id="gallery">** tag.

3. Add **spry:region="ds1"** as an attribute of the **<p>** element:

`<p spry:region="ds1"></p>`

4. Place your cursor within the content area of the **<p>** element and type "**{PictureTitle}**":

`<p spry:region="ds1">{PictureTitle}</p>`

The attribute **spry:region** tells the browser that the contents of this element will be processed by the Spry framework, and to use the declared dataset as the source for the dynamic content—in this case the dataset name is **ds1**.

In order to identify exactly what piece of content of the element is dynamic, the Spry framework uses the {} notation. In other words, when it sees a set of curly brackets, it looks into the corresponding dataset to find a piece of data with this name (the column name). In this example, we're telling it to find the first row of data in the dataset ds1 and display the piece of that data identified as PictureTitle.

5. Save the artist_detail.html page and preview it in a standards-compliant browser.

You might have been shocked when you saw your page—providing everything worked for you. If you didn't get a result like that in Figure 6.32, check to make sure that you have, in fact, copied the

JavaScript files into the SpryAssets folder—and make sure that the permissions on your folder are set to Read & Write.

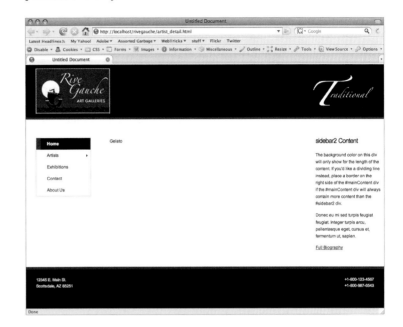

FIGURE 6.32 The Spry framework has successfully enhanced the page, so we know everything is working properly.

What happened to the page content that we had before? We're only seeing a piece of text where we previously had our nice gallery of images. This is the essence of a progressive enhancement to the page. Because we are using a standards-compliant browser capable of processing the JavaScript, the Spry framework has removed the element on the page identified as our HTML dataset and rendered only the result of the processing—in our case a single `<p>` element with the name of the first data item.

The Spry Sliding Panels widget

Now that we know that everything is working, we can add the Spry Sliding Panel widget to the page.

The Spry Sliding Panel widget is simply a div which contains panels (actually nested div elements) that slide either vertically or horizontally to reveal themselves within the confines of the declared width and height of the parent div.

All Spry widgets have a defined structure that must be adhered to. Check the Spry documentation for a description of the structure of each widget. For the Spry Sliding Panels widget the structure is as follows:

```
<div id="slidingGallery" class="SlidingPanels">
  <div id="galleryContentGroup" class="SlidingPanelsContent
Group">
    <div id="panelContents" class="SlidingPanelsContent">
    [contents of the panel]
    </div>
  </div> </div>
```

In other words, the widget is made up of three nested `<div>` elements. The first `<div>` identifies the bounding box of the visible overall panel area on the page. The second `<div>` identifies the bounding box of the contents within the panel that will be sliding. If this `<div>` element's width matches the width of the first `<div>`, the elements within it will slide vertically. If its width is wider than the first `<div>`, contents will slide horizontally until they reach the edge of their bounding box and then begin to slide vertically. Don't worry if this doesn't seem clear right now, we'll experiment with these values in a minute.

The third `<div>` is the actual contents of an individual pane or piece of content. We'll repeat this `<div>` for the number of items that we wish to scroll through the panel.

All of this will become clear as we work our way through the next few steps—so let's build it!

Creating the Structure for the Spry Sliding Panels

1. Delete the `<p>` element that we added to the page for testing, and in its place add the following code:

```
<div id="slidingGallery" class="SlidingPanels">
  <div id="galleryContentGroup" class="SlidingPanelsConten
tGroup">
    <div id="panelContents" class="SlidingPanelsContent">
    </div>
  </div> </div>
```

We've already discussed the significance of this code, so we now need to define what the content of each of the panels will be.

2. Add the following code to be used as the contents of each panel:

```
<div id="slidingGallery" class="SlidingPanels">
 <div id="galleryContentGroup" class="SlidingPanelsContent
Group">
   <div id="panelContents" class="SlidingPanelsContent">
     <div class="galleryItem">
     <p class="thumbnail">{Thumbnail}</p>
     <p class="pictureTitle">{PictureTitle}</p>
     <p class="pictureArtist">{Artist}</p>
     <p class="picturePrice">{Price}</p>
     </div>
   </div>
 </div> </div>
```

We've defined a container that will hold each of the individual images and their related data. Notice that we used the same classes that we've already created—this saves time since we won't have to create any new rules for the panel's actual content.

FIGURE 6.33 The placeholder for our sliding panels in Design view.

If you were to check the page in the browser, you'd notice that it doesn't seem to be working—the new `<div>` element is simply sitting on the page along with all of the other content and no dynamic data is appearing. (It's okay—we know you want to do it, so go ahead and save the page and preview it in a standards-compliant browser!)

Our placeholders aren't being replaced because the browser doesn't understand that it needs to pass this area of the page to the Spry framework for processing. We need to add an attribute to the element to clue the browser in.

3. Switch back to Code view and add a `spry:region` attribute to the `<div#slidingGallery>` element:

```
<div id="slidingGallery" class="SlidingPanels"
spry:region="ds1">
```

4. Save the page again and preview it in the browser.

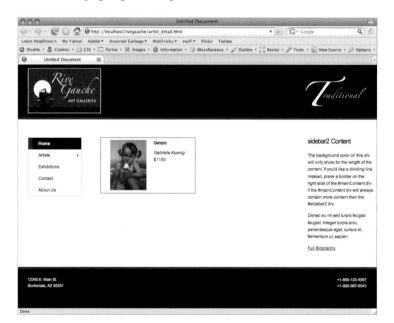

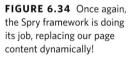

FIGURE 6.34 Once again, the Spry framework is doing its job, replacing our page content dynamically!

Okay, so things are working, but where's the rest of our content? Well, so far we have only told the Spry framework that we're interested in one item from the dataset, not all of the items. We need to instruct it to loop over the dataset and duplicate the `<div#panelContents>` element for each entry in the dataset. We do this using another Spry attribute known as repeat, telling it which dataset it should loop through.

5. Add the following code to the `<div#panelContents>` element:

```
<div id="panelContents" class="SlidingPanelsContent"
spry:repeat="ds1">
```

6. Save the page and preview it again in the browser.

Amazing! We're back to where we started—or so it seems... In reality, we're not looking at the same page. The data on the page has actually been generated dynamically via the Spry framework. But since we've not yet constrained the sliding panel area, the browser is simply repeating the individual items from the dataset down the page.

In order to constrain the items so that we can "slide" through them, we'll create some simple CSS classes.

8. Create a new rule for the `<div>` with an ID of `#slidingGallery`:

```
#slidingGallery {
    float: left;
    height: 160px;
    border: solid 1px #AD2027; }
```

This rule constrains the height of the sliding panel to 160px and places a red line around the area to give the visitor some visual feedback that this is a distinct page element.

9. Create a new rule for the `<div>` with the ID `#galleryContent-Group`:

```
#slidingGallery #galleryContentGroup {
    width: 1000em; }
```

This `<div>` defines how the content is sliding. We've set the width to 1000em to accommodate all of our panel items in a single line. Without this width defined, the items within the panel area would simply exhibit the standard wrapping effect that occurs when multiple left floated elements reach the side of their parent container—they would continue on on the next horizontal band.

10. Create a descendant selector for the `<div>` within the `#slidingGallery` with a class of `.SlidingPanelsContent`:

```
#slidingGallery .SlidingPanelsContent {
   float: left;
   width: 260px;
   height: 160px; }
```

This rule establishes the width and height of the individual sliding items within the panel.

We need to override some of the styling that we initially established for the galleryItem elements. We'll use a descendent selector.

11. Create a rule for the .galleryItem's contained within the slidingGallery:

```
#slidingGallery .galleryItem {
   border: none;
   width: 247px;
   height: 142px;
   padding-top: 12px;
   border-right: solid 1px #AD2021; }
```

Because we've already established a red border around the entire sliding panel area, we've removed the old border and are simply placing a right border to give a visual separation between the items. We're also overriding the width (previously 16em) and giving it a fixed pixel width. We've also assigned a fixed height to the items.

Finally, we need two classes defined with a relative position in order to make the widget work a bit later.

12. Create a compound rule as follows:

```
.SlidingPanels, .SlidingPanelsContentGroup {
   position: relative; }
```

You'll recognize the names of these classes as they were defined as part of the overall sliding panel structure. The SprySlidingPanels.js file looks for these classes in order to perform the sliding animation.

13. Save the page and preview it in the browser.

FIGURE 6.35 Umm… something's not quite right here.

Egad!!! What's going on with the page now?! Well, most of our CSS seems to have kicked in—our items are arranged in a single line and they've taken on the other defined properties, but they're running out of the page!

Before you throw the book out the window, calm down. The browser is simply doing its job. You see, while our CSS is working, we're missing one final element. We need to tell the Spry framework that it should hide any of the elements that do not fit within the defined panel area.

This is a built-in function of the Spry Sliding Panels widget— and we've not yet told the browser that one of these elements is on the page. Let's do that now. You'll recall that we created a link to the SprySlidingPanels.js file. We'll now instruct the browser to use this file to create the sliding functionality.

14. Back in Code view, scroll to the very bottom of the page.

You'll notice that "someone" has already added a JavaScript to the bottom of the page:

```
<script type="text/javascript"> <!--
var MenuBar1 = new Spry.Widget.MenuBar("MenuBar1",
{imgRight:"SpryAssets/SpryMenuBarRightHover.gif"}); //-->
</script>
```

This script was added to our page when we added the Spry Menu Bar. In fact, if you open up the index.html page, you'll find the same code at the bottom of that page.

The JavaScript is executed after the page completely loads in the browser—hence its position as the last element before the closing **<body>** tag. When placed within a page, the JavaScripts that create a Spry widget must be the last element processed by the browser.

15. Add the following line to the script:

```
<script type="text/javascript"> <!--
var MenuBar1 = new Spry.Widget.MenuBar("MenuBar1",
{imgRight:"SpryAssets/SpryMenuBarRightHover.gif"});
var sp = new Spry.Widget.SlidingPanels("slidingGallery");
//--> </script>
```

Once again, we're declaring a variable, this time named **sp**. This will be a new instance of a Spry.Widget.SlidingPanels. We then tell the Spry framework which unique (ID) element on the page will become a sliding panel.

16. Save the page and preview it in the browser.

FIGURE 6.36 Much nicer—now if we could figure out how to make the panels actually slide, we'd be really excited!

Now that looks a lot better, but you may have already asked yourself "Um, self, how do the panels slide?". Well, you're not crazy…
they don't slide. Or at least they don't slide yet. We need to establish some navigation to tell them how to slide.

Navigating Through a Sliding Panel

Head back over to the page in Dreamweaver's Code view and
locate the opening `<div#gallery>` tag.

1. Insert the following code between the closing `<div>` tag for
    the `#slidingGallery` element and the opening `<div>` tag of the
    `#gallery` element:

    ```
    <p id="panelNav" class="fltlft">
      <a href="#" id="firstPanel">First</a> |
      <a href="#" id="previousPanel">Previous</a> |
      <a href="#" id="nextPanel">Next</a> |
      <a href="#" id="lastPanel">Last</a> </p>
    ```

    We're going to use simple anchors (links) to control the scroll-
    ing of the sliding panels. While the Spry Sliding Panel widget
    allows us to move in steps, i.e. three or four items at a time,
    we've chosen to use a simple "first/previous/next/last" naviga-
    tion scheme. The next and previous links will move the panels
    forward or backward, one item at a time. The first and last
    links will slide the items back to the starting position or to the
    end of the items respectively.

    In order to make the Spry framework react to the clicking of
    the links, we'll need a bit more JavaScript—this time attached
    to each link itself.

2. Add the following `onclick` handlers to the links:

    ```
    <p id="panelNav" class="fltlft">
      <a href="#" id="firstPanel" onclick="sp.
    showFirstPanel(); return false;">First</a> |
      <a href="#" id="previousPanel" onclick="sp.
    showPreviousPanel(); return false;">Previous</a> |
      <a href="#" id="nextPanel" onclick="sp.showNextPanel();
    return false;">Next</a> |
      <a href="#" id="lastPanel" onclick="sp.showLastPanel();
    return false;">Last</a> </p>
    ```

An `onclick` handler is simply an inline JavaScript that tells the browser to do something when the link is clicked. In our case, we are calling out to the Spry Sliding Panels widget **sp** that we created in the script at the bottom of the page. We're telling it to execute one of those built-in functions for each click of the link(s).

3. Save the page and preview in the browser.

FIGURE 6.37 The functioning Spry Sliding Panel—a very cool enhancement to the page!

You have to admit, that's pretty cool!

Adding a Detail Image

In our non-JavaScript version of the page, each thumbnail has a link to the high-resolution version of the image. But we're still missing the ability to click the thumbnail and see the hi-rez version of the image in this JavaScript version of the page.

This relationship between the thumbnails and the hi-rez images is known as a master/detail relationship. We want the elements within the sliding panel to function as the master and when one of them is clicked, we want a detail area to react accordingly—in our case, to show us the image.

Do you remember the `<p>` element that simply contained the name of the high resolution version of the image? We hid this element from view using the `display:none` property, but it's time to use that element.

1. Create a `<div>` element above the `.slidinggallery`, but still inside the mainContent element and assign it an ID of `"detailArea"`:

   ```
   <div id="detailArea"> </div>
   ```

2. Create a `<div>` within this element to contain the detail image—assign it a class of `"detailImg"`:

   ```
   <div id="detailArea">
    <div class="detailImg"></div> </div>
   ```

3. Add an image element to the `<div.detailImg>` element along with a `<br>` element to clear the float:

   ```
   <div id="detailArea">
    <div class="detailImg"><img src="images/{HiRez}"
   alt="{PictureTitle}"  width="330" /><br class="clearfloat"
   /></div> </div>
   ```

   Notice that instead of identifying a specific image file, we've defined a Spry variable `{HiRez}`, which will tell the Spry framework to look at the dataset and figure out which element to display. Additionally, the alt attribute, using the `{PictureTitle}` variable, will dynamically generate an image name for accessiblity.

   We've also added a `clearfloat` class to the `<br>` element to push the content down the page based upon the height of the contents of the `<div.detailImg>`.

   We need to create a couple of rules to style these new elements.

When working with images it's usually best to define the container for the content with a fixed height. The reason for this is that the rest of the content on the page might have to shift due to the taller or shorter content. This can cause a "page flicker" very similar to a page refresh which sort of defeats the purpose of our Ajax (ie, no page refresh) approach. To see this for yourself, remove the height from the `#mainContent #detailArea` rule.

4. Create a new rule for the detailArea in mainStyles.css as follows:

```
#mainContent #detailArea {
    width: 40em;
    margin-right: auto;
    margin-left: auto;
    padding: 0px 0px 20px 0px;
    height: 460px;
    text-align: center; }
```

Let's "pretty-up" the detail image with a border.

5. Create a rule for the detail image itself:

```
#detailArea img {
    padding: 4px;
    margin: 0px 10px;
    border: solid 1px #AD2021; }
```

All that's left to do is to identify the elements that we've just created for the Spry framework, indicating that the image itself should change when a thumbnail is clicked.

We'll do this by adding two more Spry attributes to the page.

6. Add the `spry:detailregion` attribute to the detailArea:

```
<div id="detailArea" spry:detailregion="ds1">
```

The `spry:detailregion` attribute tells the Spry framework to look at the current dataset to determine what needs to be displayed on the page. This attribute works in conjunction with `spry:setrow` to find the "row" of data in which we are interested.

7. Add the `spry:setrow` attribute to the panelContents element:

```
<div id="panelContents" class="SlidingPanelsContent"
spry:repeat="ds1" spry:setrow="ds1">
```

8. Save the page and preview in the browser.

FIGURE 6.38 The detail image is placed above the sliding panel.

Raise your hand if it worked flawlessly… Hmm… nobody? Well, truth is, ours didn't work either. We have a detail image when we come to the page, but when we click upon another image in the sliding panel area, we're taken to the high resolution image itself. That's not right! But if we look at our code, it's logical.

```
<p class="thumbnail"><a href="images/7025.jpg"><img
src="images/7025_thumb.jpg" width="104" height="138" /></a></p>
```

As we created our dataset, we told the Spry framework to look at every `<p>` element within an individual `<div.galleryItem>`. The `<p>` element above contains our thumbnail image—but notice what is surrounding the image. It's an anchor (link). So, when we click upon the image, the browser is doing what it thinks is natural and taking us to the image file.

If we could just get the browser to ignore the anchor when we're looking at the spry version of the page...

Bet you saw this coming, "yes, Spry can provide this functionality too!"

One of the JavaScript files we added a link to was SpryDOMUtils. js. This collection of JavaScript methods allows us to manipulate the DOM (Document Object Model). In other words, we can add attributes, change attributes or remove attributes, change styles and much more. (See the Spry documentation for a complete list of its capabilities.)

We'll use a method called `removeAttribute` to remove the `href` attribute from the anchor when the page is viewed with JavaScript turned on.

1. Return to the page in Dreamweaver, and scroll to the bottom of the page. Add the following line to our script:

    ```
    <script type="text/javascript"> <!--
    var MenuBar1 = new Spry.Widget.MenuBar("MenuBar1",
    {imgRight:"SpryAssets/SpryMenuBarRightHover.gif"});
    var sp = new Spry.Widget.SlidingPanels("slidingGallery");
    Spry.$$(".thumbnail a").removeAttribute("href"); //--> </
    script>
    ```

    After the page is loaded into the browser, but before it actually renders, our script tells the browser to let the Spry framework find a selector on the page. In our case, it specifically says to find all of the `<a>` elements within an element with a class of `thumbnail`. Then the script instructs the browser to remove the specified attribute—in our case, the `href` attribute.

2. Save the page again and preview your masterpiece in the browser.

    Hopefully you're really excited now! But we're not quite finished...

Getting the Validation Gold Star

One of the primary criticisms from the web standards' community upon the initial release of the Spry framework for Ajax was the method in which Spry interactions happen within the page (including the methods we've implemented up to this point). Custom attributes and inline scripts, such as we've used, cause the page to fail when run through a validator. They make it easy to look at the page and understand what's happening, but the standards-approach is to separate presentation and content. In other words, JavaScript belongs in a external file, not embedded within the page.

Fortunately, the Spry team at Adobe implemented a method of development within Spry 1.6 known as **unobtrusive JavaScript**. In a nutshell, this approach puts all of the Spry functionality into an external JavaScript, leaving our page in its purest form. The result allows the page to validate just like any other well-structured XHTML and CSS document with all of our progressive enhancements occurring via this externally linked file.

So, to finish off our project, let's externalize our enhancements.

Creating an Unobtrusive JavaScript

Begin by creating a new JavaScript file.

1. Select File > New and choose JavaScript from the Document type column in the dialog.

2. Save the file into your site structure as externalJavaScript.js.

3. Switch back to the artist_detail.html page and scroll to the top of the document.

4. Locate the piece of JavaScript that we used to create our HTML dataset:

   ```
   var ds1 = new Spry.Data.HTMLDataSet(null, "gallery",
   {rowSelector:"div.galleryItem", dataSelector:"p",
   columnNames:["Thumbnail", "PictureTitle", "Artist",
   "Price", "HiRez"]});
   ```

5. Cut this line out of the document and then paste it into the externalJavaScript.js file. Leave the comment tags out, though.

When our externalJavaScript.js file is processed by the browser, it will create the dataset just as it did when it was in the page.

6. Remove the empty `<script type="text/javascript">` block from the document—and don't forget the closing `</script>` tag and the comments too.

We can now tell the browser to get ready to use the Spry utilities found in the SpryDOMUtils.js file.

7. Add the following code block to externalJavaScript.js:

```
Spry.Utils.addLoadListener(function() {
  });
```

This utility function is a **listener**—it listens for something to happen, and when the right something does, it executes the function.

Our listener is a `LoadListener`: it is listening for the loading of the page to complete. Upon loading the page, the browser will ask the LoadListener if it needs to do anything, and will then carry out the instructions we give it via the function.

8. Assign the `spry:region` and `spry:detailregion` attributes to the appropriate elements on the page by adding the following code to the function that we've just created: Spry.Utils. addLoadListener(function() {

```
  Spry.$$("#slidingGallery").setAttribute("spry:region",
"ds1");
  Spry.$$("#panelContents").setAttribute("spry:repeat",
"ds1");
  Spry.$$("#panelContents").setAttribute("spry:setrow",
"ds1");
  Spry.$$("#detailArea").setAttribute("spry:detailregion",
"ds1"); });
```

N *For the non-programmers among you, a function is nothing more than a block of code, or instructions, that get executed together.*

9. Switch back to the artist_detail.html page and remove the spry:region, spry:repeat, spry:setrow and spry:detailregion attributes from their respective elements leaving that area of our page as:

```
<div id="detailArea">
<div class="detailImg"><img src="images/{HiRez}"
width="330" /></div> </div>
<div id="slidingGallery" class="SlidingPanels">
   <div id="galleryContentGroup" class="SlidingPanels
ContentGroup">
      <div id="panelContents" class="SlidingPanelsContent">
```

10. Add the following lines to the function in externalJavaScript.js:

```
Spry.Utils.addLoadListener(function() {
Spry.$$("#slidingGallery").setAttribute("spry:region",
"ds1");
   Spry.$$("#panelContents").setAttribute("spry:repeat",
"ds1");
   Spry.$$("#panelContents").setAttribute("spry:setrow",
"ds1");
   Spry.$$("#detailArea").setAttribute("spry:detailregion",
"ds1");

   Spry.$$("#firstPanel").addEventListener("click",
function(){sp.showFirstPanel(); return false;}, false);
   Spry.$$("#previousPanel").addEventListener("click",
function(){sp.showPreviousPanel(); return false;}, false);
   Spry.$$("#nextPanel").addEventListener("click",
function(){sp.showNextPanel(); return false;}, false);
   Spry.$$("#lastPanel").addEventListener("click",
function(){sp.showLastPanel(); return false;}, false); });
```

Our external JavaScript now enables the clicking of the panel navigation links. You'll also notice that we have another listener eavesdropping on us. The EventListener, like the LoadListener, is listening for a defined event to occur. Within the parentheses you can see that we're defining the click event followed by another function. Or simply stated "listen for the visitor to click this link and then carry out the instructions".

11. Back in the artist_detail.html page, locate the links that we are using for the panel navigation and remove the **onclick** events from each of the anchors. You should be left with:

```
<p id="panelNav" class="fltlft">
  <a href="#" id="firstPanel">First</a> |
  <a href="#" id="previousPanel">Previous</a> |
  <a href="#" id="nextPanel">Next</a> |
  <a href="#" id="lastPanel">Last</a>  </p>
```

Finally, we'll pull the script out of the bottom of the page that we used to create the menu bar and sliding panel, and to remove the href attribute from the anchors around the thumbnails when we placed them in the sliding panels.

12. Scroll to the bottom of the page and locate the **<script>** block.

13. Cut the three lines of code from the script (then delete the remaining **<script>** block from the page) and paste it into the external JavaScript.

```
Spry.Utils.addLoadListener(function() {
Spry.$$("#slidingGallery").setAttribute("spry:region",
"ds1");
Spry.$$("#panelContents").setAttribute("spry:repeat",
"ds1");
Spry.$$("#panelContents").setAttribute("spry:setrow",
"ds1");
Spry.$$("#detailArea").setAttribute("spry:detailregion",
"ds1");
Spry.$$("#firstPanel").addEventListener("click",
function(){sp.showFirstPanel(); return false;}, false);
Spry.$$("#previousPanel").addEventListener("click",
function(){sp.showPreviousPanel(); return false;}, false);
Spry.$$("#nextPanel").addEventListener("click",
function(){sp.showNextPanel(); return false;}, false);
Spry.$$("#lastPanel").addEventListener("click",
function(){sp.showLastPanel(); return false;}, false);
var MenuBar1 = new Spry.Widget.MenuBar("MenuBar1",
{imgRight:"SpryAssets/SpryMenuBarRightHover.gif"});
var sp = new Spry.Widget.SlidingPanels("slidingGallery");
Spry.$$(".thumbnail a").removeAttribute("href"); });
```

We've now successfully moved the entire Spry-related functionality out of the page. All that's left is to "wire it up."

14. In order to tell the framework to do all the things in the function, we need to add a final line to the script before the closing "});":

```
Spry.Data.initRegions();
```

15. Save the JavaScript file.

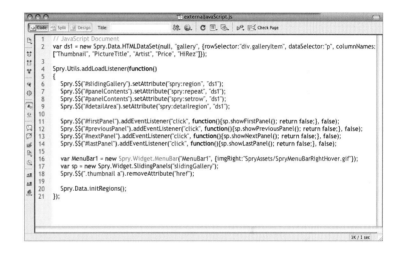

FIGURE 6.39 With all of the Spry functionality moved to an external file, we are almost ready to bill the client.

16. Scroll to the top of artist_detail.html where we have links to the external Spry JavaScripts such as SpryData.js.

17. Create a final link to the external JavaScript file:
```
<script src="externalJavaScript.js" type="text/
javascript"></script>
```

18. Save artist_detail.html and preview in the browser.

We are now able to run the artist_detail.html page through the W3C validator without errors, as all of the progressive enhancements have been completely removed from the actual HTML and CSS.

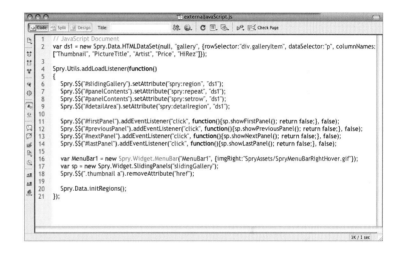 *If you want, you can go back to the index.html page and remove the Spry Menu Bar script from the bottom of the page. Then link the page to externalJavaScript. js as we've done in this section. That will ensure that index.html also will pass your validation tests.*

FIGURE 6.40 The artist detail page complete with all progressive enhancements delivered via an unobtrusive JavaScript.

Crossing the "T's" and Dotting the "I's"

At this point, you may think that we're finished—but before we reach for the champagne and party hats, what happens if we visit the page with JavaScript disabled in the browser, or with an older browser such as Internet Explorer 5.5, which we know can't interpret our more advanced JavaScript?

Let's find out…

 *If you are using Firefox, Chris Pederick has developed a widely-used extension known as the Web Developer's toolbar. This is an incredibly useful tool for any web designer/developer. It can be found at* http://chrispederick. com/work/web-developer/. *Using the toolbar, we can easily turn JavaScript off to see the effects on the page. A similar, and equally good extension, is Firebug by Joe Hewitt which can be found at* https://addons.mozilla.org/ en-US/firefox/addon/1843/.

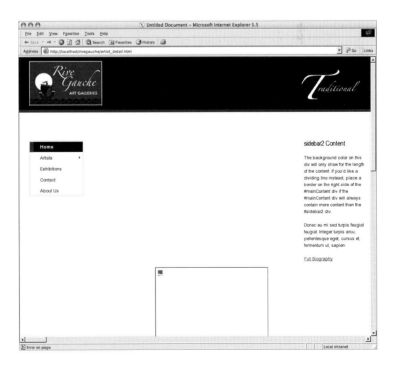

FIGURE 6.41 Our page doesn't look as good with JavaScript turned off!

FIGURE 6.42 The results in Internet Explorer 5.5 are equally disappointing.

Oh no! This is definitely not acceptable. Didn't we do all this work in order to deliver a satisfactory experience to visitors to the site that have no JavaScript capabilities?! The problem is that when the JavaScript isn't processed, the placeholders for our dynamically generated content are still visible on the page.

A couple of quick modifications can fix this.

1. Return to artist_detail.html in Dreamweaver and switch to Design view, where you might notice that the page is definitely looking a bit strange.

    Dreamweaver has no way of processing the JavaScript, so it's showing us pretty much what we saw with JavaScript turned off. Therefore, we'll use Design view to help us get the page looking better for those non-JavaScript enabled browsers.

    The simplest fix to our problem is to hide the dynamic areas when JavaScript is not enabled. And we can do that using CSS!

2. Click to select the detail image placeholder on the page and in the CSS panel's Rules section, select the `#mainContent #detailArea` selector.

3. Click the Add Property link in the Properties section and add `display:none` to its rule.

4. Do the same for the slidingGallery selector.

    This just leaves the `<p>` element that contains the panel's navigation. When we created the element, we assigned it an ID of `panelNav`.

5. Create a new rule in mainStyles.css for `panelNav` and assign its display property to **none**.

    ```
    #panelNav {
        display: none; }
    ```

6. Save mainStyles.css and preview artist_detail.html in Firefox with JavaScript disabled.

That's a much better result! The CSS has hidden the areas of the page that we aren't interested in seeing since they are only processed when JavaScript is enabled.

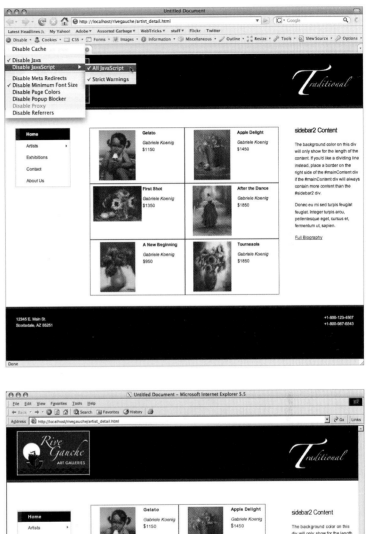

FIGURE 6.43 Now, that's more like it—the unprocessed dynamic areas are hidden from view.

FIGURE 6.44 An equally satisfying result in Internet Explorer 5.5!

As we begin to exhale and contemplate a "Tom Cruise on Oprah" moment, a final check of the page in Firefox, now with JavaScript enabled again, has us completely panicked!

FIGURE 6.45 The page is a bit too clean now! Where are the pictures?!

Because our CSS has hidden the Spry areas of the page, the browser has no way to know that we actually want to see them! Stupid browser!

1. Return to Dreamweaver and open the externalJavaScript.js file.

2. Add the following lines of code to the function above the `Spry.Data.initRegions();` line:

```
Spry.$$("#slidingGallery").
setStyle("display:block"); Spry.$$("#detailArea").
setStyle("display:block"); Spry.$$("#panelNav").
setStyle("display:block");
```

We're telling the Spry utilities that we used earlier to remove the `href` attribute to change the display property for our three selectors from **none** to **block**—allowing them to return to the page.

3. Save externalJavaScript.js and preview artist_detail.html in a standards-compliant browser with JavaScript enabled.

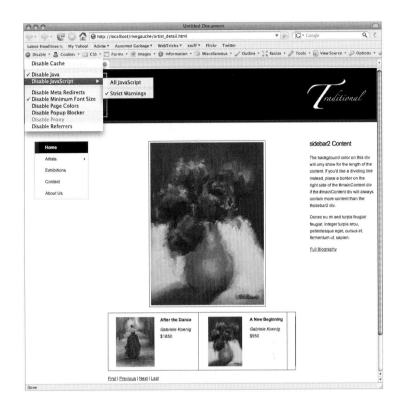

FIGURE 6.46 With the display property switched, we're back in business.

4. Our last step should really be to constrain the width of the page for Internet Explorer in order to avoid any weird float drop issues. Add the following lines of code to the IECC:

```
.thrColHybHdr #container {
  width: expression(Math.max((document.documentElement ?
document.documentElement.clientWidth : document.body.
clientWidth)/16, 1024/16)+'em');   }
#slidingGallery {width:99%;}
#mainContent #detailArea {width: 24em}
```

This constrains the page to the same width (64em) as we see in standards-compliant browsers. The rule for the #slidingGallery of 99% is to accommodate the 2px of border placed on the element. (You might remember that IE has a problem with a width set to 100% when there is a border present—it adds the width to the 100%.) Finally, we've created a rule to narrow the detailArea to fit into the allotted space when the page becomes narrow.

A Final Bit of Polish

As often happens—and you might have even noticed this already, while we were creating our menu—we forgot to double check its look against the look of the comp. Close inspection shows that we need a thin dotted line between the entries of the menu bar. Thankfully, this is an easy and quick fix.

1. Place your cursor in any of the entries in the menu and in the CSS panel, select the last `ul.MenuBarVertical` entry in the CSS cascade.

2. Change the border property to `border-top: 1px dotted #CCC`.

3. Add a bottom border to all of the entries in the list by adding `border-bottom: 1px dotted #CCC` to the `ul.MenuBarVertical li` rule.

4. Repeat the process for the flyout menu: `ul.MenuBarVertical ul` and `ul.MenuBarVertical ul li`.

5. We'll change the page indicator button by moving the ID #selected from the home button to the artist button.

We've zeroed the first element in both our side columns, so as discussed in chapter one, we no longer need the top padding for either of the side columns.

1. In both your artist_detail.html and index.html pages, remove the rules with the padding-top that are included by default with the CSS layouts.

   Be sure to keep the `zoom: 1` for the #mainContent rule.

2. Create a new CSS document called ie_fixes.css.

3. In the head of the artist_detail.html page, cut out the rules within the IECC and paste them into the new CSS documents. Remove the `<style>` block within the IECC.

4. In the head of the index.html page, do the same.

   You'll notice the `zoom: 1` rule is duplicated in both pages, but with each page's unique prefix. We only need one and it can apply to both pages.

T *One final suggestion— don't keep your Internet Explorer Conditional Comments (IECC) in the head of your document. Externalize them. This makes it much faster and easier to update them if you need to add some later. It's a simple process for our site since our IECC rules are all set to be seen by all current versions of Internet Explorer.*

T *Remember that the Spry engineers have no way to add an IECC to your page, so the IE fixes are left in the bottom of the style sheet. Anytime you can, remove them and place them in your IECC so your page will validate.*

5. Remove the prefix from either one of the `#mainContent` rules, and completely remove the other rule. You should be left with this: `#mainContent { zoom: 1; }`

6. Open the SpryMenuBarVertical.CSS and, at the very bottom, remove the section that begins with "BROWSER HACKS". Paste that into your ie_fixes.css document.

7. Finally, add the link to the CSS file you just created within each page's IECC:

```
<!--[if IE]>
<link href="ie_fixes.css" rel="stylesheet" type="text/css"
/>
<![endif]-->
```

8. Save the page and preview it in as many browsers as you want—you've created a beautiful layout that is progressively enhanced according to a browsers capabilities and which validates perfectly.

Now feel free to have that "Tom Cruise" moment! And thanks for spending what we're sure has been a lot of time with us—we hope you've learned a lot and had a fun time doing it!

Index

. (period), in class identifiers, 12, 28
(hash mark)
  in color values, 56
  in ID names, 12, 35
  in link field, 164, 219, 295–296
  in list items, 229
!important operator, 16
  character, 168
2 column fixed layout, 4
3 column liquid, header and footer layout, 156

A

a:active link state, 13, 89, 223
abbr attribute, 255
<abbr> tag, 255
absolute positioning, 26, 34–40, 65–67, 141
accent marks, 7
access keys, 242
accessibility
  and alt attribute, 161
  and data tables, 253, 256–258
  defined, 201
  designing for, 5, 199
  and em-based layouts, 210
  guidelines, 200
  importance of, 201
  and JavaScript, 290
Acme Internet Machines site, 105–153
  cleaning up nested tables in, 119–137
  CSS issues, 107–118
  index page, 106
  organizing footer for, 146–149
  rebuilding Member Login area for, 137
  rebuilding page header for, 138–144
  removing table markup from, 144–152
:active link state, 13, 88, 89, 223
:active pseudo class, 173–174
Adobe
  CSS Advisor site, 99, 167
  Fireworks. See Fireworks
  Photoshop. See Photoshop
Advanced selector type, 12–15, 223, 254
a:focus link state, 13, 89, 223

a:hover link state, 13, 89, 223
Ajax, 249, 263, 277, 290, 320
a:link link state, 13, 89
All mode, CSS Styles panel, 23
All Rules pane, CSS Styles panel, 23
alpha transparency, 78
alt attribute, 66, 161, 226
anchor styling, 88, 167–168
anchors, 88. See also links
anti-discrimination laws, 201
AP elements, 26, 142
Apply Source Formatting command, 59
arrow graphic, 188–189
art gallery site, 263–335
  building gallery page for, 296–303
  building initial framework for, 266–269
  combining CSS layouts for, 290–296
  comps for gallery pages, 265
  design requirements, 263
  main content area for, 269–276
  navigation for, 277–289
  original version of, 264
  positioning images for, 275–276
  progressive enhancement of, 304–322
  selecting starter layout for, 264–266
  styling sidebars for, 295–296
  validating, 323–335
articles
  box model, 21
  "Boxes in Columns," 44
  "Creating Liquid Faux Columns," 178
  inheritance/cascade/ specificity, 19
  "Practice of CSS Column Design," 44
  "Rendering Mode and Doctype Switching," 7
ASCII, 7
Assistive Technology, 5, 66, 226
Asynchronous JavaScript and XML, 277. See also Ajax
Attach Style Sheet command, 17

attributes, consolidating, 114–118
Attributes tab, Tag Inspector, 257
author style sheets, 15, 16–18, 169
auto margins, 42, 150
a:visited link state, 13, 89

B

background color, 53, 157, 160, 266
background images
  in faux columns, 60–61
  in fixed-width layouts, 59–64
  in headers, 160–161
  in liquid layouts, 160–161
  in sidebars, 60–61
  styling list using, 123
background property, 56, 61, 67, 218, 295
badge image, 183–185
Bergevin, Holly, 7, 21, 44
best practices, web site, 5. See also web standards
black background, 266, 288, 289
block elements, 7–8, 19
<blockquote> tag, 203, 232, 233, 234, 235
blogs, 47
body element, styling, 52–54
border property, 56, 69
box model, 19–21, 96–97
"Boxes in Columns" article, 44

 tags, 148–149
breaks, line, 148
browser chrome, 65
browser style sheets, 15, 16
browsers. See web browsers
bugs
  IE doubled margin, 167
  testing for common, 96–99
bulleted lists
  positioning, 130–131
  styling with CSS, 121–125
business principles, accessibility and, 201
buttons, styling anchors as, 167–168

C

capitalization, 115
caption element, 259
cascade, 15–18
Cascading Style Sheets, 5. *See also* CSS
centering layouts, 41–44, 59
Change Tag action, Find and Replace dialog, 120
character encoding, 6–7
character entities, 7
character sets, 6–7
Check Browser Compatibility feature, 98–99
Check Page icon, 98
Checkpoint 3.4, 200
cite attribute, 232
<cite> element, 231–232, 234
class identifiers, 28
"class-itis," 107, 112
class selectors, 11–12
classes
    finding and replacing, 108–109
    for layout types, 50
clear property, 29, 41
clearfloat class, 29–30, 83, 171
clearing elements, 29–31, 40–41, 83, 171
code comments, 55
code completion, 52
Code Format preferences, 58
code hinting, 52
code snippets. *See* snippets
ColdFusion, 300
color property, 23, 117, 206, 222
color shorthand, 161, 206
color values, determining, 158
columns
    with absolute positioning, 34–40
    clearing floated, 40–41
    creating faux, 59–61, 178
    evening, 93–94
    floating, 37–40
    modifying, in liquid layouts, 176
    percentage-based, 156
    rounding, 70–74
    tweaking, 180–182
comma-delimited lists, 222
comments, code, 55

Community MX
    box model article, 21
    IECC extension, 22, 80
    inheritance/cascade/ specificity article, 19
    liquid faux columns article, 178
    rendering mode/doctype switching article, 7
company logos. *See* logos
compound selectors, 13, 222, 223, 293
comps
    for art gallery site, 265
    for Chamber of Commerce site, 155
    determining color value of, 158
    preparing, 51–52, 159
    slicing, 52
    for travel agency site, 200
Conditional Comments, 21. *See also* IECC
conflict resolution, 18
consolidating attributes, 114–118
contact form, 240–251
    coding, 241–244
    indicating required fields in, 247–248
    styling, 245–248
    validating, 249–251
container <div> tags, 129
#container rule, 143, 158
containers
    floating, 171
    setting width of, 210–211
content, 5. *See also* mainContent div
content/design equation, 4
copyright symbol, 7, 192
corners, rounded, 70–74
Create New File command, 17
"Creating Liquid Faux Columns" article, 178
CSS
    and accessibility, 5
    advice for new users of, 3
    basic concepts, 3–27
    benefits of using, 5
    and incomplete doctypes, 6
    layouts. *See* CSS layouts
    liquid layouts. *See* liquid layouts

meaning of acronym, 10
    migrating table-based layout to, 105–106. *See also* table-based layouts
    minimalist approach to, 107
    positioning techniques, 24–27, 65
    rules. *See* CSS rules
    selector types, 10–15. *See also* selectors
    snippets. *See* snippets
    styling lists with, 121–125
    syntax, 10
    using shorthand properties in, 55–59
CSS Advisor, Adobe, 99, 167
.css extension, 16
CSS Layout Outlines option, 33
CSS layouts
    centering, 41–44
    combining in single site, 263, 290–296
    consistency across, 41
    deciphering class for, 50
    elastic. *See* elastic layouts
    fixed-width. *See* fixed-width layouts
    liquid. *See* liquid layouts
    migrating table-based layouts to, 105–106. *See also* table-based layouts
CSS properties, displaying list of, 116
CSS rules
    components of, 10
    consolidating attributes, 114–118
    deleting duplicate, 292–294
    duplicating, 213, 222
    establishing order for, 112–113
    finding and replacing, 108–110
    minimalist approach to, 107
    moving, 111–112
    organizing, 110–112
    weight of, 18–19
CSS Source Format Options dialog, 58
CSS Styles panel, 23
Current mode, CSS Styles panel, 23

D

data tables, 252–260
  accessibility issues, 253
  adding headers to, 256–258
  adding rows/columns to, 254
  inserting in page, 252–254
  selecting rows/columns in,
    254
  setting width of, 254–256
  standards-compliant, 252
  styling, 259–260
  ways of using, 252
Davis, Paul, 22, 80
declaration blocks, 10
declarations, 10, 114
declaring media types, 100–102
deprecated elements, 6
descendant selectors, 13–15
design comps
  for art gallery site, 265
  for Chamber of Commerce
    site, 155
  determining color value of,
    158
  preparing, 51–52, 159
  slicing, 52
  for travel agency site, 200
Design-time Style Sheets, 168,
    220
disabilities, accommodating
  people with, 201. *See also*
  accessibility
`display:block` declaration, 167
div-inside-a-div technique,
  84–85
div sizing, in elastic layouts,
  208–210
divs
  defined, 9
  dividing page with, 32–34
  purpose of, 9
  wrapping links in, 131
  wrapping table in, 129–130
doctype
  and deprecated elements, 6
  identifying web page's, 6
  purpose of, 5, 6
  and rendering mode, 6, 7
  resources, 7
document flow, 7
Document Object Model, 322
document standards, 5

document tree, 13–14
Document Type Definition, 5.
    See also doctype
DOM, 322
doubled margin bug, 167
Draw AP Div tool, 141–142
Dreamweaver
  autocomplete feature, 162
  CSS management features,
    176
  CSS preferences, 57–59
  default character encoding, 7
  default doctype, 6
  defining site in, 48
  Design-time Style Sheets,
    168, 220
  editing CSS in, 160, 165
  exporting styles from, 111
  finding and replacing rules
    with, 108–110
  Photoshop integration, 184
  selecting elements in, 216
  Snippets, 204–205
  Spry capabilities, 305. *See also*
    Spry framework
  using regular expressions in,
    110, 115–116
drop caps, 94–95, 99
DTD, 5, 6. *See also* doctype
DTSS, 168, 220
`dtss.css` file, 169, 170, 221

E

Edit CSS Style dialog, 224
Edit Font List dialog, 53
elastic layouts, 199–261
  adding background to list
    items in, 229–230
  adding inline navigation to,
    218–220
  adding scrollbar to, 205
  adjusting margins/padding
    in, 224–225
  creating new document with,
    201–207
  creating/styling data tables
    in, 252–260
  creating/styling forms in,
    240–251
  defined, 200
  defining type elements in,
    211–212

div sizing in, 208–210
  and em units, 207–208
  inserting/formatting images
    in, 225–227
  main content area in, 224–228
  main site navigation in,
    228–237
  resetting CSS defaults for,
    202–203
  simplifying CSS for, 202–203
  sizing sidebars in, 227–228
  styling footer in, 238–239
  styling header in, 215–217
  styling headings in, 213–214
  styling inline navigation in,
    219–220
  styling links in, 230–231
  styling sidebars in, 236–238
  text sizing in, 208
  type adjustments in, 210–214
  using <cite> element in,
    232–236
element selectors, 10. *See also*
  tag selectors
em-based columns, 85
em-based forms, 240–251
  coding, 241–244
  indicating required fields in,
    247–248
  styling, 245–248
  validating, 249–251
em-based layouts
  benefits of, 210
  forms in, 240
  how they work, 207–208
  images in, 210, 225–227
  limitations of, 210
<em> tag, 247
em units
  benefits of, 208
  defined, 207
  div sizing in, 208–210
  for margins/padding, 224
  relative nature of, 207
  text sizing in, 208
embedded styles, 17
escaping margin effect, 44
`EventListener` function, 325
`expression` property, 271–272
external style sheets, 16–17,
  107, 292
`externalJavaScript.js` file, 332
Eye icon, 33

F

faux bottom technique, 72–74
faux column technique, 9, 59–61, 136, 178
feedback, user, 256–257, 288–289
fieldset tool, 242
fieldsets, 240, 242
Find and Replace dialog, 109, 115, 120–121
Firebug, 329
Firefox, 20, 78, 177, 329
Fireworks
    creating background images in, 137
    flattening nested tables in, 138
    image optimization in, 183
    modifying graphics with, 126–128
    and png format, 78
    preparing comps in, 51–52, 159
    web optimization in, 52
first letter pseudo-element, 94
fixed positioning, 26–27
fixed-width layouts, 47–103
    adding bottom of page in, 74–81
    adding drop caps to, 94–95
    adding links to, 88–90
    adding logo to, 67–69
    adding outer page wrapper in, 75–77
    changing source order in, 85–87
    characteristics of, 47
    creating "faux" right column in, 60–61
    creating header in, 64–69
    creating new page with, 48–54
    creating outer glow in, 62–64
    creating pod in, 81–82
    creating print style sheet for, 100–102
    declaring media types for, 100–102
    example of, 48
    footer for, 77, 96
    and png format, 78–81
    popularity of, 47
    positioning graphics in, 77–78

preparing HTML document for, 50–51
rounding side column in, 70–74
styling body element in, 52–54
styling headings in, 91–93
float creep, 83
float property, 39, 84, 151, 220
floating
    columns, 37–40
    containers, 171
    images, 27–29, 275–276
    list items, 166–167, 192, 220–221
    mainContent div, 85–87
floats
    vs. absolutely positioned elements, 83
    clearing, 84–85
    forcing div to contain, 83
    printing considerations, 102
.fltlft rule, 17, 28, 29, 276, 292
.fltrt rule, 82, 268, 276, 292
fly-out menus, 277, 290
:focus link state, 13, 88, 223
:focus pseudo class, 173
font cascades, 54, 91
font property, 55–56
font size
    and em units, 207, 208
    manipulating in browser, 199
    testing default, 54
fonts, Windows/Mac, 54
footers
    for Acme Internet Machines site, 146–149
    background color for, 157
    for Chamber of Commerce site, 191–193
    floating list items in, 192
    for horticulture site, 77, 96
    and margin collapse, 45
    for travel agency site, 238–239
form validation, 249–251
forms, 240–251
    coding, 241–244
    indicating required fields in, 247–248
    styling, 245–248
    terminology, 240
    validating, 249–251

frameworks, 277. See also Spry framework
functions, 324

G

Gallant, John, 21, 44
gallery pages, 265, 296–303. See also art gallery site
gif format, 77, 81
Gillenwater, Zoe, 19, 178
graphics. See also images
    modifying, with Fireworks, 126–128
    positioning, 77–78, 275–276
    and transparency, 77–78
graphics programs, 51–52, 60, 71, 159

H

handheld media type, 100
hash mark (#)
    in color values, 56
    in ID names, 12, 35
    in link field, 164, 219, 295–296
    in list items, 229
hasLayout property, 24, 97–98
headers
    adding background image to, 140, 160–161, 217–218
    adding inline navigation to, 218–220
    adding logo to, 67–69, 161–162
    for elastic layout, 215–216
    for fixed-width layout, 64–69
    for liquid layout, 159–162
    and margin collapse, 45
    positioning navigation in, 141–144
    for table-based layout, 138–144
headers attribute, 256–258
headings, styling, 91–93, 195, 213–214
"headless Fireworks" optimization engine, 183, 184
height property, 180
Hewitt, Joe, 329
horizontal navigation bar, 163–175
    adding depth to, 163

creating CSS for, 164–167
creating hover state for, 173–175
fixing horizontal scroll in, 172–173
floating list items in, 166–167
semantic XHTML structure for, 163–164
stacking of words in, 168
styling anchors as buttons in, 167–168
tweaking, 169–172
use of images in, 163
horizontal scrollbars, 42, 172–173
horticulture site, 47–103
adding bottom of page to, 74–81
adding drop caps to, 94–95
adding links to, 88–90
adding logo to, 67–69
adjusting for IE5, 96–97
changing source order in, 85–87
checking for bugs, 96–99
creating "faux" right column for, 60–61
creating header for, 64–69
creating outer glow for, 62–64
creating pod in, 81–82
creating print style sheet for, 100–102
declaring media types for, 100–102
footer for, 77, 96
positioning bottom flower graphic for, 77–78
preparing comp for, 51–52
preparing HTML document for, 50–51
rounding side column for, 70–74
screen shot, 48
styling body element for, 52–54
styling headings for, 91–93
:hover link state, 13, 88, 89, 223
:hover pseudo class, 173–174
href attribute, 322, 332
HTML 4.01 Strict doctype, 6
HTML dataset, 305–308

HTML documents. *See also* (X) HTML documents
and content/design equation, 4
for fixed-width layout, 50–51
humanistic principles, accessibility and, 201
hybrid layouts, 266, 270, 291

I

ID selectors, 12, 147
identifiers, 12, 28
IE. *See* Internet Explorer
IECC
basic syntax for, 21–22
and Eric Meyer's CSS reset, 240
externalizing, 334
fixing bugs with, 99
and margin collapse, 45
meaning of acronym, 21
overriding styles with, 99
and png format, 78
purpose of, 21
IECC extension, 22, 80
Image Placeholder dialog, 27
Image Tag Accessibility Attributes dialog, 161
images. *See also* graphics
background, 59–64, 160–161
in em-based layouts, 210, 225–227
floating, 27–29, 275–276
optimizing, 183, 185
positioning, 77–81, 275–276
removing border from, 68–69
scaling, 226
thumbnail *vs.* hi-rez, 318–319
wrapping text around, 27–29
@import notation, 17
!important operator, 16, 169
index.htm file, 107
index.html file, 49, 327
inheritance, 19, 43
inline elements, 7, 8
inline navigation, 218–220
inline styles, 18
Input Tag Accessibility Attributes dialog, 243
Insert Div Tag dialog, 32–33, 129

Internet Explorer
and alpha transparency, 78
and auto margins, 42
and background images, 64
and box model problem, 20, 21, 96–97
and compound selectors, 13
doubled margin bug, 167
expression property, 271–272
and fixed positioning, 27
hasLayout property, 24, 97
and JavaScript, 328
and link states, 88
and margin collapse, 45
and min-height property, 180
and min/max width problem, 271–274, 333
and png format, 78, 80
and selector types, 15
and web standards, 5
and zoom feature, 64
Internet Explorer Conditional Comments. *See* IECC
Invisible Elements option, 241

J

JavaScript
and accessibility, 290
creating unobtrusive, 323–328
and fly-out menus, 277, 290
and horizontal navigation bars, 163
and Internet Explorer, 328
Math class, 272
and png format, 78
vs. Spry framework, 277
turning off, 329
jpg format, 77–78

K

keywords, 202

L

label element, 245
"label for=" expression, 240
labs.adobe.com, 278
Layer tool, 141
Layout Mode, 125, 127, 137

layout types
combining, 50, 263, 290–296
finding and replacing, 50–51
layouts
centering, 41–44, 59
elastic. *See* elastic layouts
em-based. *See* em-based
layouts
fixed-width. *See* fixed-width
layouts
liquid. *See* liquid layouts
mixing, 156
percentage-based, 105, 178,
196. *See also* liquid
layouts
table-based. *See* table-based
layouts
two-column. *See* two-column
layouts
`legend` element, 240, 245
`li` element, 165
line breaks, 148
`line-height` property, 152
`:link` link state, 13, 88
link states, 13, 88, 223
Link to Existing File command,
17
links
color considerations, 89
placing visual separator
between, 223–224
styling, 194
underlining, 89, 296
"Liquid Faux Columns" article,
178
liquid layouts, 155–196
benefits of, 155
creating faux columns in, 178
creating header in, 159–162
creating horizontal
navigation bar in,
163–175
creating hover states in,
173–175
creating left-hand navigation
in, 185–187
creating page indicator state
in, 173–175
default file name for, 156
fixing horizontal scroll in,
172–173
inserting background images
in, 160–161

inserting logos in, 161–162
laying out main content area
in, 175–190
modifying columns in, 176
simplifying CSS selectors for,
156–159
styling anchors as buttons in,
167–168
styling footer in, 191–193
styling menu links in,
187–188
`listener` function, 324
lists
comma-delimited, 222
floating, 220–221
positioning, 130–131
styling, 121–125, 221
`LoadListener` function, 324
logos
adding to header, 67–69,
161–162
color *vs.* black and white, 102
linking to home page, 68
printing considerations, 102
LVHA (love-hate) mnemonic, 88

M

Macintosh
and color sampling, 158
and Dreamweaver
preferences, 57
font considerations, 54
and Internet Explorer, 96
and reset snippet, 204
and SpryAssets folder, 306
`mainContent` div
adjusting margins/padding
in, 37, 92, 177, 181,
224–225
adjusting sidebars in, 227–228
aligning headings in, 92
clearing content in, 85
constraining for IE, 273–274
floating, 85–87
formatting images in, 225–227
inserting pod in, 81–82
limiting line length in,
270–271
modifying columns in, 176
moving, 12
positioning background for,
178

setting width of, 97
styling, 190
two- *vs.* three-column layout
in, 15
margin collapse, 44, 45, 93, 177
margin escape, 93
`margin` property, 56–57
margins
automatic, 42, 150
browser defaults for, 125
doubled, 167
in elastic layouts, 224–225
for list items, 124–125
for `mainContent` div, 37, 92, 177,
181, 224–225
in percentage-based layouts,
180–181
shorthand for, 56–57
using em units for, 224
`Math.max` function, 273
`Math.min` function, 273
`max-width` property, 270–271
media types, declaring, 100–102
Member Login area, 137
menu, placing page indicator
on, 188–190
menu bar, 279–290
adding dotted line between
entries in, 334
creating, 279–282
giving feedback via, 288–289
and JavaScript, 290
styling, 282–287
Meyer, Eric, 203, 240
meyerweb.com, 203
`min-height` property, 179–180
`min-width` property, 271, 303
Minion Pro font, 159
mobile devices, 201
monitors, designing for large,
155
Move CSS Rules command, 111,
112
Mozilla-based browsers, 177. *See
also* Firefox

N

navigation
adding background to,
229–230
horizontal, 163–175. *See also*
horizontal navigation bar

inline, 218–220
left-hand, 185–187
positioning, 141–144
Spry-based, 279–282
styling links in, 230–231
using unordered list for,
228–229
vertical, 277
nested tables, 107, 119–137, 138
Netscape, 20, 21
New CSS Rule dialog, 10–14
News and Events sidebar,
236–237
non-breaking space, 168
number sign (#), 35. *See also*
hash mark (#)

O

octothorpe (#), 12. *See also* hash
mark (#)
opening/closing tags, 33
Opera, 20, 21
optimizing images, 183, 185
outer glow, 62–64

P

‹p› element, wrapping links in,
131
padding
browser defaults for, 125
in elastic layouts, 224–225
for list items, 124–125
and margin collapse, 45
in navigation bars, 167–168
in percentage-based layouts,
180–181
shorthand for, 56–57
using em units for, 224
padding property, 56
page flicker, 320
page indicator, 174–175,
188–190, 194
page wrappers, 75–77
PC
and color sampling, 158
font considerations, 54
and reset snippet, 204
Pederick, Chris, 329
percentage-based layouts, 105,
178, 180, 196. *See also* liquid
layouts

period (.), in class identifiers,
12, 28
Photoshop
integration with
Dreamweaver, 184
optimizing images from, 183
preparing comps in, 159
PHP, 300
pixels, 207, 224
placeholder hash mark (#), 219,
229. *See also* hash mark (#)
Pleasantville Chamber of
Commerce site, 155–196
adding badge image to,
183–185
creating header for, 159–162
creating horizontal
navigation bar for,
163–175
defining, 156
design comp for, 155
laying out main content area
for, 175–190
modifying columns in, 176
simplifying CSS selectors for,
156–159
styling footer for, 191–193
png format, 78–81
pods, 81–82
Portable Network Graphic
format, 78. *See also* png
format
positioning
absolute, 26, 34–40, 65–67, 141
backgrounds, 178–180
bulleted lists, 130–131
columns, 34–40
images, 77–81, 275–276
navigation, 141–144
relative, 25
static, 25
positioning techniques, 24–27,
65, 141
pound sign (#). *See* hash mark
(#)
"Practice of CSS Column
Design" article, 44
preferences, Dreamweaver CSS,
57–59
presentation
and content/design equation,
4
defined, 4

separating content from, 5
print media type, 100, 101
print style sheets, 100–102
progressive enhancement, 290,
304
properties, 10
pseudo selectors, 13

Q

Quick Tag Editor, 131, 148, 172,
232, 233
quirks mode, 6, 20, 96–97
quotations, 232. *See also*
‹blockquote› tag

R

radio buttons, 246
Reconstitute Table command,
127
regular expressions, 110,
115–116
relative positioning, 25
relative units, 200, 207
Remove Nesting icon, 126
removeAttribute method, 322
"Rendering Mode and Doctype
Switching" article, 7
Replace Tag action, Find and
Replace dialog, 121
required form fields, 247–248
reset snippet
creating, 204–205
reusing, 204
tweaking, 205–207
Rive Gauche Galleries site,
263–335
building gallery page for,
296–303
building initial framework for,
266–269
combining CSS layouts for,
290–296
comps for gallery pages, 265
design requirements, 263
main content area for,
269–276
navigation for, 277–289
original version of, 264
positioning images for,
275–276

progressive enhancement of, 304–322
selecting starter layout for, 264–266
styling sidebars for, 295–296
validating, 323–335
rounded columns, 70–74
rules. *See* CSS rules

S

Safari, 20, 21, 78, 208, 246
scope attribute, 255
screen media type, 100, 101
screen readers, 161, 201, 255, 290
scrollbars, 42, 172–173, 205, 210
scrolling, horizontal, 172–173
search engine optimization, 284
search engines
    and absolute positioning, 65
    and content/design equation, 4
    and headings, 91, 144
    and page titles, 202
    and source order, 85
    and text styling, 4
selectors
    and CSS syntax, 10
    grouping, 13
    purpose of, 10
    simplifying, 156–159, 203
    types of, 10–15
semantic code, 201
semantic elements, 4
semantic markup, 10
semicolon, 115, 117
shorthand properties, 55–59
sidebars
    avoiding overlap with main content and, 224–225
    rounding corners of, 70–74
    setting width of, 208–209, 227–228
    styling, 295–296
site navigation. *See* navigation
Slice tool, 128
sliding panels, 309–322
    adding detail images to, 318–322
    creating structure for, 310–317
    defined, 309
    navigating through, 317–318

snippets, 204–207
    adding keyboard shortcut to, 204
    creating, 204–205
    reusing, 204
    tweaking, 205–207
source code, searching, 115
source order, 85–87
‹span› element, 94–95, 131, 249
special characters, 7
Specific Tag option, Find and Replace dialog, 120
specificity, 18–19, 23, 203
spiders, 65, 85, 91, 144, 202. *See also* search engines
Split view, 33, 41
Spry-based navigation, 279–282
Spry form validation, 249–251
Spry framework
    downloading, 278
    and form validation, 249
    and JavaScript, 290
    and progressive enhancement, 304
    purpose of, 277
    and unobtrusive JavaScript, 323
    updates to, 277–278, 279
Spry HTML dataset, 305–308
Spry Menu Bar, 279–290
    creating, 279–282
    giving feedback via, 288–289
    and JavaScript, 290
    styling, 282–287
Spry Sliding Panels widget, 304, 305, 309–322
SpryAssets folder, 306, 309
SpryDOMUtils.js file, 322, 324
standards-based design, 4. *See also* web standards
standards-compliant browsers, 5, 20, 78, 271
standards mode, 6
states, link. *See* link states
static positioning, 25
Strict doctype, 6, 201, 233, 244
style sheets
    author, 15, 16–18, 169
    design/placement of elements in, 10
    hierarchy in, 15
    linking, 17
    print, 100–102

resolving conflicts in, 18
    user, 15, 16, 169
    "zeroing out" default values in, 16, 45
styling
    anchors, 167–168
    containers, 210–211
    footers. *See* footers
    forms, 245–248
    headers, 215–217. *See also* headers
    headings, 91–93, 195, 213–214
    inline navigation, 219–220
    links, 194
    lists, 221
    mainContent div, 190
    menu links, 187–188
    navigation links, 230–231
    sidebars, 237, 295–296. *See also* sidebars
    Spry Menu Bar, 282–287
    text elements, 45
submit buttons, 246

T

table-based layouts, 105–153
    cleaning up nested tables in, 119–137
    CSS issues, 107–118
    rebuilding page header for, 138–144
    removing table markup from, 144–152
‹table› tag
    finding and replacing, 120–121
    removing, 126
    selecting, 119
tables
    accessibility issues, 253, 256–258
    adding headers to, 256–258
    adding rows/columns to, 254
    inserting in page, 252–254
    nested, 107, 119–137, 138
    selecting rows/columns in, 254
    setting width of, 254–256
    standards-compliant, 252
    styling, 259–260
    ways of using, 252
Tag Chooser, 148

Tag Inspector, 217, 244, 256, 257
tag selectors, 10–11, 32, 119
testimonials, 231–234
text
    color, 205–206
    limiting line length of,
        270–271
    sizing, in elastic layouts, 208
    styling, 45
    underlining, 89, 194, 296
`text-align` property, 43
`text-decoration` property, 117
TheRoadAhead site, 200–261
    adding inline navigation to,
        218–220
    adding scrollbars to, 205
    basic page structure for, 207
    comp for, 200
    completed page, 261
    creating/styling contact form
        for, 240–251
    creating/styling data tables
        for, 252–260
    defining type elements for,
        211–212
    main content area for,
        224–228
    main site navigation for,
        228–237
    News and Events section,
        236–237
    resetting CSS defaults for,
        202–203
    selecting CSS layout for,
        201–202
    setting text color for, 205–206
    styling container for, 210–211
    styling footer for, 238–239
    styling header for, 215–217
    styling headings for, 213–214
    styling inline navigation for,
        219–220
    Testimonials section, 231–234
`thrColElsHdr.css` file, 202
`thrColLiqHdr.css` file, 156, 170
three-column liquid layouts,
    156, 290
Three Pixel Text Jog bug, 99
transparency, 77–78
transparent gif, 77
travel agency site, 200–261
    adding inline navigation to,
        218–220

adding scrollbars to, 205
basic page structure for, 207
comp for, 200
completed page, 261
creating/styling contact form
    for, 240–251
creating/styling data tables
    for, 252–260
defining type elements for,
    211–212
main content area for,
    224–228
main site navigation for,
    228–237
News and Events section,
    236–237
resetting CSS defaults for,
    202–203
selecting CSS layout for,
    201–202
setting text color for, 205–206
styling container for, 210–211
styling footer for, 238–239
styling header for, 215–217
styling headings for, 213–214
styling inline navigation for,
    219–220
Testimonials section, 231–234
TRBL (trouble) rule, 56–57
two-column layouts
    and box model problem, 21
    combining with three-
        column, 290
    creating, 4
    preparing comp for, 51–52
type selectors, 10. *See also* tag
    selectors

U

`ul` element, 164–165, 192–193
underlined text, 89, 194, 296
Unicode, 7
universal accessibility, 5. *See
    also* accessibility
universal character encoding, 7
unobtrusive JavaScript, 323–328
unordered lists, 120, 136, 164,
    192. *See also* bulleted lists
Unscrollable Content Bug, 99
user feedback, 256–257
user style sheets, 15, 16, 169
UTF-8, 7

V

validator, W3C, 6, 327
values, 10
vertical menu, placing page
    indicator on, 188–190
vertical navigation bar, 277
viewport, 26
vision problems, 199, 226. *See
    also* accessibility
`:visited` link state, 13, 88, 89
Visual Aids
    CSS Layout Backgrounds
        option, 170, 172
    CSS Layout Outlines option,
        33, 181
    Invisible Elements option, 241
visual indicators, 188–189, 288

W

W3C
    and `!important` operator, 16,
        169
    and margin collapse, 45
    meaning of acronym, 6
    selector type information, 15
    validator, 6, 327
    Web Accessibility Initiative,
        200
    Web Content Accessibility
        Guidelines, 200
WAI, 200
Walking Tour badge, 183–185
WCAG, 200
web accessibility. *See*
    accessibility
Web Accessibility Initiative, 200
web browsers. *See also* specific
    browsers
    checking for compatibility
        with, 98–99
    and comma-delimited lists,
        222
    manipulating font size in, 199
    and page width, 65
    resolution considerations,
        64–65
    and selector types, 15
    standards-compliant, 5, 20,
        78, 271
    zeroing out default settings
        in, 202–203

Web Content Accessibility
     Guidelines, 200
web design
   and accessibility, 5, 199, 201.
        See also accessibility
   and content/design equation,
        4
   monitor considerations, 155
   professional *vs.* amateur, 105
   standards-based, 4
Web Developer's toolbar, 329
web pages
   changing source order of,
        85–87
   checking for browser
        compatibility, 98–99
   dividing into discrete areas, 9
   positioning elements on,
        24–27
   printing, 101–102
   stripping class names from,
        50–51
   using drop caps in, 94–95
   validating, 6
web sites
   defining in Dreamweaver, 48
   standards-based, 5
web standards, 5, 323
weight, of CSS rules, 18–19
white background, 160, 266
white space, 59, 138, 157
Windows fonts, 54
World Wide Web Consortium.
        See W3C
wrappers, page, 75–77

X

XHTML 1.0 Strict doctype, 6
XHTML 1.0 Transitional doctype,
   6
(X)HTML documents
   and alt attribute, 161
   building with divs, 9
   and character encoding, 6–7
   and content/design equation,
        4
   creating well formed, 5
   and doctype, 5–6
   inline *vs.* block elements in,
        7–8
   natural flow of, 7
   setting em-unit font sizes in,
        208